Philosophical-Political Profiles

Studies in Contemporary German Social Thought
Thomas McCarthy, General Editor

Philosophical-Political Profiles

Jürgen Habermas
translated by Frederick G. Lawrence

The MIT Press, Cambridge, Massachusetts, and London, England

First paperback printing, corrected by the author, 1985

This translation © 1983 by the Massachusetts Institute of Technology. These essays originally appeared in German as parts of Habermas's books *Philosophisch-politische Profile* (© 1971 by Suhrkamp Verlag) and *Kultur und Kritik. Verstreute Aufsätze* (© 1973 by Suhrkamp Verlag). The translation herein published is based on the revised edition of *Philosophisch-politische Profile* (© 1981 by Suhrkamp Verlag, Frankfurt, Federal Republic of Germany).

This book was set in Baskerville by The MIT Press Computergraphics Department and printed and bound by Halliday Lithograph in the United States of America.

Library of Congress Cataloging in Publication Data

Habermas, Jürgen.
  Philosophical-political profiles.

  (Studies in contemporary German social thought)

  Revised translation of: Philosophisch-politische Profile.
  1. Philosophy—Addresses, essays, lectures. I. Title. II. Series.
B3258.H32113 1983   193   83-42517
ISBN 0-262-08133-4 (hard)
      0-262-58071-3 (paper)

Contents

Translator's Introduction

Philosophy rests on the texts it criticizes. They are brought to it by the tradition they embody, and it is in dealing with them that the conduct of philosophy becomes commensurable with tradition. This justifies the move from philosophy to exegesis, which exalts neither the interpretation nor the symbol into an absolute but seeks the truth where thinking secularizes the irretrievable archetype of sacred texts.
T. W. Adorno, *Negative Dialectics*

This epigraph might serve as a motto for philosophical practice on the European continent, though there is a tendency in some quarters to exalt interpretations or symbols into absolutes. In any case, it does capture the characteristic approach to traditional texts of the first generation of Frankfurt School theorists. As will be clear to any reader of this collection, it is hardly less true for Jürgen Habermas. Criticism, as distinct from commentary, is his stock in trade; thus, his aim as a writer stands in sharp contrast to the various forms of text fetishism that are fashionable in academic circles today. Habermas is less concerned with reconstructing what the author intended to say to the original audience or using the text as a pretext for his own play. Rather, he seeks to grasp the subject matter and to judge the correctness and evaluate the worth of the author's views thereon. His outstanding quality as a writer is his critical sensibility.

Because of Habermas's penchant for using texts in order to get beyond them to their subject matter, the essays in which he critically assesses other thinkers are also a record of his own intellectual life.

Clear cases in point would be Habermas's two *Literaturberichte* dealing with the philosophical literature on Marx and Marxism (1957) and the literature on certain issues in the logic of the social sciences (1967). In these lengthy essays, characteristics of the intellectual journal are in evidence: a direct confrontation with the leading representatives of a wide range of concerns, orientations, and interests; a forthright coming to grips with the central issues of a topic via the authors or approaches treated; and a marked selectivity in relation to the issues under discussion. Thus, in his later foreword to the Suhrkamp edition of *On the Logic of the Social Sciences*, Habermas admonishes the reader that what is at stake in the essay is not so much "results" as a "process of self-understanding."[1] In other words, he is using the works under review to take soundings and get his bearings in relation to the overall objective of his own work. Consequently, however striking one might find Habermas's critical assessments of the authors and issues he discusses, the real point is his exploratory and provisional articulation of what would in time come to be part of his own position on the subject.

Habermas's unflinching orientation toward the subject matter, which he demonstrates so skillfully in the genre of the *Literaturbericht*, is matched in the essays in this volume. Whatever authors Habermas happens to be discussing, his overriding concern is always to see how they relate to his interest in emancipatory social theory. Intentionally or not, these essays, no less than the works that fall officially under the genre *Literaturbericht*, present us with what might be called polished fragments from an intellectual journal.

Connected with Habermas's relentless concern for the subject matter is another overriding tendency: He is less concerned with textual interpretation, in the sense of doing full justice to the author's meaning insofar as this is amenable to philological expertise, than with judging the correctness and evaluating the worth of the author's meaning. That is, he is less worried about making a case for the accuracy of his interpretation of an author's meaning than about stating just what he thinks is to be taken seriously in that author's work. Habermas's great popularity—which so contrasts with the inherent complexity and difficulty of both his manner of thought and the objects of his concern—is due in no small measure to the way he goes beyond the interpretation that understands to the further interpretation that discriminates. We sense that Habermas is really encountering the authors he writes about; that he wants to appreciate the values they represent as well as to criticize their defects. We sense that he is willing to allow himself to be challenged by their words and deeds to the degree that they strike him as in line with the reality of the subject matter in which he is interested.

Habermas's concern to see where he stands and to find out how to change his standpoint is quite clear in his exchanges with Hans-Georg Gadamer.[2] Habermas makes no bones about what he takes to be the limitations of hermeneutic philosophy in relation to the demands placed on critical reflection by domination and distortion. But neither his discussion of Wilhelm Dilthey in *Knowledge and Human Interests* or his independently worked out communication theory would have taken the shape they did if he had not also learned a great deal from Gadamer. Again, and what may be more significant in regard to his intellectual biography, Habermas is critical of Hegelian philosophy for having, as it were, speculatively tamed the French Revolution.[3] Yet it is quite evident in Habermas's critiques of instrumental reason, his emphasis on social interaction,[4] and his theory of social evolution that Hegel has been a sort of role model for his thinking.[5] These instances show how Habermas is usually transformed by his critical encounters. However, he also transforms what he learns from them into what he needs. He is not content just to present a dialectical illumination of alternative understandings or convictions; he takes sides and uses whatever he can from an author to articulate his own horizon.

The earliest of the thirteen essays collected here stem from the 1950s. In the preface to the first German edition, Habermas characterized them as the product of a quite bourgeois mode of philosophical journalism. Indeed, with the exception of the introductory essay, all of the writings gathered here are "occasional"—that is, they were elicited by occasions honoring older but contemporary philosophers or by the publication of significant philosophical works. Moreover, these studies document an epoch in philosophy that Habermas believes is coming to an end; the age in which thought is so incarnated in single great figures that one has to encounter the thinkers in coming to terms with their ideas. These early essays register the impressions these figures made on a much younger man who would eventually promote a transition from the old type of philosophy, which was concretized in great individual teachers, to a new style conceived of as intrinsically interdisciplinary and collaborative.

For anyone daunted by the theory-laden density of Habermas's *Legitimation Crisis* or his *Communication and the Evolution of Society*, the highly personal tone and texture of the essays collected here will offer a special attraction. Habermas has had contact with most of the thinkers discussed, either in lecture halls or seminar rooms or as a junior colleague. However, no matter how personal the tone of the essays, they are unmarred by sentimentality or elegy. Habermas always does more than just assess a thinker's influence and situate him in the context of the history of ideas; he praises him by showing us what he has learned from encountering him. Consequently, besides being an opportunity to see great thinkers and writers through the prism of one of the most penetrating minds of the succeeding generation, these essays provide a chance to see Habermas, provoked by them, constantly working out his own problematic and assembling the elements of his own theoretical framework. To be sure, the essays collected here make up a relatively small portion of Habermas's literary output between 1958 and 1979,[6] yet the major stages of his intellectual development are in evidence here. The earliest essays come from a period when Habermas was heavily influenced by Karl Löwith's rendition of the Young Hegelian movement,[7] and so the idea of philosophy as a socially transformative project already holds sway. Then there are essays from the time when Habermas had become a critical theorist much more in the tradition of the Frankfurt School. Finally, there are more-than-embryonic manifestations of his most recent shift toward communication theory.[8]

There is surely no author discussed in this collection with whom Habermas has less sympathy than Martin Heidegger,[9] who epitomizes the style of philosophy Habermas considers passé. As its title suggests, the essay on Heidegger departs less from substantive issues within Heidegger's oeuvre than from its great influence. That influence extends beyond academic philosophy and ranges from such scientists as Heisenberg and Weizsäcker to lay professionals in diverse fields, such as the well-known circle of favorites in Hamburg. Habermas takes care to distinguish the more authentic followers among Heidegger's disciples (for example, Oskar Becker and Eugen Fink) from the less authentic, and when he does come to confront Heidegger's thought he features the notion of the dialectic of correspondence [*Entsprechung*] culled from one of the more reliable and less misleading commentators, Walter

Schulz. Habermas criticizes the remoteness of that figure of thought from concrete suffering and displacement. He faults Heidegger's overall fundamental ontology for this as well. Nor does Habermas deem such remoteness innocent; indeed, his association of Heidegger's style of thought with Ernst Jünger, Gottfried Benn, and Carl Schmitt makes the suggestion of guilt by association unmistakable.

Habermas recognizes that Heidegger's two-phased revolt against the once-dominant Neo-Kantian style of philosophy, first in a blend of Husserlian transcendental phenomenology with Dilthey's historical mindedness and then in the so-called turning [*Kehre*], involved a radicalization of the antitechnocratic orientation common in post–World War I cultural criticism—an orientation with which Habermas is in profound sympathy. But Habermas senses that this unique chance to become liberated from the biases of Neo-Kantian transcendental philosophy was not redeemed by Heidegger, in whose work critique seems to succumb to myth in the pejorative sense. He notes quite pointedly how Heidegger had grappled unsuccessfully with the problematic that has vexed the other major figures of continental philosophy since Kant, himself included: the relationship between *a priori* conditions of possibility and the concrete history of social evolution.

Habermas clearly has a good deal more in common with Karl Jaspers, a fellow student of Friedrich Wilhelm Joseph von Schelling, than with Heidegger. They share such traits as wide and voracious reading and a certain expertise in extraphilosophical fields (psychology in Jaspers's case, social science in Habermas's). Each has a profound admiration for the achievement of Max Weber. But it is perhaps the idea of truth as intrinsically communicative that forges the deepest link between them. Habermas's discussion of Jaspers's philosophy of symbol (which was derived by combining Kant's third critique with ideas taken from Schelling) and its limitations, as well as his summary of Jaspers's overall philosophical project (existentialism as a form of Neo-Kantianism), is the more telling for having been written from a standpoint of basic sympathy. Indeed, if one were to transpose the privileged locus of intersubjective conversation from Jaspers's "metaphysical republic of scholars" into the concreteness of the dialectic of world history one might get a glimmer of the *raison d'être* of Habermas's own social philosophy.

Something like the same dynamic of sympathetic affinity and trenchant critique is at work in the essays on Ernst Bloch and Karl

Löwith. These essays are more ambitious in scope than the ones already mentioned, or perhaps Habermas just feels more at home with these men. His dissertation on Schelling had prepared him to recognize the Schellingian nature of Bloch's Marxism. Furthermore, in his discussion of Bloch we encounter a motif that will recur again and again in the rest of the collection: the subterranean impulses that came to German thought from the Kabbalah, and the strain of Jewish messianism transmitted from the Kabbalah through Jacob Böhme and Schelling to Karl Marx.

Habermas obviously resonates with Bloch's Schellingian Marxism; he could make his own the motto he proposes for Bloch: "Reason cannot bloom without hope, hope cannot speak without reason, both in a Marxian unity—all other science has no future, all other future no science." Habermas, who realizes the challenge of the Nietzschean *amor fati*, shares Bloch's optimistic utopianism. However, he cannot bring himself to accept Bloch's leap "past any sociological-historical investigation of objective possibilities promoted dialectically by the social process," and he is far from agreeing with Bloch's appeal to a *natura naturans* as a world soul or "universal substratum within the world process itself," even though he acknowledges the salutary effects of Bloch's "melancholy of fulfillment." He does appreciate Bloch's way of bringing out the difference between the arrival of material prosperity and the advent of utopia. For Habermas, though, Bloch's materialism "remains speculative" and his dialectic of the enlightenment "passes beyond dialectic to the doctrine of potency." No, even such a Schellingian version of Left Hegelianism cannot meet the demands of a critical theory.

Habermas's discussion of Karl Löwith is similar in vein to his critique of Bloch. Löwith was not less dismayed by Heidegger's attitudes toward the errant dispensations of being than Habermas was. Indeed, it was Löwith who introduced Habermas to the "revolutionary break in the thought of the nineteenth century," when philosophy had "taken up its own inexorable interest into reflection itself, utterly renounced its classical claim, and completely withdrawn from ontology into critique."

As I have already suggested, Habermas saw in the isolated character of Heideggerian *Ursprungsphilosophie* a key to its vulnerability to the delusion emanating from National Socialism, and so he has been motivated to pursue philosophy not as a theory of being but as a critique that tries to carry forward the impulse of the Left Hegelians. Löwith—

who had seen through the Heideggerian miscarriage and analyzed the movement from Hegel to the Left Hegelians with what Habermas calls "a clarity that left nothing to be desired"—headed in just the opposite direction from Habermas. For Löwith, philosophy has to keep theory and practice distinct and uphold the primacy of the former. Prescinding from whatever is fleeting, relative, and contingent, Löwith nonetheless deploys an unusually subtle historical consciousness, but he set his sights all the more insistently on *physis* (the cosmos as natural in the sense of the ancient Greeks). His great mentor, Heidegger, unintentionally demonstrated to him the pernicious effects of substituting historicism, pragmatism, and existentialism for philosophy as *theoria* in the classic sense.

Habermas's delineation of Löwith's position lets him express his own concerns and his own suspicion about "the absolute relevance of what is most relative, temporary, and contingent." He cannot help wondering "whether the self-understanding of human beings does not pertain *essentially* to that which they *are*; whether what people think of themselves is not determinative of the way they comport themselves." And so, in contrast with Löwith, he asks

Is not the nature of the human necessarily mediated by the second nature that is spelled out in the historically generated forms of his labor; in the historically developed and acquired rules of cooperative living, of commanding and obeying; in the historically discovered ways of experiencing, making sense, and gaining mastery which have been fixed in language and fostered or repressed, or lost; and which therefore have been embodied in the images that diverse societies have had of themselves? We find ourselves in a situation in which the conditions for survival have become so exorbitant, in the course of being incompatible with the forms of life that have taken on the bewitching appearance of quasi-naturalness by persisting for millennia. In such a situation of analytically debatable alternatives between mortal dangers and changes in just such nature like forms of life, historical experience of the plasticity of human nature should not get shoved under the cover of the taboos supplied by a doctrine of invariants.

Both Löwith and Ernst Bloch were more or less secularized, culturally assimilated Jews. In one of the most beautiful essays in this volume, Habermas uses the invitation to contribute to a radio series on Germans and Jews as an occasion to meditate on the "abysmal and yet fertile relationship of the Jews with the Germans." Artfully interweaving quotations from diverse sources, he ranges through a series of great Jewish philosophers since the time of the "emancipation." The affinity of Lutheran Christians for Kantian philosophy is well known; Kant has long provided a favorite haven for the mind of the secularized Protestant. The line that stretches from Marcus Herz and Salomon Maimon to the greatest thinker of Marburg Neo-Kantianism, Hermann Cohen, demonstrates that, in their "free attitude of rational criticism and cosmopolitan humanity," many cultivated Jews have been no less attracted to Kant.

Those familiar with Gershom Scholem's famous essay "Jews and Germans"[10] will appreciate the sensitivity, honesty, and delicacy with which Habermas treats the issues surrounding Jewish emancipation and assimilation and the differing reactions to the plight of being Jewish in German society. Habermas illuminates the many hues of this spectrum by giving us portraits of thinkers with an explicitly religious orientation (Frans Rosenzweig and Martin Buber), of a thinker consciously mediating between Judaism and enlightened German culture (Cohen), of secularized Jews (Ernst Cassirer and Georg Simmel), and of persons as difficult to categorize as Walter Benjamin and Ludwig Wittgenstein. The essay is full of suggestive aperçus, as when Habermas speculates about the link between the Jew's need for role playing in German society and the German-Jewish penchant for sensitive aesthetic reflection, "from Rosenkranz and Simmel . . . by way of Benjamin and Lukács, down to Adorno." Finally, it is clear that, to whatever extent Habermas is disposed to receive what Peter Berger has called "signals of transcendence," they are likely to have been transmitted to him by Jews.

If Löwith had exposed Habermas to the Left Hegelian maneuver of doing philosophy as critique, his mentor Theodor Adorno introduced him to the dialectic of the enlightenment and the correlative critique of instrumental reason, which were to become for him a heuristic device for a critique of modernity. As Adorno put it in *Negative Dialectics*,

That reason is something different from nature and yet a moment within it—this is its prehistory, which has become part of its immanent determination. As the psychic force branching out for the purposes of self-preservation, it is natural; however, once it has been split off and contrasted with nature it also becomes the other of nature. Reason, cutting nature down to size in an ephemeral way, is identical and nonidentical with nature, dialectical in accord with its own concept. Yet the more unrestrainedly reason is made into an absolute over against nature within that dialectic and becomes oblivious to itself in this, the more it regresses, as self-affirmation gone wild, into nature; only as nature's reflection would it be supernature.

The essay on Adorno, probably the most intimately personal one in this book, was written upon his death, after student activists had been attacking him for not being Marxist enough and for being irretrievably bourgeois. Habermas warns against foresaking "the right that the untrue bourgeois subjectivity still retains in the process of disappearing in relation to its false negation." He points out how Adorno revived Hegel's dialectic of the universal and the particular in his own way to evoke the contours of a "life together in communication that is free from coercion": "The reconciled state would not annex the alien with a philosophical imperialism, but would find its happiness in the fact that the alien remained distinct and remote within the preserved proximity, beyond being either heterogeneous or one's own." At the same time, Habermas is critical of the totalizing tendency in Adorno's conception of the dialectic of the enlightenment, which he says keeps Adorno from moderating the ideal of reconciliation, with all its theological overtones, into an ideal of human autonomy and responsibility.

If the essay on Adorno is the most personal in tone, the one on Arnold Gehlen takes the laurels for the most waspish. Though Gehlen is not yet very well known in the United States, this social anthropologist and follower of Max Scheler is one of the most highly esteemed theorists in Germany. In the essay devoted to him we find one of the best and clearest elaborations of the sort of reflection that moved Habermas in the direction of a theory of communicative competence. The waspish tone enters as Habermas underlines the irony in the relation between Gehlen's theory of anthropological ethics and the extremely antihumanitarian stances he takes in his social and cultural criticism: "Venerable proverbs about life and theoretically interesting assumptions are mixed in with the typical stock in trade of an out-of-step intellectual of the Right who is no longer up to the biographical aporias of his role." The implications of Gehlen's hypothesis of four distinct, biologically rooted ethical programs become all too clear when he applies them to empirical trends—for example, in his thesis that "humanitarianism," as an ethical derivative of the ethos properly rooted in the family, has in recent times been driving out the (institutional) "ethos of the state." For Gehlen this trend represents a foolhardy and dangerous overexpansion of the family ethos into domains where it is not appropriate.

Habermas first subjects Gehlen's explanatory distinctions to internal critique, then goes on to lay out his own conception of the development of moral consciousness. With the help of Emile Durkheim, George Herbert Mead, and, above all, Jean Piaget, Habermas conceives this evolution in terms of the progressive internalization and universalization of value systems. The core (but not the *terminus ad quem*) of this development is Kant's rather "disembodied" ethics. As Habermas sees it, self-legislation with neither heterogeneous motives nor external sanctions is "the central notion of European Enlightenment." On this view, Kantian morality dissolves the need for global interpretations of nature and society (in local myths or high religions) that legitimate authoritarian controls, even though Kant himself did not get completely beyond ontology. Kant's "intelligible ego," the still-ontologized subject of a completely universal and internalized morality, is isolated from communication with the multiplicity of concrete subjects. Hence, according to Habermas, it is unable to reconcile the universality of norms with the individuality of single persons. Moving beyond Kant, Habermas argues that this can be achieved by "mediation through discourse, that is, through a public process of formation of will that is bound to the principle of unrestricted communication and consensus free from domination." In this way, "the structure of possible speech, the form of the intersubjectivity of possible agreement, becomes . . . the *single* principle of morality." The individual maxim subjected to the test of the categorical imperative is thereby "socialized" into a norm subjected to scrutiny within an unrestricted discussion free from coercion.

The various aspects of the relationship between art and politics taken up in the essay on Herbert Marcuse remain as timely today as when they were written, in 1973. According to Habermas, in *Counterrevolution and Revolt* Marcuse undertook to articulate a "categorial shift in political activity." From Hobbes to Marx, the technicization of politics had concentrated on the power to satisfy material needs. The successes of modern societies in this dimension, however, have tended to unleash "the 'transcending,' nonmaterial needs, which late capitalism cannot satisfy." Marcuse assessed the potential of art for expressing these nonmaterial needs in a way that negates the repressiveness of organized capitalism variously in the course of his career, but at the later stages he saw art as inextricably linked to the human capacity to distinguish "between true and false, good and evil, beautiful and ugly, present and future." In the essay on Marcuse, Habermas uses Marcuse's sometimes contradictory theses to raise the problem of how autonomously distinct a medium art is or should be in relation to revolutionary practice overall, and to articulate "the meshing of various processes of dedifferentiation" of hitherto distinct realms. He is clearly sympathetic with Marcuse's "arguments for a new political praxis that integrates sensuality, fantasy, and desire" and with his "radically new interpretation of needs."

The essay on Hannah Arendt[11] demonstrates the great affinity that exists between her thought and Habermas's. There is in Arendt the classical distinction between purposive rational action (*poiesis*) and technical expertise (*techne*), on the one hand, and intersubjectivity engendered by discourse (*praxis*) and practical enlightenment (*phronesis*) on the other; there is the open texture of the discriminating judgment of Kant's third critique, which she transposes into the political sphere; and there is the centrality of consensus formation through free communication. All these features of Arendt's thought have been taken up in modified form by Habermas. In this particular essay, he sets forth her concept of power as the "capacity to agree in uncoerced communication on some community action" and uses it as a springboard to introduce further distinctions into the notion.

Habermas begins by setting Arendt's idea of power in relief against those of Weber's action theory and Parsons's systems theory, in both of which "successful outcome" rather than "agreement" is what counts. For Arendt, "the basic phenomenon is not the instrumentalizing of another's will for one's own purposes but the formation of a common will in communication aimed at agreement." The latter depends on "that peculiarly coercion-free force with which insights prevail." Its sole criterion is the "rational validity immanent within speech," which Habermas, when he wrote this piece, already differentiated into the truth of statements, the rightness of norms, and the truthfulness of expressions. The three-dimensional framework of Kant's critical project is obvious.

Arendt, in dissociating her notion of power from the conception of purposive rational action in Weber, stakes out the domain of communicative action, which has become central to Habermas's most recent thought. With deceptive boldness, Arendt tries to transform the basic presuppositions of liberal political theory. For Hobbes and Locke, power in the form of oppression is the most basic political phenomenon; in the state of nature as war we are its prey, whereas in the state of civil or political society this power is moderated or qualified by consent. Arendt calls the former kind of power (that unmediated through consent) *violence*; she restricts the use of the term *power* to whatever is mediated by reasonable consent. Apparently taking her bearings from an ancient Greek reading of the American experiment, she begins with legitimation, since natural equality is based (for her) not in the virtual ability of each to kill the other (as was true for Hobbes) but on "the rational claim immanent in speech." The latter is actualized, on her view, in the "public sphere," about which Habermas, too, has written extensively.[12]

In the course of a brief yet breathtaking summary and illustration of Arendt's main theses on power Habermas tells us that she made "the image she painted of the Greek polis" into "the essence of the political," and that she uses this construct in a somewhat Procrustean fashion to analyze the phenomena connected with depoliticization within modern bourgeois society and the modern state. This leads him to a reformulation of the concept of power that does not relegate to "violence" all forms of legitimate political strategic action, remove politics from its economic and social conditions, or make politics incapable of dealing with structural violence.

In regard to strategic action (or "the capacity to keep other individuals from perceiving their interests"), Habermas points out that its use in modern democracies has been both *de facto* and *de jure* when it comes to the acquisition and assertion of power, if not its engendering. But to come adequately to terms even with the engendering of power, Arendt's heuristic in terms of action theory needs to be integrated with ideas from systems theory, since power is engendered within structures that are not reducible to the intentions of the agents who are involved. Once the specifically structural aspect of violence is clearly recognized, one can go on to unmask the "unnoticed yet effective barriers to communication" erected by ideologies, which thus assume the power that, according to Arendt, should emerge from "an opinion upon which many are in public agreement." Here we approach the core of Habermas's disagreement with Arendt. For her, the arrival at a public consensus cannot be rational in the strict sense, because it is practical and not theoretical. At best, it can be "representative" thought. Accordingly, power is confined "to the force of mutual promise or contract." In contrast, Habermas argues that through tests of the validity of norms in relation to generalizable needs *cognitive* claims can be redeemed in the realm of practice, and that in this way a standard is reached for "discriminating illusionary and nonillusionary convictions." For Arendt, then, the communicative theory of action devolves into a form of natural-right theory, whereas for Habermas communication theory issues in a critique of ideology.

Habermas's obvious antipathy to Heidegger does not lead him to simply write him off. How far he is from doing so may be seen in his speech of praise for Hans-Georg Gadamer, delivered on the occasion of the latter's reception of the Hegel Prize and entitled "Urbanizing the Heideggerian Province."[13] The conceit of a contrast between the virtue of urbanity and the vice of provincialism sets the tone for Habermas's terse summation of the contributions of a philosopher who has participated with him in one of the most celebrated debates of recent years.

Habermas sees Gadamer, the father of what has come to be known as philosophical hermeneutics, as having accomplished a translation into terms accessible to the contemporary academic discussion of the rather arcane and rough-hewn reorientation of thought achieved by Martin Heidegger. He has tried "bridging three chasms that have opened up between ourselves and the philosophy of the Greeks: . . . the breaks brought about in the nineteenth century by historicism, in the seventeenth century by physics, and at the start of modernity by the transition to the modern apprehension of the world." His painstaking elaboration in terms of the philologically retrievable tradition of Heidegger's meditation "about the Being which is not supposed to be the being of a circumscribable entity" has yielded real dividends for contemporary science and scholarship: "It demonstrates . . . that hermeneutics has contributed precisely to the self-enlightenment of methodological thinking, to the liberalizing of the understanding of science, and even to the differentiation of the practice of research." Beyond this, it "furthers the enlightenment concerning the depth structures lying at the base of the life world" by "highlight[ing] the linguistic intersubjectivity that unites all communicatively socialized individuals from the outset." These forms of enlightenment are in complete consonance with Habermas's own aims, but Habermas does not let us forget that "the Enlightenment, the universalist eighteenth century" is more important to his reconstruction of the humanist tradition than it has been to Gadamer's. This essay demonstrates how open the conversation between Gadamer and Habermas remains.

Anyone who reads Habermas's eightieth-birthday tribute to Gershom Scholem[14] will not be surprised that Habermas was later chosen to represent the Federal Republic of Germany at the ceremonies in Israel following Scholem's death. The depth of feeling that Habermas manifests in this essay is, I believe, not due just to the fateful relationship between Germans and Jews discussed so stunningly in Scholem's famous 1966 article on the subject. It has more to do with Habermas's long-standing empathy with German-Jewish thinkers, with his indebtedness to Scholem for uncovering the roots of Schelling and Marx in the Kabbalah, and with his interest in Scholem's account of how one strain of Jewish thought sought to overcome historicism by means of mystical exegesis.

The poignancy of Habermas's response to Scholem's discussion of Germans and Jews is matched only by the boldness with which he sketches the implications of Scholem's portrayal of the transformation within the mystical tradition of the Jewish notions of revelation, tradition, and teaching. Habermas's approach here is based on maintaining the centrality of the subject matter of the authoritative text for all philological procedure. For one who, like Scholem, does not claim "an immediate, intuitive access to the divine life process," the only access to the ineffable subject matter of the authoritative texts of Jewish revelation, tradition, and teaching is, as Habermas explains, "a theory of the object." The "object" in this case includes the entire complex of relationships among God, the revealing subject; the authoritative Torah; the human transmission of meaning, both in the original formation of the Torah and in the forms of commentary; and, finally, the human realization of meaning in relation to the eschaton. Habermas develops this theory of the object with respect to issues in epistemology and the philosophy of history.

The keystone of the mystical interpretation of the way these elements are related to one another is the doctrine of the self-contraction of God in the act of continuing creation. The effective-historical upshot of this doctrine has been threefold: the materialist doctrine of nature, the revolutionary theory of history, and the nihilism of the post-revolutionary movement. The first, which is supposed to have begun with God's self-diremption in creation and continued throughout the course of natural and historical evolution, formed the underpinning for Schelling's speculations in *Ages of the World* and for Hegel's *Logic*. The second, in which God's self-banishment transforms the messianic task of redemption into a purely human one, emerges in secular fashion in Marx and the succeeding tradition, with the interpretation "no revolutionizing of nature without a revolutionizing of society." The nihilistic trend has its origin in God's creative act of descent into darkness and is transmogrified into a doctrine of redemption through sin. This doctrine has borne fruit not only in religious practices throughout the centuries but also in secular forms ranging from authentic nihilism to modern-day terrorism.

Having noted that Judaism has been in the forefront of involvement with the "universalist values of emancipatory movements, bourgeois as well as socialist," Habermas evidently finds congenial Scholem's interpretation of Judaism as "a moral concern, a historical project that cannot be defined once and for all"; as "a spiritual enterprise that lives out of religious sources." It is clear, moreover, that Habermas does not fully credit Scholem's characterization of himself as a mere historian living with the question of whether Judaism can survive the secularization of its religious sources. He obviously overhears something more when, in a reply to a question about the significance kabbalistic thought might have for contemporary Judaism, Scholem responds: "God will appear as non-God. All the divine and symbolic things can also appear in the garb of atheistic mysticism."

Walter Benjamin might well be a candidate for the title of an atheistic mystic in our day. Habermas's essay[15] on this friend of Adorno and associate of the Frankfurt School, sometime friend of Brecht, and enigmatic friend of Scholem may well be the richest piece in this collection; it is surely the most difficult. It stands as a watershed in the burgeoning literature on Benjamin. However, it is also a radical coming to terms on Habermas's part with a thinker who may represent the most serious challenge to his emancipatory enterprise.

Benjamin's thought is notoriously elusive, almost evanescent. Its characteristic oscillation between Marxist materialism and Jewish religious motifs is hard enough to follow without the changing valences he assigned to art and surrealist thought at different times. And though Benjamin was quite sensitive to the abuses of Marxism and Judaism in their inauthentic forms of positivism and magic, respectively, he tended to fall into them himself at times. The tension in his work between the two (as Scholem would have it, opposed) orientations, and the intermix of their debased forms, make his thought almost impossible to systematize, let alone appropriate. Habermas takes his cue from the image in Benjamin's "Theses on the Philosophy of History" of the theological dwarf and the Marxist puppet of historical materialism. Benjamin, he argues, tried to enlist historical materialism in the services of a theology of history.

After laying out the main classifications of the literature on Benjamin, Habermas begins his account by concentrating on various aspects of Benjamin's philosophy of art, brilliantly setting Benjamin's ideas against the similar yet perhaps less profound ideas of Marcuse and Adorno. Here we meet such notions as 'aura,' 'secular illumination,' and 'dialectical images.' Not the least virtue of Habermas's rendition is the way he registers Benjamin's own ambivalence toward the phenomenon of aura, according as it is ritualized or deritualized.

One constant feature of Benjamin's thought is the experience correlative to what in the "Theses on the Philosophy of History" he calls the *Jetztzeit* [now time]: an experience of time that breaks up the continuity of homogeneous time or of time as a raceway of instants. Habermas points out the centrality of Benjamin's theory of experience as unspoiled and unmutilated—"of people living close to nature, madmen, seers, and artists"—and of his project of a criticism that rescues, that "transpose[s] the beautiful into the medium of the true, by which transposition 'truth is not an unveiling which annihilates the mystery, but a revelation and a manifestation that does it justice.' " Experience in this sense enters upon "a field of surprising correspondences, between animate and inanimate nature . . . wherein things, too, encounter us in the structure of vulnerable intersubjectivity." "In such structures," Habermas continues, "the essence that appears escapes the grasp after immediacy without any distance at all; the proximity of the other refracted in the distance is the signature of a possible fulfillment and a mutual happiness." Habermas observes that for Benjamin such experience is like religious or mystical experience. However, the intent of Benjamin's "rescuing critique" is to render an experience that had been solitary and esoteric into one that is public and universal.

Habermas discusses how Benjamin's theory of experience is moored in a mimetic theory of language whose crucial aspect is a semantic potential in the light of which humans can interpret their needs and make the world accessible to experience. The primordial mimesis consists in the imaginal representation of "natural correspondences," which serve without exception to "stimulate and awaken the mimetic capacity in the human being that responds to them in human beings." This original expressive stratum of language constitutes a potential out of which human historical self-interpretation is nourished. Like the "Jews who were prohibited from investigating the future" and "instructed in remembrance," rescuing critics would dig retrospectively until they penetrated the taproot of this semantic potential by "grasp[ing] the constellation [their] own era has formed with a definite earlier one." Thus, rescuing critique establishes a conception of the present as "the time of the now," which is "shot through with chips of messianic time." Benjamin believed that this procedure would benefit from the use of historical materialism as a heuristic device.

Habermas appreciates how historical materialism kept Benjamin from reducing politics to show in a merely surrealist fashion, and the way the messianic strain in his thought engendered a "prophylactic doubt" that kept his dialectical theory of progress from reducing utopia to prosperity and so short-circuiting the revolutionary content of universal freedom and happiness into a regime of meaninglessness. Here, however, on the threshold of Nietzsche's "last man," Habermas does not think Benjamin's semantic materialism—his synthesis of historical materialism and theology—is successful. Its standard is too 'Manichaean,' too totalizing, to take proper account of partial emancipations under secular auspices "in the products of legality, if not even in the formal structures of morality."

Habermas has provided a remarkable statement of Benjamin's challenge. The course of modern history has increased the dimensions of catastrophe and heightened a certain eschatological consciousness; it has left us in the situation of crisis portrayed in Benjamin's philosophical-historical thesis on *Angelus Novus*. We can discern from Habermas's essay "Does Philosophy Still Have a Purpose?" that he wants to confront the contemporary crisis of modernity, as did Weber, Heidegger, Adorno, Horkheimer, and others, by reraising the question of rationality. He understands in all its subtlety the changed constellation of philosophy since Hegel's death—as regards the unity of philosophy and science, the relationship between philosophy and tradition, the interplay of philosophy and religion, and the new position of philosophy with respect to the life world. But however nonabsolutist, collaboratively nonelitist, and interdisciplinary Habermas thinks philosophy will have to become, he is not willing to resign himself to the suggestion that the light of reason was no more than a temporary resting place of the Greeks or of the Enlightenment. Instead, he addresses the question of rationality today as if one could still discover how things really are. One hopes that his receptiveness to Benjamin will keep him from underestimating the darkness of spirit in which reason now has to learn.

In closing, I wish to acknowledge my deep indebtedness to Thomas McCarthy for all the time and painstaking labor he has devoted to improving this translation. However much he virtually deserves to be called co-translator, I take full responsibility for all the book's shortcomings. As Hans-Georg Gadamer once said to me by way of consolation, "There are no translations free from error."

Frederick G. Lawrence

Notes

1. Habermas, *Zur Logik der Sozialwissenschaften* (Frankfurt, 1970), p. 7.

2. See essays by Habermas and Gadamer in *Hermeneutik und Ideologiekritik* (Frankfurt, 1971).

3. See especially Habermas, "Hegel's Critique of the French Revolution," in *Theory and Practice* (Boston, 1971).

4. Habermas, "Labor and Interaction: Remarks on Hegel's Jena 'Philosophy of Mind,' " in *Theory and Practice.*

5. Habermas, "Können komplexe Gesellschaften eine vernünftige Identität ausbilden?" in *Zwei Reden* (Frankfurt, 1974).

6. For an exhaustive bibliography including English translations see Thomas McCarthy, *The Critical Theory of Jürgen Habermas* (Cambridge, Mass., 1978).

7. See Axel Honneth, Eberhard Knödler-Bunte, and Arno Widmann, "The Dialectics of Rationalization: An Interview with Jürgen Habermas," *Telos* XX (1981): XX–XX.

8. On the periodization of Habermas's thought see T. McCarthy, "History and Evolution: On the Changing Relation of Theory to Practice in the Work of Jürgen Habermas," in *PSA 1978*, Proceedings of the 1978 Biennial Meeting of Philosophy of Science Association, vol. 2, pp. 397–423; W. Zimmerli, "Jürgen Habermas: Auf der Suche nach der Identität von Theorie und

Praxis," in *Grundprobleme der grossen Philosophen*, ed. J. Speck (Göttingen, 1981); J. Schmidt, "Jürgen Habermas and the Difficulties of Enlightenment," *Social Research* 49 (1982): 181–208.

9. See Habermas, "Martin Heidegger. Zur Veröffentlichung von Vorlesungen aus dem Jahre 1945," in *Philosophisch-politische Profile* (Frankfurt, 1971).

10. Gershom Scholem, "Jews and Germans," in *On Jews and Judaism in Crisis: Selected Essays*, ed. W. Dannhauser (New York, 1976).

11. Originally published as "Hannah Arendts Begriff der Macht," *Merkur* 30 (1976): 946–961.

12. Habermas, *Strukturwandel der Oeffentlichkeit. Untersuchungen zu einer Kategorie der bürgerlichen Gesellschaft* (Berlin, 1965) (to appear in English in this series).

13. Originally published in Habermas and Gadamer, *Das Erbe Hegels. Zwei Reden aus Anlass des Hegel-Preises* (Frankfurt, 1979). Gadamer's contribution, "The Heritage of Hegel," appears in Gadamer's *Reason in the Age of Science* (Cambridge, Mass., 1981).

14. Originally published as "Die verkleidete Tora. Rede zum 80. Geburtstag von Gershom Scholem," *Merkur* 1 (1978): 96–104.

15. Originally published as "Bewusstmachende oder rettende Kritik. Die Aktualität Walter Benjamins," in *Zur Aktualität Walter Benjamins*, ed. S. Unseld (Frankfurt, 1982); also in *Kultur und Kritik* (Frankfurt, 1973).

Does Philosophy Still Have a Purpose? (1971)

Almost nine years ago, Adorno answered the question "Does philosophy still have a purpose?" as follows: "The only philosophy we might responsibly engage in after all that has happened would no longer make any pretense of being in control of the absolute. Indeed, it would have to forbid itself to think the absolute, lest it betray the thought. And yet it must not allow anything to be taken away from the emphatic concept of the truth. This contradiction is its element."[1] Now, this contradiction has been an element of any philosophy that is to be taken seriously since the death of Hegel. The question taken up by Adorno does not arise by accident; since the end of the great philosophy, it has accompanied all philosophy like a shadow. Of course, in this shadow four (maybe five) generations of philosophers have survived Marx's dictum on the elimination of philosophy. Today the question whether the shape of the philosophic spirit has changed a second time presses upon us. If at that time what was in retrospect called great philosophy had met an end, today the great philosophers themselves seem to share this fate. Even after the systematic claim to a continuation of the *philosophia perennis* was relinquished, the type of philosophy propounded by influential teachers has continued in the last century and a half. Now the signs are growing that this type of thought embodied in individual philosophers is losing its power.

Even Heidegger's eightieth birthday was only a private event. The death of Jaspers left no trace. Primarily theologians seem to be interested in Bloch. Adorno has left a chaotic terrain behind him. Gehlen's most recent book is hardly of more than biographical value. This is all, of course, a provincial, German perspective. However, if I am correct, in the Anglo-Saxon countries and in Russia philosophy has for decades been at that stage which the title of Germany's official journal of philosophy, *Zeitschrift für philosophische Forschung*, announces for the discipline: the stage of research in which scholarly progress is collectively organized. I do not at all wish to lament this condition, but it justifies my beginning with the German example. The phenomenon in which we are interested seems to have taken shape here in a conspicuous way: the transformation of a spirit which, till yesterday so to speak, moved in the medium of the older philosophy. Of course, I am not pursuing this question for the sake of an edifying retrospective. The goal of these reflections is not an elegy to philosophy but an exploration of the tasks legitimately posed for philosophy today, when not only has the great tradition come to an end but so (in my view) has the style of thought bound to individual erudition and personal testimony.

1

I would like to set out from four observations that can be made in view of German philosophy during the last half-century.

1. First of all, one is struck by the astonishing continuity of the schools and the chief problematics. The theoretical approaches that dominated philosophical discussion in the 1950s and the 1960s had already arisen in the German-speaking world in the 1920s. At that time basically five philosophic impulses succeeded against the imperial status of Neo-Kantianism, whose influence reached far beyond Germany's boundaries: with Husserl and Heidegger a phenomenology oriented partially toward transcendental logic and partially toward ontology; with Jaspers, Litt, and Spranger a *Lebensphilosophie* that linked up with Dilthey and was tinted by existentialism and by Neo-Hegelianism; with Scheler and Plessner (and in a certain way with Cassirer, too) philosophical anthropology; with Lukács, Bloch, Benjamin, Korsch, and Horkheimer a critical philosophy of society harking back to Marx and Hegel; and with Wittgenstein, Carnap, and Popper the logical positivism centered in the Vienna Circle. After World War II (that is to say, after the exile and suppression of the better part of German philosophy) these traditions did not break up at all; instead they returned in slightly changed constellations, often in the same persons, theories,

and schools. The lone exception was Neo-Positivism, which had become the dominant philosophy in the Anglo-Saxon countries and had evolved and diversified in an unusually fruitful way. In the 1950s this form of philosophy started to react on Germany from outside and indirectly gained great influence in the philosophy departments here: Not one of the successful "Viennese" emigrants returned. But all the central figures who determined the philosophical scene in Germany in the last two decades—Heidegger, Jaspers, Gehlen, Bloch, Adorno, Wittgenstein, and Popper—may easily be located in the traditional molds of the 1920s.

2. The continuity of development is reinforced by the uninterruptedly personalized form of appearance taken by philosophical thought. It is no accident that the philosophical constellations can be characterized without great difficulty in terms of names. Up to our own day philosophic thought has moved in a dimension in which the form of presentation does not remain extrinsic to the ideas. The factual unity of theoretical and practical reason that till now has been expressed in this sort of individualized thinking requires communication not just on the level of propositional content but also on the metacommunicative level of interpersonal relations. In this respect philosophy has never been a science; it remained constantly bound to the person of the philosophical teacher or author. It is itself noteworthy that up till now philosophy in Germany has preserved the rhetorical element, even among those who raise a hue and cry against it in the name of scientism.[2] Of course, among us there are signs of a depersonalization of philosophy as well. Probably in a few years the posture taken for granted in the past will strike us as old-fashioned. I am speaking of the rhetorical gesture with which Heidegger, Jaspers, Gehlen, Bloch, and Adorno have expounded, paraded and spread their ideas as academic teachers before their students and the literary public, in political publications, and even in the mass media. As the example of Jaspers shows, an expressive or highly stylized language is by no means always needed for this, although the selection of key words in philosophy, no matter how desiccated the German of the lectern may otherwise be, always has more than a merely terminological significance; it also has an expressive quality for the purposes of indirect communication. Maybe among the general public the place of this philosophy appearing in representative persons will be taken by the synthetic scientific "world

view" projected in ever-new versions by popularizers among the spec-ialized scientists or by journalists of science who are not dilettantes.

3. Fascination with the recent historical phenomenon of fascism is worth noting as far as the evolution of philosophy in Germany is concerned. The violence of this objective process polarized all camps. Even the philosophers and philosophies of the 1920s and the early 1930s are forcibly shifted into the perspective of the spiritual prehistory of fascism; they cannot claim an indifference to what came to pass. The innocence of a neutral self-understanding was all over after 1945 anyway. Political biography separates those exiled and returned (such as Bloch, Horkheimer, and Adorno) from the "inner" emigrants of many shadings (such as Jaspers and Litt) and from the intellectual outriders or temporary emergency auxiliary of the regime (such as Heidegger, Freyer, and Gehlen). Of course, this biographical mortgage would not have remained important for more than two decades were it not that the problem of an indirect intellectual authorship of political crimes, and the general problem of the practical consequences and by-products of philosophizing, had persisted and indeed had not been taken care of as a systematic question. In spite of the question of guilt and collective liability, which Jaspers raised and then let trickle away, none of the participants has investigated the spiritual causality between the content of a philosophical doctrine and its legitimating function for the actions of others who appeal to it, even with respect to a neutral example such as Rousseau or Nietzsche. On the one hand, the unintended consequences are no more to be subjectively imputed (as we put it) to the philosophical teacher than to any other author; on the other hand, the objective effective-historical context is no more extrinsic to a philosophic work than to any other. This can still be grasped fairly well in terms of Hegel's distinction between morality [*Moralität*] and ethics [*Sittlichkeit*] or of Marx's category of false con-sciousness. The questions are these: How, if the biographical con-sciousness of the author and the historiographical awareness of those coming after are not to be well-meaningly separated through time and social role? How, if the teaching and the experience of the un-intended political consequences coincide in the self-reflection of one and the same person, and, moreover, have to be worked through with a view to future praxis? How are radical thinking and a teaching with manifold political consequences possible, in such a way that the one doing the philosophy neither overextends his responsibility by mor-

alizing (and grows rigid in horror before anticipated indeterminate eventualities) nor abandons himself to the objective lack of responsibility and proceeds lightheartedly toward activism or toward abstinence from praxis? Only a satisfactory response to this question would give us a chance of identifying the errors that beset philosophical thinking on the precarious level of effective history and of bringing the risk of error under control. Until now, loss of identity seems to have been the punishment for admitting errors; at any rate, this explanation makes intelligible the uniquely resistant behavior of all those who could have given succor to something they did not want.

4. Doing philosophy in Germany is characterized by a critical relationship to the times, which stands in unique contradiction to its academicism. Regardless of their useful research, none of the schools that feel obligated to their traditions and want to pursue something like 'pure' philosophy—whether it be the continuation of ontology (as Neo-Scholasticism and Nicolai Hartmann did), or in connection with the philosophy of reflection (as in the outcroppings of Neo-Kantianism), or on the basis of a new codification of the more recent analytical philosophy—has produced first-rate interpretations and really productive minds in the same measure as the philosophical orientations that do not cultivate such a sublime shyness about being affected by things. The more productive schools have broken with the claim to autonomy of a philosophy of origins [*Ursprungsphilosophie*] perched on some ultimate grounding. Philosophical anthropology and (within the context of philosophy of history) critical social philosophy both attempt to integrate the material contents of the human sciences. Hermeneutic phenomenology and existentialism, wherever they explicitly engage traditional questions (say, the question about the being of whatever is) also break out of the framework of self-sufficient theoretical philosophy. Even Neo-Positivist theory of science and linguistic criticism basically express a practical interest in enlightenment and a rational way of life, despite their scientistic self-understanding. Thus, there was no philosophical position worth naming that was not implicitly joined to a (if you will) normative theory of the present age. In contradistinction to the academically domesticated business of teaching in other parts of the world, in postwar Germany the leading philosophical teachings have contained (often at the price of analytic purity) an explosive potential for a critique of the present age, ranging from authoritarian institutionalism, through the cultural criticism stylized in terms of the

history of Being and the cultural pessimism on the Left, to a radical utopian critique of society. This critique of the times ran against the grain of the objective trends of the development of the epoch in a remarkable way: In its deepest intention, not one of the philosophies named conforms to the current social and political order. That holds as true for the irrationalist impulses of Heidegger and Gehlen as for the dialectical critiques of Bloch and Adorno. However, not only a backward-looking escapism into the immediacy of Being or into the great institutions, and not only a future-oriented thinking with emancipatory intent lacks the complacency of a philosophy that has been established self-confidently in its *juste milieu*, that knows itself to be at one with the progress of the epoch, or that has regressed in self-satisfaction into specialized research; in Germany such identifications are lacking even in liberal thought. This can be seen in the subterranean Jacobinism of a Jaspers just as clearly as in the abstract, enlightened rigidity of those influenced by Popper (e.g., Topitsch and Albert).

The fourth observation, like the third, refers to the specifically German context in which a unique contour of the spirit that had already collapsed in other places could be conserved during the last half-century. This peculiar combination of capacity for insight and autism, of stubbornness and sensitivity, belongs in the context of a development characterized by retardation and noncontemporaneity. Three mutually compatible theories of noncontemporaneity construe the same phenomenon as typically German: the theory of retarded capitalist development,[3] the theory of the belated nation,[4] and the theory of postponed modernity.[5] Within this framework, room is found for special assumptions about the social descent and the political situation of the German bourgeois cultural establishment, especially the officialdom.[6] For all these theories the key phenomena are the setbacks of the peasants, the establishment of an official Protestantism as the national church, the territorial fragmentation of the Reich and the belated attainment of national unity, the slow infiltration of the new modes of production, the delayed and then explosive unfolding of industrial capitalism, the class compromise between a bourgeoisie without political independence and a nobility unshaken for a long time in its social foundations and in its bureaucratic-military positions of leadership, the pseudo-religious redemptive function of cultural humanism, a radicalized but apolitical inwardness, bureaucratic bondage of the spirit, intellectual aristocratism and state ideology, the rigid authoritarian structures of the bourgeois nuclear family, inhibited urbanization, and so on. This list may be lengthened arbitrarily with superficially characteristic clichés. It circumscribes a complex of historical developments that stand out like geological faults in comparison with the processes of modernization in England and France. If the theories of noncontemporaneity (for which the parallel development of neighboring states serves as the norm) are right, there may be a correlative ambivalence; in Adorno's pointed words,

As the meshes of the civilizational network—of bourgeoisification— were not in fact so finely spun over long stretches of time in Germany, a store of unseized natural power was maintained. It generated the unswerving radicalism of the spirit as much as the permanent possibility of regression. Consequently, just as Hitler is scarcely to be ascribed as a fate to the German national character, so it was hardly accidental that he made his climb to power in Germany. Hitler would not have been able to thrive without that German seriousness which is stirred by the pathos of the absolute and without which the best would not be. In Western countries where the game rules of society have penetrated the masses more deeply, he would have fallen prey to laughter.[7]

The same ambivalence is expressed in the philosophical spirit. The angular stance toward a process of sociation that itself deviates from the normal course of capitalist development, of the formation of the nation-state, and of modernization makes this spirit sensitive to the loss of human substance which the violent advance of rationalization demands of a society (which even so persists in its quasi-natural antagonisms) but also to the necessity of forcing this progress in a retarded country in order to lessen the barbarism within archaic realms of life, which only comes into appearance against the background of possible rationalization. The subtle balance of these simultaneously achieved insights—which means insight into the dialectic of the enlightenment— is most difficult wherever philosophy is incapable of appreciating itself and its situation with respect to the real process, for the philosophy that claims to be master of what is absolutely primary and strikes the pose of a demiurge has to derail dialectic from its insight. In the name of some evoked primal time or depth or remoteness or strength, it then resists the advance of rationality; or in the name of an overarching faculty of reason [*Vernunft*], it sacrifices the intellect [*Verstand*] to utopian visions—this is another relic of mystical rapture. "The holy seriousness," as Adorno concludes the reflection quoted above, "can pass over into the bestial seriousness, which in virtue of its hubris is literally projected as the absolute and rages against everything that does not yield to its claim."[8] This frenzy of philosophic thinking was often the price paid in Germany for an insight that was surely more easily gained here, precisely on account of this angular stance, than from a triumphant common sense: the insight that the absolutism of intellect [*Verstand*] transforms method into raving madness.

If there does exist a connection between the observed peculiarities of German philosophy and the peculiarities of socio-economic and political development that theories of noncontemporaneity claim to explain, then the suspicion that that type of thinking will soon come to an end attains the force of a prognosis, for in the meantime the Federal Republic (which, ironically, was prepared for by upheavals of the social structure under the Nazi regime) has made up for the non-contemporaneities during this postwar period of reconstruction. Under administratively regulated capitalism, Germany (the Federal Republic) has, for the first time in centuries, become a contemporary of Western Europe. Superstitiously one still fears to say it out loud: We are living today in one of the six or seven most liberal nations and in one of the six or seven social systems with the fewest internal conflicts (however great they may be). What were once specifically German conflicts have, in spite of the division of the nation, almost completely disappeared. It seems that those conflictual tensions that once were intellectually productive (in that they led to feelings of a more delicate sensibility) and were transposed into stimuli and spiritual provocations are shifting to America in the wake of a thoroughly comfortable Swissification of Europe; at any rate, in the United States the talk is about a Europeanization, even a Germanization, of culture.[9] There is growing there, among other things, a curious interest in problematics and traditions in which we can recognize philosophical approaches of the 1920s.

If that prognosis is correct, and we cannot pretend more than a certain plausibility for such loosely interwoven speculations, the question whether philosophy still has a purpose arises anew and with still greater urgency. If the problem of the context of the emergence (and preservation) of a specifically German tradition of thought is supposed to be defused, could a simply critical interest be satisfied with the prospect that doing philosophy in our country will become at once more uninteresting and less risky? Beyond the good feeling of getting rid of national idiosyncrasies, the unsettling question remains whether, after the downfall of systematic philosophy and now even the retreat of philosophy itself, it is still possible to do philosophy, and, if it is, for what purpose philosophy is needed. Why should not philosophy, like art and religion, fall victim to the world-historical process of rationalization described in historical terms by Max Weber and expressed conceptually by Horkheimer and Adorno in their dialectic? Why should not even philosophy itself fade away in the graveyard of a spirit that can no longer affirm and realize itself as absolute? Does philosophy still have a purpose today, and will it tomorrow?

2

To find at least a tentative answer, we ought to look closely at the structural changes initiated in philosophical thought with the break in tradition signaled by Hegel's death and investigated by Löwith (in *From Hegel to Nietzsche*) and Marcuse (in *Reason and Revolution*). To this end, I would like to put forward and elucidate four quite oversimplifying assertions about philosophy, and indeed about the basic intentions it pursued from its beginnings until Hegel. These affirmations are based on the familiar view that Greek philosophy brought to validity for the first time "the claim of the *Logos*," whatever that may mean, as against the mythic form of world interpretation. Philosophy, like mythology, was a system of interpretation that comprehended nature and the human world at once. It apprehended the cosmos—being as a whole. In this respect, philosophy could replace myth. Of course, it did not tell naive stories but inquired methodically after reasons. Although philosophy never entirely stripped away the traces of sociomorphic world images (Topitsch), there followed necessarily from its theoretical claim a depersonalization of the interpretation of the world. The plausible ordering of phenomena requiring explanation into contexts of interaction among acting and speaking quasi-persons equipped with superior powers no longer satisfied the explanatory claim of philosophy. Then, too, philosophy had to give up the link of mythical narrative with ritual action. A certain form of cultic practice survived in highly sublimated forms (even in the operations of university departments), but it was not to be permitted in a thematic way. Consequently, philosophy could not replace myth in its stabilizing function for the practice of life. Its own relationship to practice had instead to be secured in a mediated fashion by means of initiation into a theoretical form of life.

Setting out from these global observations, I would like to defend the following affirmations:

a. The unity of philosophy and science was not called into question in principle until Hegel. With the beginnings of philosophic thought, the notion was formed of theoretical knowledge for whose validity reasons could be made explicit; philosophy and science were one without question. The initial specialization of particular spheres of knowledge proceeded until the late Middle Ages as an internal differentiation; disciplines (e.g., mathematics and physics) remained part of philosophy insofar as they could pose a theoretical claim. Insofar as they pursued a sheerly descriptive intent (as did historiography or geography) they were banished to an empirical sphere bereft of theory, but they were defined exactly in virtue of this negative relation to philosophy as the authentic science. This changed only with the rise of the modern natural sciences, which could still be conceived of as primarily *philosophia naturalis*. But even in contrast with them philosophy did not withdraw into the sphere of competence of merely formal science or to complementary fields such as ethics, aesthetics, and psychology; it affirmed the claim to provide ultimate foundations for all theoretical knowledge with which metaphysics stands or falls. Philosophy remained the foundational science right into the nineteenth century.

b. Until Hegel the unity of philosophical doctrine and tradition, in the sense of a tradition that legitimates domination, was not called into question in principle. Philosophy is a figure of the spirit that emerges only under conditions of high civilization (that is, in social systems where the ruling power is centralized in a state); there the need for the legitimation of the political system is met in general by world views with origins in myth or in the high religions. Although the truth claim of philosophy competes with the normative claim of these traditions, and although certain philosophies entered repeatedly into public conflict with the particular claims of tradition, philosophical criticism never completely left the context of tradition behind. As long as philosophy pretended to apprehend being as a whole, it afforded a derivation of basic socio-cosmic assumptions which themselves could take over functions in relation to the legitimation of domination. In bourgeois society, rational natural right dissolved the Christian justifications of political domination.

c. Until Hegel, philosophy and religion always claimed to fulfill different functions. Since late antiquity, philosophical thought was compelled to specify its relationship to the saving truth of the Judeo-Christian redemptive religion. Its theoretical solutions varied from a fundamental critique of biblical tradition, through declarations of indifference and incompatibility, to the grand attempts to identify philosophical knowledge with revelation or revelation with philosophical knowledge. But in no case, despite Boethius, did a philosophy serious about its claim want to replace the certainty of salvation of religious faith. It never offered a promise of redemption, confident expectation, or consolation. No doubt Montaigne, with the affirmation that philosophy means studying the art of dying, revived an ancient topos; however, the stoic preparation for one's own death is precisely the expression of the lack of consolation that pertains to philosophical thinking in principle.

d. Philosophy was the affair of a cultured elite; it never reached the masses. The organizational forms of philosophical teaching and the social composition of its addressees have changed during the course of the history of philosophy, but as a matter of fact and as a result of its self-understanding philosophy has from the very beginning been the preserve of those who possessed leisure—i.e., those released from productive labor. The prejudice of a spiritual aristocracy that the many are by nature incapable of philosophic insight accompanied philosophy until Hegel. In the eighteenth century it was interrupted from time to time by the representatives of the philosophy of the Enlightenment, but in those days the absence of a universal system of education meant that their problematic lacked a real basis.

If these global affirmations should happen to be right, what has changed since the death of the last systematic philosopher of undisputed rank? What structural changes justify the thesis about the end of "great" philosophy? I will try to respond to this question by commenting on the four affirmations advanced here.

ad a. The unity of philosophy and science has become problematic in the meantime. Philosophy had to give up its claim to be a foundational science in relation to physics as soon as it could develop and ground a cosmology only in dependence on the results of research in the natural sciences and no longer in virtue of its own competence.

Hegel's philosophy of nature remained the last. In the early modern period philosophy reacted to the rise of modern science in such a way that it clothed its claim to ultimate grounding in the guise of epistemology. But after Hegel the philosophy of primordiality could no longer be defended even from this position of retreat. With positivism, epistemology resigned in favor of the theory of science (in other words, the reconstruction of scientific method after the fact).

ad b. Meanwhile the unity of philosophy with the tradition has become problematic. After the release of physics from the philosophy of nature and after the breakdown of metaphysics, theoretical philosophy shrunk to the theory of science or itself became a formal science. Practical philosophy thereby lost its link with theoretical philosophy. With the Young Hegelians and with the systematic motifs developed in Marxism, existentialism, and historicism, practical philosophy became independent. Increasingly, it made do without the ontological grounding that had been taken for granted by politics and ethics since Plato. In addition, it conceded the outspokenly theoretical claims with which the philosophy of history had made the sphere of human affairs, rather than nature, into its characteristic objective field (Vico). Hence, philosophy lost the possibility of supporting socio-cosmic world views; only now could it become radical critique. The newly independent practical philosophy was drawn into the alignment of fronts in the European civil war; since that time there can be something like a revolutionary philosophy, and a reactionary philosophy as well.

ad c. The complex and shifting relationship between philosophy and religion has also changed in the meantime. On the one hand, a philosophy that had to relinquish the idea of the One or the Absolute along with its claim of ultimate grounding also had to criticize the idea of the one God that had evolved in the high religions more radically than before. Metaphysics had heretofore been in a more promising situation to either substitute for or conceptualize (in order to integrate) the competing form of world interpretation. Postmetaphysical thought does not dispute determinate theological affirmations; instead it asserts their meaninglessness. It means to prove that in the system of basic terms in which the Judeo-Christian tradition has been dogmatized (and hence rationalized) theologically meaningful affirmations cannot be set forth at all. This critique is no longer related immanently to its object; it strikes at the roots of religion and opens the way to a historical-critical dissolution of the dogmatic contents themselves, which began in the nineteenth century. On the other hand, the newly independent practical philosophy entered into the heritage of redemptive religion, where metaphysics never had been able to claim a substitute or competitive function. The ambivalent connection between the tradition of the Augustinian or Joachitic theology of history with the bourgeois philosophy that arose in the eighteenth century had prepared the way for the invasion of salvational claims into philosophy. However, only after both the cosmological and transcendental philosophical foundations for the unity of practical and theoretical philosophy were broken and a self-reflection restricted to the sphere of the history of the species entered in place of ultimate grounding did philosophy, with a characteristic turn toward the utopian and the political, take into itself an interest in liberation and reconciliation, which till then had been interpreted in religious terms.

ad d. In philosophy there was ingrained from the start a contradiction between the claim of reason to the universal validity of knowledge and the culturally elitist confinement of access to philosophy. Since Plato this contradiction has often found expression in a political philosophy that demanded power for the privileged ones who were capable of insight, thus providing both philosophical justification for the established domination and dogmatic universality for philosophical knowledge. As investigations done with some of my students have shown,[10] the motif of a spiritually grounded elite has remained influential in the humanistically cultivated social models. Of course, this finding is itself an indicator of a development that started with the extension of higher education in the nineteenth century in a way that was prototypical in Germany. Through the education of *Gymnasium* [high school] teachers in the "philosophical" faculties of the new universities, which were set up in accord with Humboldt's reforms, philosophy was established as both a specialty and a background ideology of the emerging *Geisteswissenschaften* and became widespread in the sections of the bourgeoisie that understood themselves as cultured. Without any revision of its culturally elitist self-understanding, an institutionally secured diffusion of philosophy tailored to the academy got started just at the moment when philosophy had given up its authentic systematic claim. On this basis, philosophy became a ferment within the formation of bourgeois ideology. In the workers' movement, philosophy attained a completely different influence by way of Marx. Here the elitist barriers by which philosophy had set itself in contradiction with itself seemed to fall away. Indeed, Marx must have had this in mind when he asserted that if philosophy were to be realized it would have to be overcome.

After Hegel, philosophical thought passed over into another medium. A philosophy that absorbs into its awareness the four structural changes mentioned above no longer conceives itself as philosophy; it understands itself as critique. Critical of "first philosophy," it dispenses with ultimate grounding and affirmative interpretations of being as a whole. Critical of the traditional determination of the relationship of theory and practice, it apprehends itself as the reflective element of social activity. Critical in equal measure of the claims to totality made by metaphysical knowledge and by religious interpretations of the world, it is, with its radical critique of religion, the basis for absorbing the utopian contents of both religious tradition and the cognitive interest in emancipation. Finally, critical of the elitist self-understanding of the philosophical tradition, it takes its stand on universal enlightenment—about itself as well. Adorno and Horkheimer understood this self-enlightenment in terms of the "dialectic of the enlightenment"; it terminates in Adorno's *Negative Dialectics*. At this point, of course, the questions arise whether on the way toward critique and self-critique philosophy has not been robbed of its content, and whether ultimately (contrary to the self-understanding of a critical theory of society[11]) it offers only the empty exercise of a self-reflection that takes up the objects of its own tradition without still being capable of any systematic idea.[12] If this is the way things stand, does philosophy still have a purpose?

3

In recent decades philosophy has gained a reluctant political influence on public awareness, although in their appearance and in their thinking philosophers themselves have been more caught up with the traditional contents and the gesture of great philosophy than with its systematic claim. Philosophical thought in its stage of critique, whether it was aware of itself as critique or not, fed on its heritage. At the same time, it opened up a new dimension for the movement of philosophical thought, namely that of a substantive critique of science.

The way philosophy has determined its relationship to modern science has been decisive for the development of modern philosophy itself. Since the seventeenth century, the impulses that have been formative and explosive of systems have in general come from epistemological questions. However, since the middle of the nineteenth century, after first philosophy had collapsed even in its epistemological form, the theory of science has taken the place of epistemology. By *theory of science [Wissenschaftstheorie]* I mean a methodology pursued with a scientistic self-understanding of the sciences, and by *scientism* I mean faith in science in itself—the conviction that we should no longer apprehend science as one form of possible knowledge but should identify knowledge with science.[13] What is scientistic is the attempt to ground the knowledge monopoly of the sciences and to provide in this sense a norm for the metatheoretical self-understanding of the sciences. This effort is carried forward today on a level of subtle argumentation by those schools within analytic philosophy that have never relinquished the basic intention of the Vienna Circle.

Just a few decades ago scientism could be regarded as an internal academic affair. This has changed since the sciences that generate technically usable knowledge began to exercise significant social functions. In advanced industrial systems, economic growth and the dynamics of total social development have become largely dependent on scientific and technological advances. In the same measure that "science" has become the most important productive force and the subsystems of research and education are credited with a functional primacy in determining the direction of social evolution (Luhmann), all of the following have taken on direct political significance: the action-orienting notions of theoretical knowledge, of scientific method, and of scientific progress; the connections between technological application and practical enlightenment and the general transposition of scientific information into the practice of life; and the interpretation of the relationships of experience, theory, and consensus-forming discourse. Therefore, the interpretation and critique of science has political consequences in equal measure.

This critique of science pursues two points of view. On the one hand, scientism has not done justice to the research practice of the historical and social sciences. As long as there is no system of basic concepts for the objective domain of systems of communicative action (concepts that are theoretically fruitful and capable of being made operational in a way that is comparable to the basic concepts for the objective domain of bodies in motion and observable events), a pseudo-normative theory of science that does not at all allow for a differentiated constitution of objective domains has to exercise a retarding effect, at least on the development of social sciences that do not produce technologically applicable knowledge but only knowledge that orients action. This is exactly the category of knowledge that is functionally necessary for a practically rational guidance of the productive power of science together with its social consequences and by-products. On the other hand, scientism establishes a universal concept of science that justifies technocratic steering mechanisms and excludes rational procedures for the clarification of practical questions. However, if practical questions no longer count as capable of truth and if deciding questions capable of being true can lead only to information that is technologically applicable (i.e., serves the orientation of purposive rational action, corresponding to the basic assumptions of scientism), then the connection between scientific-technological progress and social practice that has become relevant today is either a matter of empirical analysis and technical control or altogether unaccessible to rationalization, whether it be left to arbitrary decision or to unreflective, or quasi-natural, self-regulation. In this case, the complex of issues central to overall social development would be removed from the realm of problems accessible to discursive clarification and rational formation of consensus. Then the division of labor between the technocratic planning of state bureaucracies and giant organizations and the more or less autodidactic cultural syntheses of individual scientists or science journalists (who are supposed to maintain the legitimating power of the scientistic notion of science) would be inevitable.

If, on the contrary, democratic planning as the steering mechanism for developed social systems is not to be excluded from the outset, a critique that had entered into the heritage of philosophy would have to take over three urgent tasks (besides other things). It would have to criticize the objectivistic self-understanding of the sciences and any scientistic concept of science and scientific progress, it would have to deal especially with basic issues of a methodology of the social sciences in such a way that the elaboration of adequate basic concepts for systems of communicative action were not hindered but promoted, and it would have to clarify the dimension in which the connection of the logic of research and technological development with the logic of consensus-forming communication becomes clear. Such a critique would have to secure upon its own proper basis the contents flowing into it from the results of the empirical sciences and from the utopian traditions. In conventional terms, it would have to be a theory of the sciences and a practical philosophy at once.

There are three philosophical approaches that are characterized by this link at the present time. There is Popper's critical rationalism, which has emerged from a self-critique of both the empiricist and the formalist limitations of logical positivism. Then there is the methodological philosophy of Paul Lorenzen and the Erlanger School, which in conjunction with motifs from Hugo Dingler discloses the practical-normative foundations of the sciences and of a rational formation of consensus. And, in conjunction with Horkheimer, Adorno, and Marcuse, there is the so-called critical theory, which pursues a program of the theory of knowledge as a theory of society.

If there exists a philosophy in the face of which the question "Does philosophy still have a purpose?" need no longer be raised, then today, according to our reflections, it would have to be a philosophy of science that is not scientistic. If it communicated with the sciences and with scientists themselves, it would find in the rapidly expanding university system a broader basis of influence than philosophy had ever enjoyed before. It would no longer have any need of the organizational form of a doctrine embodied in individual philosophers. It would incur a politically effective task inasmuch as it went against the twofold irrationality of a positivistically restricted self-understanding of the sciences and a technocratic administration isolated from publicly discursive formation of will. For this precise reason, whether the approaches to a theory of the sciences with practical intent that are discernible today will attain practical influence is not within the immanent power of philosophically specialized discussion. A philosophy that idealistically credited itself with this power would have forgotten the idea over which philosophy entering the stage of critique had labored for almost a century and a half. In this respect, the future of philosophical thought is a matter of political practice.

Philosophical thinking sees itself confronted not only with the fixations of a technocratic consciousness but at the same time with the collapse of religious consciousness. Only today is it clear that the philosophical interpretation of the world confined to a cultured elite depended precisely on coexistence with a widely influential religion. Philosophy, even after assimilating utopian impulses from the Judeo-Christian tradition, has not been capable of mastering by means of consolation and trust the *de facto* meaninglessness of death in its contingency, that of individual suffering, or that of the private loss of happiness—in general, the meaninglessness of the negativity of the risks built into life—in a way that had been possible for the religious hope in salvation. In the industrially advanced societies we observe for the first time as a mass phenomenon the loss of the hope in redemption and the expectation of grace, which, even if no longer within an ecclesiastical framework, are still supported by interiorized faith traditions. For the first time the mass of the population has been shaken in the basic levels of securing its identity; in limit situations it cannot get away from a fully secularized everyday awareness and have recourse to institutionalized or at least deeply internalized certainties. Some indicators speak in favor of the fact that, in reaction to the mass loss of the religious certainty of salvation, a new Hellenism is taking shape, that is, a regression below the level of identity reached in communication with the one God in the monotheistic high religions. Many small subcultural ersatz religions are forming in marginal groups that are extraordinarily differentiated geographically, socially, and with respect to content. These ersatz religions range from transcendental meditation to new communal rituals and half-scientific training programs to collective self-help organizations (often with goals that are only apparently pragmatic) to small activist groups trying to transform the world under the sign of political theology, anarchism, or sexual politics. Perhaps all these subcultures are based on a similar motivational structure. From the perspective of the theological tradition, these new interpretations of the world and of human existence present themselves as a new paganism that finds expression in a new pluralism of idol worship and local mythologies. Such retrospectively oriented comparisons are dangerous. They are no match for the unique ambivalence lurking within the "new" potential for conflicts (I mean the ambiguity of withdrawing from motivation and of protest, the ambiguity of regressive dedifferentiation and of innovation). Perhaps these ambiguities can be demonstrated both on the level of personality structures and on the level of the group structures that hold together precisely complementary potentials.

In the face of these ambivalent phenomena attached to the collapse of ego and group identities within high civilizations, a philosophical thought in communication with the sciences and effective at large could provide no more than the fragile unity of reason, namely the unity of identity and the nonidentical that is established in rational discourse.

Notes

1. T. W. Adorno, *Eingriffe* (Frankfurt am Main, 1963), p. 14.

2. See, for example, H. Albert, "Plädoyer für kritischen Rationalismus," in *Das 198. Jahrzehnt*, ed. C. Grossner et al. (Hamburg, 1969).

3. G. Lukács, "Über einige Eigentümlichkeiten der geschichtlichen Entwicklung Deutschlands," in *Die Zerstörung der Vernunft* (Berlin, 1955).

4. H. Plessner, *Die verspätete Nation* (Stuttgart, 1959). Cf. Habermas, "Die Traktate über die Wurzeln deutschen Ungeistes," in *Philosophisch-politische Profile* (Frankfurt, 1971).

5. R. Dahrendorf, *Gesellschaft und Demokratie in Deutschland* (Munich, 1965). Cf. Habermas, ibid., p. 234.

6. F. K. Ringer, *The Decline of the German Mandarins* (Cambridge, Mass., 1969). Cf. Habermas, ibid., p. 239.

7. T. W. Adorno, "On the Question: What is German?" in *Stichworte* (Frankfurt, 1969).

8. Ibid., p. 106.

9. E.g., C. G. Schorske, "Weimar and the Intellectuals," *New York Review of Books*, May 7 and 21, 1970.

10. Habermas et al., *Student und Politik* (Neuweid, 1961).

11. A. Wellmer, *Gesellschaftstheorie und Positivismus* (Frankfurt, 1969).

12. B. Willms, "Theorie, Kritik, Dialektik," in *Über Th. W. Adorno* (Frankfurt, 1968); R. Bubner, "Was ist Kritische Theorie?" in *Hermeneutik und Ideologiekritik* (Frankfurt, 1971).

13. Cf. Habermas, *Erkenntnis und Ineresse* (Frankfurt, 1968).

The German Idealism of the Jewish Philosophers (1961)

"The Jew can play a creative role in nothing at all that concerns German life, neither in what is good nor in what is evil." This statement by Ernst Jünger has outlived the anti-Semitism of the conservative revolutionaries in whose name it was written more than a generation ago. I heard the identical assertion just a few years ago in the philosophy department of one of our great universities. As this version had it, Jews at best attain stardom of the second rank. At that time, when I was a student, I did not give it a second thought; I must have been occupied with reading Husserl, Wittgenstein, Scheler, and Simmel without realizing the descent of these scholars. However, the well-known philosophy professor who gainsaid the productivity of his Jewish colleagues did know of their origins. The stubbornness of the components of an ideology whose discrepancies could be conveyed by any lexicon is remarkable. If it were a matter of dissecting into pieces a form of the spirit such as that of German philosophy in the twentieth century, separating it out according to its parts, and putting it on the scales, then we would find in the domain supposedly reserved for German profundity a preponderance of those the same prejudice wants to assign to the outer court as merely critical talents.

It is not my intention here to offer another proof of what has long since been demonstrated. There is another situation much more in need of clarification: It remains astonishing how productively central motifs of the philosophy of German Idealism shaped so essentially by Protestantism can be developed in terms of the experience of the Jewish tradition. Because the legacy of the Kabbalah already flowed into and was absorbed by Idealism, its light seems to refract all the more richly in the spectrum of a spirit in which something of the spirit of Jewish mysticism lives on, in however hidden a way.

The abysmal and yet fertile relationship of the Jews with German philosophy shares in the social fate that once forced open the gates of the ghettos, for assimilation or reception of the Jews into bourgeois society became a reality only for the minority of Jewish intellectuals. Despite a century and a half of progressive emancipation, the broad mass of the Jewish people had not gotten beyond the formal aspects of equal rights. On the other hand, even the courtly Jews, like their successors, the Jewish bankers of the state of the nineteenth century, never became fully acceptable socially. Indeed, they had not striven so seriously to break down the barriers of their invisible ghetto; a universal emancipation would have threatened what privileges they possessed. Assimilation stretched only a thin protective layer around the permanently foreign body of Jewry. Its medium was a culture gained academically, its seal a baptism often socially coerced. If these cultivated Jews would give back to the culture intellectually as much as they owed to it, their social standing remained so ambivalent right into the 1920s that Ernst Jünger could not only deprecate their productivity as the "feuilleton prattle of civilization" but also put in question the process of assimilation: "To the same extent that the German will gains in sharpness and shape, it becomes increasingly impossible for the Jews to entertain even the slightest delusion that they can be Germans in Germany; they are faced with their final alternatives, which are, in Germany, either to be Jewish or not to be." This was in 1930, when those who could not adapt to a dubious politics of *apartheid* were already being offered the menacing promise that was so gruesomely kept in the concentration camps.

And so, precisely out of the marginal strata that had been assimilated most successfully, there emerged the spokesmen for a turning back of the German Jews to the origins of their own tradition. This movement found its political expression in Zionism and its philosophic expression in the (as it were, anticipated) existentialism of Martin Buber, who fastened onto the last phase of Jewish mysticism. The Polish and Ukrainian Hassidism of the eighteenth century had drawn its ideas from kabbalist writings, but the doctrine had retreated so far behind the personality of the Hassidic holy men that the traditional, ideal figure of the learned rabbi was pushed out by that of the folkish

Zaddik, whose existence was the Torah become entirely and utterly living. In Buber's zeal against the rationalistically stultified teaching of the rabbis and his appropriation of the religion of the people, which was full of mythic legends and mystical faces, a new pathos of existential philosophizing was enflamed:

With the destruction of the Jewish communal spirit the fruitfulness of the spiritual conflict became weakened. Spiritual force is mustered henceforth on behalf of the preservation of the people against outside influences; the strict enclosure of one's own realm, to protect against penetration by alien tendencies; the codification of values in order to fend off every shift in values; the unmistakable, unreinterpretable, hence consistently rational formulation of religion. In place of the God-filled, demanding, creative element there entered the ever more rigid, merely preserving, merely continuing, merely defensive element of official Judaism; indeed, it was directed ever more against the creative element, which seemed to endanger the status quo of the people by its audacity and freedom; it became its persecutor and life-enemy.

The Hassidic impulse first found a philosophical language in the work of Franz Rosenzweig. Rosenzweig, who with Buber translated the Bible into German, had worked on Hegel's philosophy of state as a student of Friedrich Meinecke. In his own great project he attempted—as the title of the three-volume work, *Star of Redemption*, announced from afar—an interpretation of Idealist thought out of the depths of Jewish mysticism. Not only was he one of the first to establish links with Kierkegaard; he also took up motifs of the so-called late Idealism, especially from Schelling's last philosophy; thus he divulged the lineage of existentialist philosophy decades before it was painstakingly rediscovered by the official history of philosophy. The basic question on which the Idealist self-confidence in the power of the concept shatters is this: "How can the world be contingent, although it still has to be thought of as necessary?" Thought labors in vain on the impenetrable fact that things are so and not otherwise, that they are simply contingent, that the historical existence of human beings is so profoundly bathed in enigmatic arbitrariness:

Inasmuch as philosophy . . . denies this opaque presupposition of all life; that is, inasmuch as it does not let death count as something real but makes it into nothing, it conjures up for itself the illusion of presuppositionlessness. . . . If philosophy wanted not to stop up its ears in the face of the cry of anguished humanity, it would have to start from this: that the nothingness of death is a something; that each new nothingness of death, as a new newly fruitful something, is not to be talked or written away. . . . Nothingness is not nothing, it is something. . . . We do not want a philosophy that deceives us by the all-or-nothing tone of its dance about the lasting domination of death. We want no deception.

The deception that has been seen through leads to the insight that the world, in which there is still laughter and crying, is itself caught up in becoming — the appearances still seek their essence. In the visible happening of nature is disclosed the growth of an invisible realm in which God himself looks forward to his redemption: "God, in the redemption of the world by human beings and of human beings in relation to the world, redeems himself."

Idealism only entered into competition with the theology of creation; still in bondage to Greek philosophy, it did not look upon the unreconciled world from the standpoint of possible redemption. Its logic remained in the grips of the past: "True lastingness is constantly in the future. Not what always was is lasting; not what gets renewed at all times, but solely what is to come: the kingdom." The meaning of this, of course, is only disclosed to a logic that does not, like that of Idealism, deny its linguistic body; it has to open itself up to the underlying logic deposited in the language — a resonance from the ancient kabbalist idea that language reaches God because it is sent out from God. Idealism condemned language as the instrument of knowledge and elevated a divinized art as its substitute. A Jew actually anticipated Heidegger, the *philosophicus teutonicus*, in this peculiarly heightened awareness.

Toward the end of World War I, Rosenzweig sent home the manuscript of *Star of Redemption* by mail from the field of battle. The way he conceived of the messianic vocation of Jewish exile during his time on the Balkan front is documented by a passage from one of his letters: "Because the Jewish people already stands beyond the opposition that forms the authentically dynamic power in the life of the nations, beyond the polarity of particularity and world history, of home and faith, of earth and heaven, so, too, it does not know war."

Another Jewish philosopher, Hermann Cohen, had on Christmas Day 1914 burdened the consciences of students withdrawing from their studies to the field of battle with the thought that the political expression of the messianic idea is eternal peace: "Since the prophets as international politicians recognized evil as existing neither exclusively nor especially in individuals but in the nations instead, so the disappearance of war, eternal peace among the nations, became for them the symbol of morality on earth." Cohen, who so idiosyncratically takes Kant's idea of eternal peace back into the Old Testament, stands, however, in a different camp than Buber or Rosenzweig. He represents the liberal tradition of Jewish intellectuals who were inwardly connected with the German Enlightenment and supposed that in their spirit they might be capable of feeling at one with the nation in general. Immediately after the outbreak of the war, Cohen delivered before the Kant Society of Berlin a remarkable speech ("On the Peculiarity of the German Spirit") in which he exhibited to the imperialistic Germany of Wilhelm II and his military forces the original testimony of German humanism. Indignantly he dissociated himself from the "insulting" distinction between the nation of poets and thinkers and that of fighters and state builders: "Germany is and remains in continuity with the eighteenth century and its cosmopolitan humanity."

Less cosmopolitan is the tone of his apologia: "in us there struggles the originality of a nation with which no other can compare." This kind of loyalty to the state later delivered over those who in deluded pride called themselves National German Jews to the tragic irony of an identification with their attackers.

Cohen was the head of the famous Marburg School, in which there flowed the Jewish erudition of a generation that philosophized in the spirit of Kant and transformed Kant's teachings into an epistemology of natural science. Kant (who, after all, was so amazed at the linguistic power of Moses Mendelssohn that he once stated that "if the muse of philosophy should choose a language, she would choose this one") likewise selected, as a partner in the academic disputation concerning his *Habilitationsschrift*, a Jew: the onetime physician Marcus Herz. Just as Lazarus Bendavid had done in Vienna, in Berlin Herz put his all into propagating Kantian philosophy. The first one to go beyond promulgation to appropriate the new criticism in a productive way, and to push it radically beyond its own presuppositions was the genial Salomon Maimon, who had been inspired in his youth by Spinoza. Maimon went from being a beggar and vagrant to being a scholar protected by a patron; Fichte, who was not the least bit modest, conceded superiority to him without envy. Maimon, as Fichte wrote to Reinhold, has revolutionized Kantian philosophy from the ground up "without anyone's noticing." "I believe," continued Fichte, "future centuries will bitterly mock ours." German historians have not taken any impulse from this. This first generation of Jewish Kantians entered into oblivion, as did Kant in general.

It was the polemical writing of another Jew—the cry of Otto Liebmann that "there must be a return to Kant!"—that paved the way for a second Kantianism since the middle of the last century. Cohen was able to return to the matrix of problems prepared by Maimon. Cohen's great student Ernst Cassirer summarized his teacher's intention at Cohen's grave: "The primacy of activity over passivity, of the independent-spiritual over the sensible-thinglike, should be carried through purely and completely. Any appeal to a merely given should fall aside; in place of every supposed foundation in things there should enter the pure foundations of thinking, of willing, of artistic and religious consciousness. In this way, Cohen's logic became the logic of the origin."

Besides the direct "Marburg line," however, Arthur Liebert, Richard Honigswald, Emil Lask, and Jonas Cohn played a decisive role in the Kantian-tinted epistemology of the turn of the century. Moreover, Max Adler and Otto Bauer developed a Kantian version of Marxism. In this climate there was a exuberant development of the acuity in commentary and analysis that is ambiguously ascribed to the Jews as a natural quality—and that even Martin Buber suspects of a "dissociated spirituality," "a spirituality dissociated from the matrix of natural living and from the functions of a genuine spiritual conflict, neutral, insubstantial, dialectical, that could give itself to all objects, even the most indifferent, in order to dissect them conceptually or to place them in reciprocal relationships, also without really belonging in an intuitive-instinctual way to any one of them."

Now, it may be that the theories of knowledge and science that considered themselves to be without history and presuppositions did in fact appeal to the inclinations of those Jews who once had to achieve freedom of thought by renouncing tradition. The attachment of the generations brought up in the ghetto to the condition of an enlightened culture was purchased with a break from age-old obligation, a leap into a foreign history; for example, Mendelssohn had to keep his work with German literature secret from his fellow Jews! Perhaps the physiognomy of Jewish thought was also shaped by the fact that something of the distance characteristic of an originally foreign gaze had been preserved in it. Just as once-familiar things are more naked to an emigrant who has returned home after a long time, so a peculiar sharpness of vision is characteristic of one who has become assimilated. Because he lacks intimacy with the cultural realities that have been cooled down for his appropriation, they relinquish their structures to him all the more easily.

On the other hand, the rabbinic and especially the kabbalistic hermeneutics of the Holy Scriptures had schooled Jewish thought for centuries in the exegetical virtues of commentary and analysis, and the Jewish mind was drawn whenever possible by epistemology because its method gave a rationalized shape to its long-since customary mystical problematic. The mystic obtains the stages of the theogony, the developmental history of the coming to be of the Godhead, by turning the path of his soul toward God; consequently, his knowledge is always mediated by transcendental reflection on the mode of his own experience. It is no accident that Simmel's introduction to philosophy uses the mysticism of Meister Eckhart as the key to Kant's Copernican turn.

Kant's attractiveness to the Jewish mind is naturally to be explained first of all by the way he unfolded the free attitude of criticism based on rational belief and of cosmopolitan humanity into its most clairvoyant and authentic shape (aside from Goethe). Kant's humanism influenced the convivial social interchange—assimilation without insult—that had its moment in the salons of Berlin around the turn of the nineteenth century. What is more, critique was also the means of Jewish emancipation from Judaism itself. It not only secured an urbane attitude and worldly tolerance on the part of Christians; it also offered the philosophical tool with which the grand self-dynamism of the Jewish spirit sought to master its religious and social destiny. Jewish philosophy, in all its versions, has remained critique.

Society does not permit emancipation without a break. Because assimilation assumed forms of submission, many assimilated Jews became all the more Jewish in their private lives as a rigorous identification with the expectations of their environment allowed less and less room for them to present themselves publicly as anything other than emphatically German. This tension, so transparent from a social-psychological point of view, emerges from a posthumous work of

Cohen dedicated to the memory of his Orthodox father, "Religion of Reason from the Sources of Judaism." The Kantian rationalism of the Marburg School stripped away the specific pathos it owed to its Lutheran lineage; the theory was, so to speak, secularized again. But finally the layer of "civilization" to which the *Zivilisationsjuden* (as they were called) seemed so completely to have given themselves over broke open, and the question of the bindingness of the Mosaic Word of God pushed the aged Cohen to the margins of his system. Insofar as the humanity of nations had taken on the form of a culture purified by philosophy and science, they surely shared the same religion of reason. However, the concept of reason, pictured in the image of a primordial spring, was illumined for the first time in history by the testimonies of the Jewish prophets. With utter rigor Cohen sought to salvage the autonomy of reason in relation to the positive nature of revelation. His philosophical conscience came to rest at last with the following tortuous notions: "If I am dependent upon the literary sources of the prophets for the concept of religion, so too would these remain mute and blind if I did not—under their tutelage, to be sure, but not just guided by their authority—approach them with a concept which I made the basis of my learning from them."

Of course, present-day theory of knowledge and science has not been determined by Cohen but by two other Jewish scholars. Inside Germany the phenomenology of Edmund Husserl and internationally the logical positivism inaugurated by Ludwig Wittgenstein have become a predominant in this period.

In the year of Hermann Cohen's death, Wittgenstein's *Tractatus Logico-Philosophicus* appeared, opening with the lapidary statement "The world is everything that is the case." Wittgenstein was a major influence on the Vienna Circle, in which the Jews Otto Neurath and Friedrich Waismann were prominent. Later on, Jewish emigrants contributed to the worldwide triumph of the new doctrine. In the United States, Hans Reichenbach was the main influence; in Great Britain, Wittgenstein himself. At Cambridge, Wittgenstein led the life of a reclusive *Privatdozent*. Without publishing anything, and in the quiet of his colloquia with a small circle of students, he brought about the turn from logical to linguistic analysis. The chief concern of linguistic analysis was no longer with the analysis and step-by-step construction of a universal language that would picture facts. It did not serve a systematic purpose but rather a therapeutic one of explaining any given formulations by means of language analysis and expressing their meaning in "perfect clarity." Philosophical responses were confined to recommendations of this or that mode of expression and ended in the artistry of language games that found satisfaction exclusively in themselves.

After two and a half decades of silence and shortly before his death, Wittgenstein gave in to the urgings of his friends and students and allowed a second book, *Philosophical Investigations*, to appear. He added a foreword full of resignation: "Up to a short time ago I had really given up the idea of publishing my works in my lifetime. . . . I make them public with doubtful feelings. It is not impossible that it should fall to the lot of this work, in its poverty and in the darkness of this time, to bring light into one brain or another—but, of course, it is not likely." In *Philosophical Investigations* Wittgenstein extols as his authentic discovery one that makes us capable of breaking off philosophizing at any given place. Philosophy is supposed to come to rest, so that it can no longer get put in question by questioning itself. Already in the *Tractatus* his deeper impulses had been revealed in the following statement: "We feel that, even when all possible questions have been answered, the problems of life remain completely untouched. Of course there are then no questions left, and this itself is the answer. The solution of the problem is seen in the vanishing of the problem. (Is this not the reason why those who have found after a long period of doubt that the sense of life became clear to them have then been unable to say what constituted that sense?" Wittgenstein does not hesitate to apply this insight to his own reflections: "My propositions serve as elucidations in the following way: Anyone who understands them eventually recognizes them as nonsensical, when he has used them—as steps—to climb up beyond them. (He must, so to speak, throw away the ladder after he has climbed up to it.) . . . What we cannot speak about we must pass over in silence." Such a silence has a transitive meaning. Even what has been uttered must be taken back again into the broken silence. Rosenzweig's remark that "there is nothing more Jewish in the deeper sense than an ultimate misgiving toward the power of the word and an inward trust in the power of silence!" reads like a comment on this. Because Hebrew is not the language of the assimilated Jew's everyday life but is removed from this as the sacred language, he is deprived of the ultimate and most obvious freedom from constraint in life, which is to say, in his torment, what it is that he suffers: "For this reason he cannot speak with his brother at all, with him the look conveys far better than the word. . . . Precisely in silence and in the silent sign of discourse does the Jew feel even his everyday speech to be at home in the sacred speech of his ceremonial hour."

The Kabbalah differs in a characteristic way from other mystical traditions: The written tradition is meager; there is a complete absence of mystical autobiography.Gershom Scholem, the historian of Jewish mysticism, reports that the kabbalists were bound to silence or to oral transmission alone; most manuscripts were abolished, and few of those that were still extant reached print. Seen from this vantage, Wittgenstein's use of language in speaking about the mystical appears thoroughly consistent: "There are, indeed things that cannot be put into words. They make themselves manifest. They are what is mystical."

In contrast, Husserl sought to ground philosophy as an exact science precisely on the basis of a rigorous description of phenomena that make themselves manifest "by themselves" and are "given" intuitively in unmediated evidence. Transcendental phenomenology shares its intent with logical positivism, but not its path. Both fasten on the Cartesian starting point of doubt that never despairs of itself; however, the things [*Sachen*] to which Husserl would penetrate are not semantically and syntactically analyzable sentences of natural or scientific languages but achievements of consciousness out of which the meaningful network of our life world is constructed. Husserl did not wish to derive these intentions and their fulfillments, but simply to let them be seen from their "ultimate conceivable experiential standpoint"; in this he distinguished himself sharply from the Neo-Kantians and from the older Idealism in general. One day Plessner accompanied his teacher Husserl home after a seminar; he recalls the following: "When we reached his garden gate his deeper displeasure erupted: 'I have always found German Idealism in its entirety disgusting. All my life I'—and here he drew up his slender walking stick with the silver handle and pressed it against the gateposts—'have sought reality.' In an unsurpassably plastic way the walking stick portrayed the intentional act and the posts its fulfillment."

Husserl was isolated in his Freiburg home as the political horizon began to cloud over. He could lecture publicly about his mature philosophy only outside Germany, in Vienna and Prague. (He died in 1937.) Unlike Wittgenstein, he did not withdraw the systematic claim into the self-complacency of linguistic glass-bead games or into the stillness of the mystically unspeakable. Instead he attempted a great final project that was supposed to apprehend the crisis of the European sciences as the crisis of European humanity and to overcome it. Against the waves of fascist irrationalism, Husserl wanted to erect the dam of a renewed rationalism: "The reason for the failure of a rational culture . . . lies not in the essence of rationalism itself but solely in its being rendered superficial, in its entanglement in 'naturalism' and 'objectivism.' " In a genuinely Idealist fashion, he believed he could head off the disaster if only he could successfully ground the *Geisteswissenschaften* in a phenomenologically exact way. The crisis seemed to be rooted precisely in that a rationalism rendered superficial sought its grounding in a false and perilous way, by a natural scientific reduction of all spiritual phenomena to their physically explainable substructures. Instead of this, Husserl believed that the spirit should climb back into itself and clarify the achievements of consciousness hitherto hidden to itself. Husserl placed his trust in the world-moving force of this "theoretical attitude": " . . . this is not only a new cognitive stance. Because of the requirement to subject all empirical matters to ideal norms, i.e., those of unconditioned truth, there soon results a far-reaching transformation of the whole praxis of human existence, i.e., the whole of cultural life."

Though he had a rather questionable way of phrasing it, Husserl would have liked to bestow on philosophers the vocation of "functionaries of humanity." In his earlier works he had worked out the procedures through which phenomenologists would be assured a correct cognitive attitude. A kind of derealizing of reality was supposed to dissolve their interested involvement in the process of real life in order to make pure theory possible. In this withdrawn state, which he called *epoche*, Husserl daily exercised an admirable asceticism. He meditated for months and years, and from the written reports of his meditations grew the mountains of posthumous research manuscripts—documents of a working philosophy neither lectured on nor published. What Husserl practiced, then, was a methodological exercise. When politics drew him away from contemplation, however, the old philosopher attributed to it a bearing on the philosophy of history. The theory that grew out of a withdrawal from all praxis was supposed in the end to make possible the "new sort of praxis" of a politics directed by science—"a praxis whose aim is to elevate mankind through universal scientific reason according to norms of truth of all forms, to transform it from the bottom up into a new humanity made capable of an absolute self-responsibility on the basis of absolute theoretical insights."

This little mantle of philosophy of history was already threadbare before Husserl drew it over his doctrine, which was unhistorical to the core. And yet his stance is captivating: He fought for his lost cause with pathos and with the illusion of pure theory.

How much this cause was lost became evident in 1929 in the famous dispute between Cassirer and Heidegger in Davos. The theme was Kant, but in truth the end of an epoch was up for discussion. The opposition of the schools paled beside that of the generations. Cassirer represented the world to which Husserl belonged against his great pupil—the cultivated world of European humanism against a decisionism that invoked the primordiality of thought, whose radicality attacked the Goethe culture at its very roots.

It is no accident that the Goethe cult at the start of the nineteenth century was created in the salon of Rachel Varnhagen, for it is certain that no one else strove with such intensity to live in accord with the model of Wilhelm Meister, who understood the "cultivation of personality" so peculiarly and so deceptively as an assimilation of the bourgeois to the nobleman, as did those Jews who were also called "exceptional Jews of culture." What they expected of that model has been expressed by Simmel: "Perhaps no one has lived as symbolic a life as Goethe, since he gave to each only a piece or facet of his personality and yet at the same gave 'the whole to everyone.' To live symbolically in this manner is the only possibility of not being a comedian and a role player." The interiorized Goethe promised not only the way to assimilation, but also the solution to the Jews' ordeal of constantly having to play a role without being capable of being identical with oneself. In this twofold respect, the culture of German classicism was socially necessary for the Jews. Perhaps it is precisely for this reason that we owe to them the most sensitive aesthetic reflections, from Rosenkranz and Simmel, through Benjamin and Lukács, down to Adorno.

In the course of the conversations at Davos, a student put three questions to Cassirer; each of his responses closed with a Goethe citation. Heidegger, however, polemicized against the flaccid aspect of a human being who merely made use of the works of the spirit;

Heidegger wanted "to cast [things] back upon the toughness of fate." The discussion came to an end with Heidegger's refusal to take Cassirer's outstretched hand. What Heidegger announced four years later, at the Leipzig election rally of German scientists in the name of Hitler's party, reads today like a continuation of these events: "We have broken with the idolization of a thinking without grounding and power. We are seeing the end of a philosophy capable of serving it. . . . The primordial courage in the confrontation with what is—either to grow from it or to be shattered by it—is the innermost motivation behind the inquiry of a science rooted in a national people (*völkischen Wissenschaft*). For courage lets us go forward; courage releases us from what has held true up to now; courage risks the unaccustomed and the incalculable." It was this incalculable factor that Cassirer had at that very moment to escape. Emigration led him to the United States by way of Sweden and England. There he wrote his final work, *Myth of the State*, whose closing chapter deals with the technique of modern political myths and ends with a commentary on a Babylonian legend: "The world of human culture could not arise before the darkness of myth was vanquished and overcome. But the mythical monsters were not definitively destroyed."

Heidegger's questionable victory over the humanitarian intellectuality of Cassirer takes on a special inexorability from the fact that he convicted the enlightened position of a real weakness as well: In the face of the thought now proclaimed as "radical," the roots of the eighteenth century do not reach sufficiently deep. Before the eighteenth century there was no Jewish West, only the Middle Ages of the ghetto. A return to the Greeks, whenever it was attempted by Jews, always had about it something of a lack in power. Power secretly resided only in the depths of their own tradition, the Kabbalah.

Over the centuries the kabbalists had elaborated the technique of allegorical interpretation, before Walter Benjamin rediscovered allegory as the key to knowledge. Allegory is the counternotion of symbol. Cassirer had conceived every content of myth, philosophy, art, and language as the world of symbolic forms. In that world's objective spirit, human beings communicated with one another, and in it alone were they able to exist at all, for in the symbolic form—as Cassirer believed himself capable of saying with Goethe—the inconceivable is wrought, the ineffable is brought to speech, and the essence is brought to appearance. But Benjamin recalled that history—in all that it contains from the outset of the untimely, the painful, the failed—is shut off from expression through the symbol and from the harmony of the classical pattern. Only allegorical representation succeeds in portraying world history as a history of suffering. Allegories are in the realm of thoughts what ruins are in the realm of things: "To preserve the unfreedom, imperfection, and brokenness of the sensible, the beautiful physis, was essentially denied to classicism. Precisely this, however, the allegories of the baroque, hidden beneath their bold pomp, bring out with hitherto unanticipated emphasis."

Before the gaze schooled in allegory the innocence of a philosophy of symbolic forms is lost; before it is disclosed the fragility of that foundation—firmly and conclusively established, so it seemed, by Kant and Goethe—of an enlightened culture of beauty. It was not as though Benjamin had given up its idea, but he saw in its roots the schizoid nature of precisely those "cultural values" and "cultural treasures" that Jews were discussing so naively. In truth, history was the triumphal procession of the rulers over those lying on the ground: "According to traditional practice, the spoils are carried along in the procession. They are called cultural treasures. . . . There is no document of civilization that is not at the same time a document of barbarism. And just as such a document is not free of barbarism, barbarism taints also the manner in which it was transmitted from one owner to the other." [Benjamin, *Illuminations* (New York, 1969), p. 256]

Benjamin took his own life in 1940 when, after his flight through southern France, the Spanish border officials threatened to deliver him over to the Gestapo. The theses on the philosophy of history that he left behind are among the most moving testimonies of the Jewish spirit. In it the dialectic of the enlightenment, which in its broken progress dominates the as yet undecided course of history, is held fast in the form of an allegorical interpretation. The ninth thesis says

A Klee painting named "Angelus Novus" shows an angel looking as though he is about to move away from something he is fixedly contemplating. His eyes are staring, his mouth is open, his wings are spread. This is how one pictures the angel of history. His face is turned toward the past. Where we perceive a chain of events, he sees one single catastrophe which keeps piling wreckage upon wreckage and hurls it in front of his feet. The angel would like to stay, awaken the dead, and make whole what has been smashed. But a storm is blowing from paradise; it has got caught in his wings with such violence that the angel can no longer close them. This storm irresistibly propels him into the future to which his back is turned, while the pile of debris before him grows skyward. This storm is what we call progress. (*Illuminations*, pp. 257–258)

Benjamin was not the first to break through the circle of Jewish thought devoted to the theory of science and to epistemology, which later was expanded to encompass the philosophy of history. Already Simmel, who had been a friend of George and Rilke as much as of Bergson and Rodin, had crossed the boundaries of the then dominant academic philosophy: "There are three categories of philosophers: one group hears the heartbeat of things, a second only that of human beings, a third only that of concepts; a fourth group, the philosophy professors, hears only the heart of the literature."

In Simmel's posthumous writings there is a characteristic fragment on the art of the drama that deals with an experience that often lends a nervous dynamism to the private lives of assimilated Jews. Hannah Arendt, the clever historian of anti-Semitism, has described how the philo-Semitic circles in *fin de siècle* Paris accepted cultivated Jews with the curious compliment that one could no longer even tell their descent; they were supposed to be Jews, but not be like Jews:

In this ambiguous back and forth each of the individuals in question was an accomplished actor; it was only that the curtain that should have normally brought the play to an end would never again be lowered and the people who had made a theatrical role out of their entire lives no longer knew who they really were, even in solitude. If they entered into society, they instinctively detected those who were like them; they recognized one another automatically from the unusual mixture of arrogance and anxiety that had determined and fixed each of their gestures. Out of this there arose the knowing smile of the clique—which Proust discussed at such length—which . . . only indicated secretly what everyone else present had long known, namely that in every corner of the salon of Countess So-and-so there was sitting another Jew who was never allowed to admit it, and who without this in itself insignificant fact would oddly enough never have arrived in the much sought after corner.

On top of this, Jews who were held personally responsible for the pitilessness of their environment in terms of an "enigmatic demonism of mask changing" could not but become sensitive to the role character of human existence in general. If I bring one of Simmel's insights into connection with this sharpened sensibility, this does not bring its validity into doubt. It goes as follows:

We not only do things to which culture and the blows of fate induce us from without, but we inevitably represent something that we really are not. . . . It is very seldom that a person determines his mode of behavior in complete purity out of his very own existence; usually we see a preexisting form before us which we have filled with our individual conduct. Now this: that the human being experiences or represents a predesignated other as the development entrusted to him as most centrally his own, so that he does not simply abandon his own being, but fills the other with this being itself and guides its streams into those manifoldly divided arteries whose paths, though running a preset course, absorb the whole inner being into this particular shape—this is the pre-form [*Vorform*] of the art of theater. . . . In just this sense we are all somehow actors.

Helmut Plessner, too, developed his general anthropology out of his "anthropology of the actor." The human being does not merely live in the midst of his body, like the animal. Without being able to eliminate this centering, he also falls outside it; he constantly has to relate to himself and to others, to lead a self-enacted life in accord with the "director's instructions" of the society:

As a relation-to-himself the actor is the person of a role, for himself and for the spectator. In accord with this relationship the players and spectators only repeat, however, the distancing of people from themselves and one another that pervades their daily life. . . . For what is this seriousness of everydayness in the end but realizing-oneself-bound-to-a-role which we want to play in society? To be sure, this role-playing does not want to be a performance. . . . the burden of image-projecting for our social role is taken from us by the tradition into which we were born. Nonetheless, we, as virtual spectators of ourselves and the world, have to see the world as a stage.

An anthropology that apprehends the human in terms of his compulsion to play a role finds its continuation without any break whatsoever in sociology. Simmel, like Plessner, worked in a sociological mode; so, too, did Max Scheler, the real founder of philosophical anthropology. During his last years, Scheler taught sociology at the University of Frankfurt, which had gained fame, in virtue of the influence of Franz Oppenheimer, Gottfried Salomon, Carl Grünberg, and Karl Mannheim, as a center of sociological research. There Max Horkheimer united his chair in philosophy with the directorship of the Institute for Social Research, and even Martin Buber became a sociologist.

The Jewish spirit dominated sociology from the days of Ludwig Gumplowicz on. The Jews' experience of society as something one runs up against was so insistent that they carried along a sociological view, so to speak, right from their doorsteps. In neighboring disciplines, too, it was they who were the first to employ a sociological point of view. Eugen Ehrlich and Hugo Sinzheimer founded the sociology of law. Ludwig Goldscheid and Herbert Sultan were the leading sociologists of finance.

The imagination of Jewish scholars in general was sparked by the power of money—Marx, especially the young Marx, was an example of this. In this regard the intimate enmity of the cultured Jews toward the moneyed Jews—that sublime intra-Jewish anti-Semitism against the stratum whose *imago* was minted by the Rothschilds—might have been a motive. Simmel, himself the son of a salesman, even wrote a "Philosophy of Money." In Simmel, however, one also finds the other typically Jewish interest besides the sociological: the interest in a philosophy of nature inspired by mysticism. His diary includes this: " . . . treat not only each human but also each thing as if it were an end in itself that would result in a cosmic ethics." The mystical link between morality and physics is again encountered here, in Kantian terminology. Simmel's friend Karl Joel wrote about the "Origins of Philosophy of Nature from the Spirit of Mysticism." In the 1920s, David Baumgardt undertook to repair the so-called injustice done to Baader, whom a positivistic age had forgotten so completely. In Baumgardt's "Franz Baader and Philosophical Romanticism," a Jew comes across the golden vein of those speculations on the ages of the world— so pregnant for a philosophy of nature—that lead from Jacob Böhme via Swabian Pietism to the Tübingen seminarians Schelling, Hegel, and Hölderlin. Even before this, Richard Unger had recognized in Hamann's tension-filled relationship to the Enlightenment the "realistic strain" of Protestant mysticism, which, with its acceptance of a ground of nature in God, is differentiated from the spiritualistic mysticism of the Middle Ages.

Even Scheler's and Plessner's sketches of a philosophy of nature exhibit a certain strain of this tradition. Despite all their sober elaboration of materials from the particular sciences, they still betray a speculative bent that stems from nature mysticism; Scheler's cosmology even reverts explicitly to a God that becomes.

However, all these Jewish scholars seem not to have attained full awareness of what force had set them on the path of this special tradition. They had forgotten what was still generally known at the close of the seventeenth century. As Scholem reminds us, Johann Jacob Spaeth, a disciple of Böhmean mysticism, overcome by the consonance of this doctrine with the theosophy of Isaac Luria, went over to Judaism. A few years later, the Protestant pastor Friedrich Christoph Oetinger (whose writings Hegel and Schelling as well as Baader had read) sought out in the ghetto of Frankfurt the kabbalist Koppel Hecht in order to be initiated into Jewish mysticism. Hecht responded that "Christians have a book that speaks about the kabbalah more clearly than the Zohar"; what he meant was the work of Jacob Böhme.

It was this kind of "theology" Walter Benjamin had in mind when he remarked slyly that historical materialism would be a match for anything if only it would take theology into its service. This reception actually happened with Ernst Bloch. In the medium of his Marxian appropriation of Jewish mysticism, Bloch combines sociology with the philosophy of nature into a system that today is borne along as is no other by the great breath of German Idealism. In the summer of 1918 Bloch published *The Spirit of Utopia*, which holds up a Marxism confined to economics to a mirror. *The Spirit of Utopia* is comparable to a *Critique of Pure Reason* for which the *Critique of Practical Reason* still needed to be written. Bloch writes

Here the economy is sublated; but what is missing is the soul, the faith for which room is to be made; the clever, active gaze has destroyed everything, to be sure, much that needed destroying. . . . Also it disavowed with good reason the all-too-arcadian socialism, the utopian-rationalist socialism that had reemerged since the Renaissance in the secularized guise of the Thousand-Year Reich, and often enough merely as a formless drapery, the ideology of very sober class goals and economic revolutions. But of course the utopian tendency is not adequately conceived in all this; nor is the substance of its wish images met and judged; and it certainly does not rid us of the primordial religious desire . . . to share in the divine essence, finally to be installed chiliastically in the goodness, freedom, and light of the *telos*.

In Lurianic mysticism the idea is developed of the universe's arising in virtue of a process of shrinkage and contraction; God withdraws into an exile within himself. In this way the primordial impenetrability and power of matter is explained, as well as the positive character of evil, which can no longer be facilely evaporated into a shadow side of the good. On the other hand, this dark ground remains a nature in God; the nature of God remains a divine potency, the world soul or *natura naturans*. Into these depths reaches the notion Bloch lays at the basis of speculative materialism: Matter is in need of redemption. Since the time of that theological catastrophe described by the Zohar in the image of a shattering of a vessel, all things bear within themselves a break; they are, as Bloch expresses it, abstracted forms of themselves. The process of restoration was almost already completed when Adam's fall once again threw the world down from its proper stage and threw God back into exile. This new age of the world, with the ancient goal of the redemption of humanity, of nature, and indeed of the God knocked off his throne, is now the responsibility of humans. Mysticism becomes a magic of interiority, for now the outermost reality depends on what is most inward. (An old saying from the Zohar guarantees the redemption as soon as only a single community does perfect penance.) Prayer becomes a manipulative activity with significance for the philosophy of history.

For Bloch, political praxis replaces religious practice. The chapter "Marx, Death, and Apocalypse" also bears the subtitle "On the Way of the World, How What is Turned Inward Can Get Turned Outward." In this chapter is found the following statement:

For ages matter has been an embarrassment not only for those seeking knowledge, but an embarrassment in itself; it is a demolished house within which the human being did not come forth; nature is a rubbish heap of deceived, dead, rotted, confused, and wasted life. . . . Only the good, thoughtful person holding the key can usher in the morning in this night of annihilation, if only those who remained impure do not weaken him, if only his crying for the Messiah is inspired enough to stir up the saving hands, to ensure for himself in a precise way the grace of attainment, to arouse in God the forces drawing us and himself over, the inspiriting and grace-filled forces of the Sabbath reign, and thus to swallow up in victory the raw, satanic, breathtaking moment of conflagration of the apocalypse and straightaway to vanquish it.

Bloch's five-part work *The Principle of Hope* contains his clearest elucidation of this early vision and of its place in intellectual history. He has now sublated the Schelling of *Ages of the World* into the Marx of the *Paris Manuscripts*:

Human abundance as well as that of nature as a whole . . . , the real genesis, is not at the beginning, but at the end; and it starts coming to be only when society and human existence become radical, that is, take hold of themselves at the roots. The root of history, however, is the toiling, laboring human being, who develops whatever has been given and transforms it. Once he has apprehended himself and grounded being without estrangement and alienation in real democracy, there thus arises in the world something that appears to everyone during childhood and yet within which no one ever was: home.

Because Bloch recurs to Schelling, and Schelling had brought from the spirit of Romanticism the heritage of the Kabbalah into the Protestant philosophy of German Idealism, the most Jewish elements of Bloch's philosophy—if such categories have any meaning at all—are at the same time the authentically German ones. They make a mockery of the attempt to draw such a distinction at all.

Just as Bloch (from the Schellingian spirit) and Plessner (from the Fichtean spirit) appropriated German Idealism and made good its prescient insights in relation to the present state of the sciences, so too it was Jewish scholars (friends of Walter Benjamin) who thought out Hegel's dialectic of the enlightenment to a point where the ongoing beginning opens up a view of the still outstanding end: Theodor Adorno, Max Horkheimer, and Herbert Marcuse, preceded by the early Georg Lukács.

I wrote this piece for a series of radio programs devoted to "Portraits from German-Jewish Intellectual History." Thilo Koch, to whose initiative the series must be credited, requested all contributors to record in concluding the experiences they had as authors during the course of working on their theme. My conclusion follows.

Wherever genuine philosophizing begins mere reportage comes to an end, and my task was only the latter. I had hesitations about undertaking it. Would not this undertaking—despite the high hopes with which it was planned—pin a Jewish star on the exiled and the beaten once again?

At the age of 15 or 16 we sat before the radio and experienced what was being discussed before the Nuremburg tribunal; when others, instead of being struck silent by the ghastliness, began to dispute the justice of the trial, procedural questions, and questions of jurisdiction, there was that first rupture, which still gapes. Certainly, it is only because I was still sensitive and easily offended that I did not close myself to the fact of collectively realized inhumanity in the same measure as the majority of my elders. For the same reason, the so-called Jewish question remained for me a very present past, but not itself something present. There was a clear barrier against the slightest hint of distinguishing Jews from non-Jews, Jewish from non-Jewish, even nominally. Although I had studied philosophy for years before I started on this study, I was not aware of the lineage of even half of the scholars named in it. Such naiveté is not adequate today, in my opinion.

Scarcely twenty-five years ago the cleverest and most important German theorist of state law—not just some Nazi, but Carl Schmitt himself—was capable of opening a scientific conference with the horrible statement that "we need to liberate the German spirit from all Jewish falsifications, falsifications of the concept of spirit which have made it possible for Jewish emigrants to label the great struggle of Gauleiter Julius Streicher as something unspiritual." (I assume you know who Streicher was.) At that time Hugo Sinzheimer responded from his exile in Holland with a book on the Jewish classics of German jurisprudence. In his conclusion, Sinzheimer turns his attention to this same Carl Schmitt: "If one attends to the origins of the scholarly activity of the Jews at the time of the emancipation, it is not a matter of an influence of the Jewish spirit on German scientific labor. . . . Perhaps nowhere else in the world has the spiritual life of Germany celebrated greater triumphs outside its origins than precisely in this period when the ghetto was opened up and the intellectual powers of the Jews, held in check for so long, encountered what were the heights of the culture of Germany. It is the German spirit that lies at the basis of the Jewish influence."

To repeat this truth and to confirm it once again in connection with the fate of the Jewish philosophy is, of course, not unimportant, and yet it is still based on a question dictated by the opponent. Meanwhile the question of anti-Semitism itself has been disposed of—*we* have disposed of it by physical extermination. Hence, in our deliberations it cannot be a matter of the life and survival of the Jews, of influences back and forth; only we ourselves are at stake. That is to say, the Jewish heritage drawn from the German spirit has become indispensable for our own life and survival. At the very moment when German philosophers and scientists started to "eradicate" this heritage, the profound ambivalence that so eerily colored the dark ground of the German spirit was revealed as a danger of barbarism for everyone. Ernst Jünger, Martin Heidegger, and Carl Schmitt are representatives of this spirit in its grandeur, but in its perilousness as well; that they spoke as they did in 1930, 1933, and 1936 is no accident. And that this insight has not been realized a quarter of a century later proves the urgency of a discriminating kind of thinking all the more. This has to be one with that fatal German spirit and yet split with it from within to such an extent that it can relay an oracle to it: it must not cross the Rubicon a second time. If there were not extant a German-Jewish tradition, we would have to discover one for our own sakes. Well, it does exist; but because we have murdered or broken its bodily carriers, and because, in a climate of an unbinding reconciliation, we are in the process of letting everything be forgiven and forgotten too (in order to accomplish what could not have been accomplished better by anti-Semitism), we are now forced into the historical irony of taking up the Jewish question without the Jews.

The German Idealism of the Jews produces the ferment of a critical utopia. Its intention finds no more exact, more worthy, more beautiful expression than in the Kafkaesque passages at the end of Adorno's *Minima Moralia*:

Philosophy, in the only way it is to be responsive in the face of despair, would be the attempt to treat all things as they would be displayed from the standpoint of redemption. Knowledge has no light but what shines on the world from the redemption; everything else is exhausted in reconstruction and remains a piece of technique. Perspectives would have to be produced in which the world is similarly displaced, estranged, reveals its tears and blemishes the way they once lay bare as needy and distorted in the messianic light. To gain such a perspective without caprice and violence, utterly from sympathy with the objects—this alone is important to the thinker. It is the simplest thing of all, because the situation cries out urgently for such knowledge, yes, because the completed negativity, once it is brought entirely into view, includes the mirror script of its opposite. But it is also something utterly impossible, because it presupposes a vantage point, even though it might concern a minute matter, which is removed from the range of human existence, whereas, of course, any possible knowledge does not have to be bullied merely by that which is in order to prove normative; but precisely for this reason it is itself fraught with the same distortion and neediness it intended to evade. The more passionately thought girds itself against its conditionedness for the sake of the unconditional, the less consciously and hence more perilously does it fall to the world. It even has to conceive its own impossibility for the sake of possibility. In relation to the exigency that thereby impinges upon it, the question about the reality or unreality of redemption itself is almost a matter of indifference.

Karl Jaspers: The Figures of Truth (1958)

Truth, Jaspers has it, can be proved only by the depth, the authenticity, and the rank of its existential presentation; philosophically, it cannot be established rationally in an unequivocal way that is binding for all. The manifoldness of the figures of historical truth is indissoluble; any one of them is immediate to God. No one can share in all or even in several of them as their born representative, so to speak, but one can tolerate them and attend to them as possibilities in which the truth makes itself known to others. To this end, Jaspers believes himself quite capable of joining the intention of complete tolerance with the mood of unconditional resoluteness. Whoever does not wish to communicate with "alien" truths in this attitude only confirms his own lack of truth. So all philosophical ideas are subject to the question whether they hinder or promote communication; this is their highest criterion. Jaspers's involuntary isolation under the Nazi regime exacerbated earlier experiences and made the breakdown of communication appear to him as the absolute evil.

The "parliamentarian" process by which an American professor of philosophy, Paul Arthur Schilpp, gives the floor to the "living philosophers" in the series entitled Library of Living Philosophers could have been invented just for Jaspers. Following an autobiographical introduction, 24 authors discuss the teachings of a living philosopher, raise objections, ask questions, and pursue their own line of thought farther, and at the end the celebrated thinker has an opportunity to respond. Besides the volumes on Cassirer, Dewey, Einstein, Russell, and others, one is devoted to Jaspers [*The Philosophy of Karl Jaspers*, ed.

P. A. Schilpp; Library of Living Philosophers, volume IX, reprint of 1957 edition (LaSalle, Ill., 1981)]. It is the optimistic assumption of this American project that the methods of parliamentary discussion may prove fruitful in philosophical discussion. On precisely this ground, Jaspers's philosophizing gives forth a peculiar echo: It is an attempt, in contrast with traditional liberalism, to develop an (as it were) historically reflective liberalism and to adequately affirm bourgeois humanity and tolerance in a world of totalitarian claims. This extremely defensive liberalism revises the classic model of a system of competing individuals who guarantee the *ratio* of the whole inasmuch as they pursue only their own *ratio*. In its place enters a model of competing powers, each of which witnesses in its representatives to its own historical truth without allowing a knowable truth of the whole. The general questions are no longer to be decided in a rational discussion that is normative for all.

Hannah Arendt, who in her contribution to the collection presents Jaspers as a "citizen of the world," tries to clarify the political intention of his philosophy. Technical and economic development, starting from Europe, has brought together the countries of the world into a global unity of commerce. For the first time all peoples live in a common present, but there is no corresponding common past. Only an unmediated pluralism (traditions that are isolated, pasts that remain alien to one another)—not the pluralism of pasts as such or the various social, political, and cultural traditions as such—might stand in the way of the solidarity of humankind. The unification of the world seems threatened at its very core by self-destructive inner strife so long as the heritage of the separate destinies, reciprocally appropriated, does not aid in realizing the common present. This end is served by communication among the world-historical traditions, which were established by great individuals in the so-called axial period (800 B.C.–200 A.D.): Confucius and Lao Tzu in China, Buddha in India, Zoroaster in Persia, the prophets in Palestine, and the Greek philosophers and tragedians in the West. What could be more equal to this task of universal communication than a way of thinking accustomed to reading philosophers as "ciphers"? The dogmatic contents are left behind, and the kernel of truth in every conceivable, rationally irreconcilable sort of metaphysics is salvaged nonetheless. Metaphysical ideas are not taken as straightforwardly true, but each stands for the truth of some realm of faith; they are true as "contents of an existential impulse."

Through a history of philosophy that functions in this way, a humanity brought together coercively, although disunited in its depths, can be supplied with the watchword of universal communication and shown a horizon in which it can grasp its chance for a solidarity come due.

In the meantime, Jaspers has published the first of the three projected volumes of his history of philosophy. He understands them as political in the broad sense, as a medium of reconciliation, analogous to the "world philosophy" of Hellenism and to the mediation among peoples of Plotinus and Boethius.

If the world is not actually to be healed by philosophy, it is still supposed to learn under philosophy's direction to maintain itself in a rational manner. The solidarity of humanity is supposed to grow out of the efforts of each individual to perfect himself in an attitude of polemical tolerance; this restricts the normativity of one's own insight and decision in favor of those from other sources. Immediately the thought of the weakness of philosophy and the impotence of the spirit shows up. Jaspers turns this into a Stoic component of his alternative in the philosophy of history. However, even if we were to succeed in some marvelous way in vigorously spreading this awareness of polemical tolerance through a worldly philosophy of communication, there would remain doubt as to whether the real oppositions within a world forced together technologically and economically demand a normative insight into the one basic complex of social development rather than the awareness of a polemical tolerance that in the end is not rationally binding—a consciousness shaped by an amiable late-bourgeois urbanity and skepticism.

Jaspers treats the history of philosophy as the history of great philosophers. Anything created in the great manner goes back to individuals; this holds true in philosophy as well. The existence of great persons, he would have it, is like a guarantee against nothingness. Any present that is not reflected in meditation on its past "greats" stays caught in a void without history. Great individuals make themselves evident wherever something novel enters into history by a leap; they are not conceivable as a possibility before they become a reality. Even in the realm of universality which they represent they are unique and irreplaceable. The import and the scope of their existence overflow the proportions of their historical context. In time, they are beyond time (not, of course, like Hegel's great philosophers, who apprehend their age in ideas and hence are raised up to a higher yet still temporal level; the circumstances of their epoch are rather external to the great thinkers). And if a thinker can be adequately grasped by historical analysis alone, he does not belong among the "greats." The latter come before us in their purity when they are released from their ties to their historical moment and are gathered into the eternal realm of the spirits. Contemporaries of the eternal, they are eternally contemporaries for us who are more mortal. The eternal element in work and life permits the great man (Jaspers does not observe any great women) to become a manifestation that can speak fundamentally at any time and to anyone. Individual is capable of "awakening" individual beyond all the bounds of history.

This spatio-temporal universality of contact is startling. Is this—if it should actually come about today—not something that becomes possible in the present situation for the first time? Whether I, situated in the traditions of European history, can really "get something started" with the tradition of Confucius or that of Buddha is hard to separate from the historical situation in which I find myself objectively. Chances for communication, even with great persons, are obviously not there for the asking; they are epochal, in the sense of being bound up with the life context of a determinate historical setup. It is no accident that one epoch reacts only to certain determinate epochs in whose past it can comprehend its own future as well as the continuity of its history, and that it is to some extent blind to all other epochs. Even in the case of Jaspers such an active relationship appears under the title of historicity. However, where it relates only to assorted existences in their individuality it becomes a historicity without history. History, then, serves as the material for inexhaustible interpretations. Each individual existence interprets itself in history in its own fashion. And yet this fashion is not supposed to be arbitrary; it is supposed to appropriate a specific past in a binding way. However, by what else is it determined than by the objective process of history itself, which, prior to all private life history and through it, is common to all individual existences in the same situation? Merleau-Ponty's objection against the existentialist philosophy of his friend Sartre holds even more true for that of Jaspers; it ignores the *milieu mixte, ni choses ni personnes*, the reality of that objective life context which is made by human beings and yet stands over against them as an alien force. Certainly even Jaspers does not regard it as a matter of utter indifference whether the "sociological form of human existence" of the philosopher is that of the nobility, that of the rentier class, that of the literary elite, that of officialdom, or that of an itinerant preacher; but the greatness of the great men bursts the bounds of historical formation, the kernel of eternity its earthly shells. If the great men are really accessible to anyone at any time, they lose precisely the normative moment that resides in their historicity, namely the ability to be the particular component of a distinct, inexchangeable history.

Not only does the world history of philosophy set its great persons free from their real context; it also conducts them into a sphere uniquely reserved for them, beyond history in the realm of the great minds— a sort of metaphysical republic of scholars where they encounter each other as did the philosophers in Raphael's *School of Athens*. To be sure, no great figure seems to be subsumable under epochs or under types; by the same token they only become 'eloquent' in the measure in which they represent "powers." The echo of Ranke's great powers is no accident. In the afterword to the new edition of the three-volume *Philosophie* [tr. E. B. Ashton (Chicago, 1969–70)] Jaspers speaks of the organism of primordial powers of truth in conflict, which take on the guise of ideas not so much in the Kantian as in the Platonic sense. And when Jaspers attempts to group the great philosophers in the light of these powers, to bestow on them a "shadowy reflection of eternal orders," then in a remarkable way we find points of contact between the organic Platonism of the younger Schelling and the historical Platonism of the older Jaspers.

The first type comprises the "paradigmatic men": Socrates, Buddha, Confucius, and Jesus. Aside from Confucius they wrote nothing, and yet with their teachings they became the starting points of powerful traditions. Philosophers in the proper sense are found only in the second type, the "continuously productive founders of philosophizing": Plato, Augustine, and Kant. They ground inexhaustible possibilities of thought rather than a tradition of finished ideas. Among the metaphysicians, there follow first those who come to rest in the vision of their ideas: Plotinus and Spinoza before all others; then those with mundane piety, such as Empedocles and Bruno; then the dreamers of truth and madness of the vintage of Böhme and Schelling; and finally the great constructors of Fichte's stripe, who are scrupulously distinguished from the great systematicians, Aristotle, Thomas, and Hegel. The "penetrating negators," including Descartes and (remarkably) Hume, stand over against the "radical awakeners," among them

Pascal and Kierkegaard. Jaspers makes the best of the psychological and biographical tools that he uses so sensitively in the presentation of the "paradigmatic" individuals, whose lives and teachings seem even now to be one and the same. He clearly feels himself linked sympathetically with the "continuously productive founders." Yet he unravels the political-historical writings of Kant with the subtlety that lends to his book on Schelling a brilliance scarcely repeated in the rest of his writings. The presentation of Kant makes especially clear how much Jaspers's existentialism is a form of Neo-Kantianism (if this hasty ascription may be permitted as a first attempt). Perhaps Jaspers's opposition to Rickert has its deeper root in this subterranean mooring. On the other side, Jaspers's nervous sensitivity to such a systematic thinker as Spinoza reveals the metaphysical intentions of a philosophy that is organized by Jaspers himself in his *magnum opus* on the model of the classic themes of rational cosmology, psychology, and theology, in terms of "world orientation," "existential illumination," and "metaphysics."

A world history of philosophy as a history of great philosophers—"the" great philosophers—lays claim to an undeceptive standard of greatness, even if not of the sort that would guarantee a comprehensive selection. Despite all the reservations that are meant to leave pronouncements about greatness or its lack in "abeyance," this history does insist on an objective ordering of spirits.

Jaspers's defense against the charge of a spiritually aristocratic arrogance is that nothing is taken away from what in the language of ciphers is called the equality of all humans in the sight of God, from the reality of the moral weight of the many. There is no absolute difference between humans, "even though the abyss separating them is so huge." Nevertheless, Fritz Kaufmann, in his contribution to *The Philosophy of Karl Jaspers*, wonders whether the stress on the neighborliness of self-reliant persons on the heights of existence may not keep Jaspers from taking fully seriously the power of compassion and love toward all. Kaufmann sets the aristocratic ethos of self-realization in relation to Protestant inwardness, to that "concern for self, which is deeply grounded and absorbs all else and in comparison with which the most self-sacrificial social work, all the work for the external welfare of humans, has to seem empty and secondary. This attitude characterized Luther's stand in the Peasants' War and Nietzsche's understanding of religion, and it resounds in the work of Thomas Mann, especially in his *Considerations of an Unpolitical Man.*" Against this, Jaspers emphasizes his double impulse toward justice. The one impulse heads toward salvaging the effectiveness of what is best, the other toward the right of every human to strive for the improvement of external life conditions by equalizing opportunity. Heidegger's ontological distinction between authenticity and fallenness comes up again in Jaspers as the distinction between the freedom of existential impetus and mere being as is (just going on living). Accordingly, the effective histories of the great men fall together and the "coin of the masses" diverges.

This dichotomous outlook will, of course, not clear up the embarrassment in the face of the destiny of great men. The philosophy of polemical tolerance loses its best asset when it has to exercise covertly what it does not admit openly: God's judgement upon humanity. Jaspers comforts himself with the statement: I do not judge any figure totally, I penetrate, but I do not have a comprehensive overview. With the attribute of greatness, however, Jaspers actually qualifies men, not merely in this or that respect but in their innermost cores. Were greatness in his sense to concern only the objectifications produced by such men, were it to concern what would ultimately be separable from them as achievements, were it to concern aspects and not the vulnerable center, then there would be no remonstrating about an order of greatness. But Jaspers relates greatness expressly to the rank ordering of human existences. But this rationale is not enough. Whoever does not accept judgments about this kind of greatness finds Jaspers imputing to himself instincts that would level off human importance in favor of sorcerers, supermen, and totalitarian leaders. Such alternatives, formulated in a variety of ways, spring from an understandable conservative impulse of reverence, but they happen to be the same ones with which others reduce fascism and democracy to a common denominator. A philosophy that personalizes the process of history can so little separate the life from the work of an individual that any judgment as to the objective meaning of an achievement becomes a pronouncement of judgment about existence. Such a philosophy is not going to understand that a contradiction between life and work can be exacted by objective forces—even though this contradiction might become, and may already be, just what is normal in a situation that alienates humans from themselves.

For Jaspers, greatness has to be positive from every point of view. That is why the question whether there might be a greatness of confusion and of madness, a greatness of illusion and of bewitchment, is so important for him. A thought for which authenticity and depth and ultimately even rank and greatness are identical with truth has to deny the greatness in untruth and evil. To be sure, Jaspers notes well something like a luciferian brilliance about the artificial structures contrived from nothingness, but in the end these must let themselves be unmasked as lacking in existence, like an enchantment. In a way similar to Schelling, Jaspers characterizes evil as a tearing loose from the matrix of existence. The isolated spirit is enchanted; its very indecisiveness between good and evil already permits a slide into evil. Evil harbors greatness only on loan. In the great there are also elements of the illusory and the negative, but for Jaspers great enchanters as such— persons great in evil, the demonic, in itself—do not exist. And great human existences as such and as a whole are not good; rather, what is good is whatever it is in them that makes them great.

Still, how are good and evil to be discriminated in great individuals if greatness is what marks such a person in his inmost essence? Once one has introduced him for the first time, the great one is justified by himself alone. How then is partisanship against menacing greatness and its threatening consequences to be envisaged in a way that is at all meaningful? Moreover, doubts arise as to the presupposition itself: Have we not experienced that vileness may be uttered in a manner that is truly great, even if not truthful? The style embodied in evil does not necessarily show fractures. In the end, does not the truth formulated existentially provide a critical dimension for the appropriation of history? Wherever it remains confined to the forms of appearance proper to greatness, does it not head toward the apologetic equation of what is ponderous with what is important and of what is important with what is right? The demand of Jaspers—in striving beyond every doctrinal partisanship to fasten upon a unique great partisanship, that of being partisan for reason, humanity, truth, and goodness— blunts its own point when it accepts the injunction to hold fast not only to this partisanship but to its lack of determinacy.

According to Jaspers, only science can claim universal validity. In contrast, philosophy appeals not to the logic of the consciousness common to all, but beyond this to the metalogic of individual human existence. It must deal objectively with the unobjectifiable, without really being permitted to do so. And it has to integrate this tension as well into its reflection—even to the "upheaval of logic." One only wonders if logic may be so easily overturned as Jaspers supposes with this absolute differentiation between scientific knowledge and philosophical faith.

Martin Heidegger: The Great Influence (1959)

"The shepherds dwelt invisible and outside the wasteland of the devastated earth, which is still supposed to be of use now only for the securing of domination by human beings. . . ." The linguistic gesture of the writer Heidegger reveals something rebuffing: The reader is challenged by the author and even compelled into a view that stretches out over the epochs of the world, but he is expected to follow down untrodden paths rather than being afforded the mutuality of conversation. This peculiar reserve is not that of a great philosopher attaching value to a proper distance; here the prophetic thinker is paying heed to a distinction of rank. Communication does not belong to the basic vocabulary of this philosophy. Even so, we shall take advantage of the favor left us by this hard-to-approach addressee and speak without regard to chronological order in order to "correspond" [*entsprechen*] to him; we shall look out from the vantage of the jubilee celebration and gaze upon a powerful effective history. In the framework of the university, Martin Heidegger is the most influential philosopher since Hegel.

To be sure, Heidegger's influence is not confined to the universities; actually, those who are most dependent on him assemble *ante portas* instead. These small circles, sometimes drawn together into sects, are spread throughout the country and are difficult to take in at a single glance. In one respect they adapt themselves to the manner of the thinker himself, who shuns the congresses of colleagues in his discipline and prefers to attend the meetings of the lay brothers. Among the latter, some captains of industry seeking relaxation on the Bühler

Heights have already attained a sort of legendary fame. Perhaps in this endearing attempt of managerial types to get interested in paths leading nowhere [*Feldwege*] the other side of Heidegger's mode of contact with reality—the one that, so to speak, lies opposite to Being (*Sein*). Some who are ill disposed toward Heidegger have regarded this as interweaving mysticism with chain mail.

Nonetheless, it is more reliable to have a look at the academic influence in its entirety. A great number of chaired professors, along with the sort who wish to be chaired professors, appeal to Heidegger as the originator of their way of doing philosophy. Many have taken up and elaborated his motifs; most of them are captivated and driven by his impulses in general. Of course, the stances of appropriation differ widely. For example, there is the attempt to retrace the path Heidegger traveled as a Jesuit seminarian from Thomas via Brentano to Husserl to a renewed Christian philosophy (Max Müller); the knowledgeable modesty that descends from the summit of metaphysics to the plain of a fragile skepticism carefully tracked back to antiquity (Oscar Becker); the resolve to abandon philosophizing itself, along with metaphysics as a mere propaedeutic to "Heidegger's mythology" (Walter Bröcker); and the start of an attempt to bring Heidegger's philosophy into the horizon of the great tradition and to reconcile them again (Eugen Fink). Some have leapt completely out of the dialectic of history into a cosmological trust in a nature that stays ever the same (Karl Löwith). Other paths lead—with Heidegger "pinned down"—back to Hegel (Bruno Liebrucks). Indeed, older students have discovered in *Being and Time* an access to Marx, which seems odd only at first glance and which enables them to translate the concepts of the analytics of *Dasein* into those of a philosophical history of the drives (Herbert Marcuse).

These positions mark off the academic influence of Heidegger from the margins. No less prominent than the outsiders are the genuine disciples—some combative "orthodox" followers, others more mild-mannered "pedagogues"—who seem to take the teaching to heart less for the sake of its purity than for the sake of guidance along the path of thought. From this circle have emerged sensitive interpretative investigations in the history of philosophical problems. Often they center around Plato or Descartes, whose heritages constitute caesuras in the history of that Being which has been so thoroughly "forgotten" until our own day; always they refer to the "self-empowering of the subject," which is supposed to sum up the unsalutary features of the present period.

The teachings of Heidegger have forged beyond German borders as far as Latin America and Japan; its impulses have been picked up in Paris above all. The return of his influence from beyond the Rhine after World War II almost made Heidegger into a reimport; at that time, *Being and Time* reached most students by way of a detour through *Being and Nothingness* via Sartre's "The Flies." A Heidegger renaissance born of the spirit of the Resistance—what a source of misunderstandings!

Naturally, in the midst of the mounting literature around him and about him, Heidegger still does not feel really understood. An outstanding work by the Tübingen philosopher Walter Schulz appears to be one of the remarkable exceptions to this rule; it is remarkable especially because it lends precision in an almost positivist manner to the course of Heideggerian thinking in a way that anyone might recapitulate for himself. What is surprising is not the interpretation as such but its soberly understated lines. The existential ornamentation falls away. Figures of thought appear in greater purity. A certain space is gained for the refinement of scholastic distinctions, and hence for the penetration of intellect (usually berated by Heidegger), rather than for thoughtful meditation.

For example, Schulz analyses the important dialectic of "correspondence" [*Entsprechung*] as follows: We can only think Being [*Sein*] and bring it to language in the measure that Being itself makes our thinking possible and lets us dwell in the house of language. My own sense of Being, which does not lie at my disposal, is what first establishes the possibility in me by which I am able to "correspond" with it. Formally considered, the same figure of thought is found in completely different constellations as well. It is present in Marx, who pushed Hegel's dialectic of reflection beyond itself to that of theory and practice. Of course, this dialectic of corresponding, through its ongoing relation to the dialectic of Hegel, has a sense quite opposed to that of Heidegger: The indirect power of society over humans is supposed to be dissolved; however, that of "Being" is to be released within humans and through their agency. Whatever may actually be the case in this connection, the reference to it here is only meant to show that the "figures" of Heideggerian thought laid bare in this way do indeed resemble ones familiar from the tradition. Their analysis, therefore, mediates a historically distanced recapitulation of this thinking that curiously slips away from its entire claim. So it seems that in the measure that Heidegger treats the well-versed correspondence with Being like a privilege—as though he alone enlarges the field of experience of the history of Being, designates which authors are relevant, and creates the key words—it is only with great difficulty that those coming after him will be able to escape the situation of the epigones: to be constrained to draw the implications of a formalism that is already laid out.

In *Being and Time* Heidegger joined essential motifs of Dilthey and Husserl. Dilthey had experienced cultures historically as objectifications of a "life" [*Leben*] that was always to be comprehended on the basis of the preunderstanding of its totality. Husserl, returning to the achievements of consciousness, had raised the "constitution of the world" (that is, of the meaning of any and every kind of entity) to a theme for pure description. Heidegger, then, seeks to ground human *Dasein* from itself both in its historicality and in its totality. *Dasein* enjoys the advantage of being, among all entities, the one that understands itself in terms of the meaning of Being: Inasmuch as humans generate and maintain themselves by labor, beings surrounding humans break forth in their significance. Beings attain this Being only within the world of humans, and their essence consists precisely in finding themselves in a world they simultaneously project. From this starting point, with penetrating insistence and truly disclosive skill, Heidegger has spun out the analytics of human existence [*Existenz*] in mighty spirals. It is the last great attempt to date at a *prima philosophia*. With the "totality of *Dasein*" it intends to secure for itself a first beginning from which the Being of all beings may be grounded; hence the name fundamental ontology. This attempt, however, only achieves its real success—if I may be permitted this crude abbreviation—with the insight into its unspoken failure. The second half of *Being and Time* was never published, because the first half had come up against a twofold limitation: Human *Dasein*—at least in the form it actually takes—is altogether incapable of ontologically grounding itself. This reveals at the same time the thoroughly historical character of truth, which proceeds from the world of humans as its open horizon. The truth, so to speak, has time at its core. As a result, philosophy as "first philosophy" [*Ursprungsphilosophie*] has also become impossible for Heidegger.

At this parting of the ways, when philosophy sees through the fragility of its original claim and renounces its claim to self-grounding, an important question arises regarding the position from which it disputes its heritage—if not from itself. Heidegger might have been able to direct his inquiry back from the ontologically fixed structures of *Dasein* (the *Existenzialien*) to the factual experiences drawn from the concrete situation (the *Existenziellen*). In doing so, he might have been able, in the manner of the critique of ideology, to place philosophy in relation to the history of this situation, to the development of the social life context. Instead he undertakes the famous "turning" [*Kehre*] toward the history of the formally existential components [*Existenzialen*] themselves, toward the history of Being.

At first glance, this can be seen in the discoloring of the language. *Being and Time* had entered deeply into the spiritual climate of the 1920s. The flagrant contagion of this philosophy far beyond the realm of philosophy can only be comprehended from this. So, for instance, on the occasion of Heidegger's sixtieth birthday, Carl Friedrich von Weizsäcker frankly admits

. . . I began to read *Being and Time*, which had been published a short time before, when I was still a student. Today I can state with a good conscience that at that time I understood nothing of it, strictly speaking. But I could not avoid the impression it made, and would even today concede to it that here, and here alone, those tasks for thinking were being engaged that I divined in the background of modern theoretical physics.

Such prephilosophical "translations" came about, as Paul Hühnerfeld points out in his biography of Heidegger, in the court of a *Zeitgeist* wearing Expressionist clothing. Moreover, one found here under the label of the everyday mode of being of *Das Man* the current concepts of cultural criticism from Oswald Spengler down to Alfred Weber, only now qualified as ontology. Correlative to this was the ingredient of Lutheran radicalism in the project of "authentic"*Dasein*, which secures its wholeness "heading provisionally toward death." This Protestantism at its nadir of secularization gave way at the start of the 1930s to a decisionism purified of Kierkegaard and theological remains and marching in the trappings of antiquity. In 1935, on the occasion of an interpretation of Sophocles, we still find the following: "The actively violent one, the creative one who moves out into the unspoken, breaks into the unthought, coerces the undone and makes the unperceived appear, this violent one stands at risk at any and every moment." If the subject that intends to ground itself is already experiencing its impotence here, since then Being gains the upper hand completely: Human *Dasein* must be received from its hand in a fateful manner. The name of the human is now shepherd and guardian of Being; he is permitted to dwell in language as the house of Being; he is called to watch over what is self-bestowing; and so on.

When one approaches the "turning" in this way (from the outside, as it were), guided by the changing linguistic qualities, the process proves to have irresistable parallels in the intellectual biographies of other peers. Gottfried Benn travelled the path from breeding the new German man to the world of artistic expression as pure form—to the "denial of history," Ernst Jünger that from the total mobilization of the worker to the reclusive freedom of the wanderer in the woods who realizes he is independent of "those in the technical-political forefront and their groups." Even with Carl Schmitt one can notice a similar withdrawal from engagement, a sublimation of original positions on a level at once higher and less decided. In Heidegger's case, this interiorization takes place in the name of an "overcoming of metaphysics." This is also the title of a collection of sketches from the years 1936–1946, which provide an outstanding documentation of the contemporary motif of *Kehre*: disappointment with what had first promised to be a German awakening through an incursion of violence into the unthought. In the meantime another act of violence—above all the totality of the world war, in all its consequences—had revealed itself to be an accomplice of what it was allegedly to overcome, as had the new order of things in general. To quote Heidegger: "One supposes that the Leaders, on their own and in the blind frenzy of a selfish quest. . . , claimed everything for themselves and set up everything in accord with their own sense of things. In truth, they are the necessary consequences of Being gone into error, within which emptiness spreads. . . ."

Thus, even the transformation of Heidegger's own philosophy would have been a reason to reverse the still dominant transcendental direction of inquiry, from the vantage of that parting of the ways reached after *Being and Time*. Fundamental ontology could then be apprehended and derived from the history of the concrete life contexts for which it was initially supposed to afford the conditions of possibility. Yet

Heidegger relativizes philosophy and the subject trying in vain to ground itself ontologically in the opposite direction—against the background history of the dominant disposings of thinking by Being. This disposing by Being is to be released from the poetic word by thinking. Heidegger turns to Hölderlin for a dialogue between thinker and poet. Above the mortals (formerly called *Dasein*) loom the gods, beneath heaven (formerly *Welt*) the earth now rests, and now the entity ingredient in this "quadrant" [*Vierung*] is "thing" [*Ding*]. The thinker surrenders himself to "simple things." In this way and only in this way does he labor against the "subjectivism" of contemporary humanity, with its destructive will to domination as manifest in "technology." Along with the "subjectivistic" ossification of received thought he also leaves behind its normativity. The evocation of myth is legitimated as a form of spiritual exercise; Heidegger wants his thinking to be understood "never normatively as a statement," but "only as a possible incentive to pursue the path of correspondence." By way of restriction he adds "The thinking of Being, as correspondence, is a very mistake-laden and very meager business." Yet seldom has the claim of thinking been set on a more lofty plane.

Among the public, the fate of a "metaphysics brought to its completion" is realized as "technology" (objectified nature and reified society are thereby conceived together). In a concealed way and among thinking persons, metaphysics has in the meantime been twisted into a new salvation. What is the case for one is not so for the other. Greek tragedy gets mixed with Breughel's hellish tumult in a vision: "Before Being can eventuate in its primorial truth, Being as will has to be broken, the world must be impelled into catastrophe, the earth into devastation, and humanity into mere labor. Only after this decline and fall does there occur in the long run the yawning duration of the beginning. . . . The downfall has already occurred. The consequences of this event are the circumstances of the history of the world of this century. They are only a draining off of what has already perished. Its course is ordered in a historical-technological fashion in the sense of the last stage of metaphysics." The apocalypse bears the signs of atomic catastrophe. "The laboring animal is left to the tumult of its own making, so that it might tear itself apart and be annihilated into the nil of nothingness."

Since the eighteenth century the power of criticism has been brought to bear against crisis. Criticism has also been opposed to metaphysics.

From Kant to Husserl it has remained as decisive a force in philosophy as it has in the theater from Schiller to Brecht; on the model of a court of judgment, it gleans the true from what is merely a matter of opinion in the dispute of conflicting parties. However, as a counterpoise to crisis and a notion to counter metaphysics, Heidegger names not criticism but mythos. His attitude toward that from which he derives all experience is not critical either. The critique of language is as alien to him as the following pronouncement of Karl Kraus: "Would there be any stronger securing in the moral realm imaginable than linguistic doubt?" (In the meantime, Karl Korn has chosen this question as the motto for an investigation that subjects Heidegger's language itself to linguistic criticism.)

Perhaps Heidegger's thought may be characterized indirectly by what it does not achieve: It understands itself just as little in relationship to social practice as it does in relation to the interpretation of the results of the sciences. As to the latter, it demonstrates the metaphysical limitations of their foundations and abandons them, along with "technology" in general, to the "mistake" [Irre]. For the shepherds dwell outside the wasteland of the devastated earth. . . .

The situation of the category of greatness is an odd one today. Its fragility is mirrored in our incapacity to set up monuments. Not even the most genuine feeling of the epoch can succeed here, as Reg Butler's "Unknown Political Prisoner" shows. The story of Heidegger's influence is great, and most would call his work itself great. Perhaps this very case makes understandable why our relationship to greatness is a broken one.

Ernst Bloch: A Marxist Schelling (1960)

If I were not a bit intimidated by Bloch's generous use of it, I might well have selected the following motto: "Reason cannot bloom without hope, hope cannot speak without reason, both in a Marxist unity— all other science has no future, all other future no science." This is one of the few epigrams of an epic thinker who, "traces" and his own inclinations notwithstanding, does not always show his strength in the miniature form of aphorism and parable. Bloch lets himself be driven by the plenitude of his thought into the breadth of the narrative. *Das Prinzip Hoffnung*,[1] written in the United States, revised and enlarged in the eastern sector of our country, and published completely for the first time in its western sector, reflects as much in its external history as in its internal one—the odyssey of a mind from the spirit of exodus. A thought in the process of undergoing experience and going astray develops and takes up that "brooding" in the dark ground of the world pointed to by Jacob Böhme. "Nothingness hungers for something," as Böhme put it, "and that hunger is desire as the first *verbum, Fiat.*" Bloch pursues the same theme when he plays off hunger as the fundamental drive against Freud's libido. The ever-renewed hunger drives people about, sets the tone for self-preservation as self-expansion, and, in its enlightened figure, is transformed into an explosive force against the prisons of deprivation in general. This informed hunger, another form of the *docta spes*, develops to the point of a resolution to eliminate all relationships under which people live as forgotten beings. Hunger appears as the elemental energy of hope. The very work Bloch devoted to hope has to it something of a hunger—from a grandiose systematizing of felt hopes it is on the way to an intended system of fully conceptualized hope.

The positivist who hears that reason cannot bloom without hope will also object that reason ought to conceive. Nonetheless, Bloch, in a manner all his own, positively appropriates what supposedly degenerates into the illusion of falsely posed questions in the face of positivism's verdict. Like positivism, Bloch criticizes myths, religions, and philosophies as illusions; however, he takes them seriously as a preappearance of something to be achieved in the future. He holds onto what, in consequence of a distinction within the modern logic of science, is a normative moment skimmed off from the facts—not, however, as an ontological component, but rather as the forecourt of intentional experiences which press on from what is currently the case to what is beyond it. Bloch does not blame previous philosophy for the courage to transcend, but for its false awareness of such courage— as if in transcending itself it disclosed what a given person was or always has been. Aristotle understood essence [*Wesenheit*] as an already-has-been-ness [*Ge-Wesenheit*]; so, too, Heidegger still understands the absent presencing of Being as the still-to-come return [*bevorstehende Wiederkunft*] of what has already been originally. Knowledge, which from Plato's anamnesis right down to Freud's analysis seems to follow the tug of recollective return, is actually related to something advancing toward us that is only objectively possible. The latter indicates the outlines of a *vérité a faire*, a truth to be realized, which is "nowhere" already real and which to that extent is utopian. At any rate, utopia, since the days when Thomas More meditating *de nova insula utopia* conferred a name upon it, has been able to develop into concrete utopia to the extent that the analysis of the historical development and its social driving forces have begun to uncover the conditions for its possible realization. Bloch is not occupied with this sort of analysis; he simply takes it as something already accomplished by historical materialism. The greater threat that within his own camp "schematizers with a treasury of quotations" and "practitioners from the empty hand" betray utopia in regard to the business of its realization seems to require of Bloch the still greater effort to grasp the dimensions of utopia itself and to fasten upon it so that it cannot be lost to the surviving generations.[2]

For the sake of a socialism that lives from a critique of tradition, Bloch wants to hold onto the tradition of what has been criticized. In contrast with the unhistorical procedures of a critique of ideology in the style of Feuerbach (who took up only half of the Hegelian meaning of "sublation" [Aufheben], and in using it proceeded with the tollere but renounced all elevare), Bloch wants to glean ideas from the ideologies, to salvage whatever may be true in false consciousness: "Every great culture till now is the preview of something attained, at least to the extent that it could be constructed in imagery and ideas upon the summits of time with a rich view into the distance." Even the critique of religion that Marx resumes in the "Theses on Feuerbach" undergoes its retrospective interpretation in this way. God is dead, but the "place" he held has survived him; the realm into which humanity had imaginatively projected God and the gods remains behind as an empty cavelike space even after the collapse of these hypostases; its "depth dimensions" [Tiefenabmessungen] (that is to say, those of atheism finitely conceived) reveal the outlines of a future realm of freedom.

In a variation on Leibniz, who for his part was doing a variation on Locke, Bloch with a wink of the eye wrestles from the economicism of a Marx sentenced to Diamat the truth still encoded in the mythologemes: Nothing is in the superstructure that is not also embedded in the basis, with the exception of the superstructure itself. A Solomonic mode of orthodoxy, here as everywhere. Still, this orthodoxy does not represent a return from Marx to Hegel, as may first appear to be the case. The phenomenology of hope does not, as does the phenomenology of spirit, pursue spirit's outdated figures. For Bloch the figures of the spirit draw the objectivity of their appearance instead from the "experimenting validity" of an anticipatorily projected novelty. Up to now philosophy has not revealed its incognito, the objective possibility of a realm of freedom: "Again and again, the mantle of Platonic anamnesis, which covered over a dialectically open eros, shut off all philosophy till now (Hegel's included) . . . in a contemplative-antiquarian dead end" (antiquarian just because it clothed what lay in the future in the guise of what was long since past; contemplative because a genesis of the sort that projected into the beginning an end that is still outstanding falsely reserved to theoretical replication what, after critical preparation, would have to be achieved by responsible praxis).

Resistances to Utopia, Literary and Psychological

The market gives little chance to a favorable outlook on utopia. Since Karl Mannheim used the sociology of knowledge to diagnose the utopian impulse as moribund decades ago, the corroborating symptoms have piled up. The more long-range military plans become, the more densely is the Western world shielded politically against the future. In West Germany the shattered revolution from the Right posthumously celebrates the literary successes of the Left. Arguments from Nietzsche can be mobilized against "pipe dreams" in the philosophy of history; on the other hand, Hegel, who is especially rigorous against mere opinion, takes his own stand on the side of progress, even if on that of the easily subjectivizable consciousness of freedom.

Two strategic lines are drawn in the campaign against utopia. On one side is a kind of direct negation of history. A sort of anthropological Platonism, which proposes constant standards for the optimal conditions of survival, of a noble or a degenerate life, heads in that direction. Along with the negation is found an aesthetic Platonism, fashioned as if to play a complementary role, which promises eternity to the crystals formed in a world of pure forms by great individuals at lucky moments in time. In both cases the swamp of history is dried up; what seems to be a realization of meaning within it evaporates in the meaningless cycles of nature. Obviously, however, world history pushes forward toward epochal breaks; before it the immutability of human nature posited at its basis shrivels into a fiction, as does the denial of any possible meaning of history in the face of the dialectic of progressive rationalization. The other line of argumentation therefore shunts aside this state of affairs as well. Instead of a direct negation, it obliquely introduces a kind of rounding off of history. Eschatological thought bets on the return of a mythological age, which can be hastened by the meditative evocation of a destiny of being, or by a botanizing philosophy of global history. Philosophy of history is outbid by metahistory, and the historically observable situation no longer has any need for a rational discussion of its objective possibilities. Such thought makes use of a consciousness burdened with the feeling of crisis merely to integrate empirical history as a whole into the cycles of a superhistory; it derails the open historical process of possible self-determination and redirects it back into the received contours of a naturelike occurrence: The book of history gets translated back into a book of geological lore concerning the ages of the world. The conservative thesis about the maintenance and equilibrium of energy, which brings physics and morality under one metaphysical common denominator, excludes novelty and excludes possible progress toward what is better—even in the smallest possible dose, that of the daydream. In contrast, Bloch notes the most fleeting excitations as the cells of a grand dream of anticipation, as the core of that hope whose principle is supposed to raise humanity "out of its rut." Ernst Jünger, representing an entire camp, has only one gesture left for this sort of thing:

. . . one hears even thinkers in our day say "If this or that were not so, then everything would be all right." It might be conceivable that, if this or that were not so, things would be exposed as even more gruesome—utterly prescinding from the fact that when one nightmare is dispelled another immediately takes its place. These theses and others like them are nurtured upon the equation of reason and morality. The world is filled with the rational persons who mutually condemn one another's lack of rationality. Things nonetheless take their course, and quite obviously it is one completely different from the one everyone intended. Whoever notices this is closer to the wellsprings than if he belonged to any parties, no matter whether they deal with the situation in a closed meeting or *in pleno*.

Bloch would recognize in this the language of the doorkeepers who, with the legitimacy of what is apparent to the naked eye, once again close off wherever possible the openness of the world—which as administered is more and more shut off anyway. Against the new Romantics he could enlist their noble forebear and model Franz Baader, who wrote

It is a basic prejudice of humans to believe that what they call a future world is a thing fashioned and completed for people, which stands without their aid like a house that has already been built, whereas surely that world is instead an edifice whose builder is this particular person and which only grows along with him.[3]

Nietzsche discovered anew the ancient idea of the eternal return in order to sanctify the "moment." In *amor fati* the will to power, as it storms the heights, reaches its zenith: If even the most fragile instant in the restless interchange of finite life energies is guaranteed a return and hence eternity (which is to say a weight of significance, as it were an inability to get lost in the flux of appearances, and an equal value with every other instant), then and only then can the entire happiness of the moment, the happiness of the entire moment, be disclosed to the disillusioned consciousness. The effort of the ultimate will, that is, cancels out its own projection into the future; it not only accepts the present as it is but also affirms it in its depths. Bloch allows himself to be guided by the same motif: "The ultimate will is that which wants to be authentically present. The human wants finally to be himself in the here and now, wants to be in the fullness of his life without postponement and distance." But his redeeming word, hope, is opposed to that of the eternal return. Through a mere reform of moral awareness—a transvaluation that would entrench what is transvalued—the darkness of the lived moment would of course become more impenetrable. Consequently, the chain of eternal return has to be burst, and the exit onto the untrodden has to be gained in a utopian way: ". . . the pressing forward has to it not only the aspect of an outlet, or of an open space, which can still be taken, still chosen, still cut off, a path already forged, a route already laid down—but off the beaten path, within the realm of the objectively possible, a correlative that is in some fashion possible for us, toward which the pressing onward does not proceed endlessly without satisfaction." The *carpe diem* becomes real only where the seal of the *amor fati* has been dissolved and the mantle of Platonic anamnesis covering the dialectically open *eros* is torn open. This relationship to Nietzsche makes Bloch into an antipode of those counterrevolutionaries who in their own way derive from Nietzsche and who would take the wind out of the sails of utopia.

Prescinding from these kinds of resistance, the reception of the work might nonetheless be influenced as well by its own *habitus*. The things for which, say, Benn in literature and Schmidt-Rottluff in painting may stand now gain representation in philosophy by way of Bloch—late expressionism, the style of the first decades of our century, maintained right into its middle (a style, gained with age, that shows signs of clarification but also of relaxing). The exploded fragments of a hyphenated terminology, the welling exuberance of a pleonastic phraseology, the strong-chested breathing of dithyrambic plangency, and metaphors that at times remind one more of Böcklin than of Benjamin still envince power and greatness of format, but they have outlasted their time. In addition, the utopian radiance is colored in the spectrum of generational experiences that today have largely lost their self-evident character. The *Jugendbewegung* cannot become old-fashioned in the serious way of a Biedermeier. Breaking out into free nature, longing for the roaming life, and sentimentality toward the circus and prostitution have undergone an aging process that does not have anything specific to do even with the growing old of the new within the enchanted circle of the modern. The psychology of youth proper to the *Wandervogel* leaves "traces" even in the concept of hope. Not altogether without reason, however, skepticism has been conferred on contemporary youth, and one wonders whether other generational experiences, which have outgrown Boy Scout Romanticism, legitimately leave their mark here—experiences that clash not with utopia but with Bloch's introduction to utopia.

The Heritage of Jewish Mysticism

Bloch has emerged unexpectedly within the zone of Bonn and upset the usual topography.

Wherever Marxism has made European philosophy its own without getting melted in the crucible of transcendental critique, it has created (at least where Bloch is concerned) an imposing mediation of philosophical traditions—especially the German—split along confessional lines. The Jewish element within Marxism makes for a particular sensitivity toward perspectives once looked after by the Kabbalah and mysticism—even toward the repeatedly severed Pythagorean and Hermetic traditions, seldom refined to the level of official philosophy. The Hellenistic skein was not really unraveled during the Middle Ages by Christian philosophy. This ancient tradition made its entry (in however clouded a form) into the awareness of the new age during the Renaissance—precisely the German Renaissance, with Paracelsus at the intersection of its wide branches—under the etiquette of Neo-Platonism. Very much alive in Böhme, and passed on to the Tübingen seminarians Hegel, Schelling, and Hölderlin by way of Oetinger's Swabian pietism after leaving behind certain tints in Leibniz's monadology, it really crossed the threshold of higher speculation only with Schelling's philosophy of nature and attained its full range with his doctrine of the ages of the world. The very names of a philosophy of "nature" and of "the ages of the world" are suggestive of the way the thought of that provenance revolves elliptically about the two centers of matter and of historical process—an apocryphal tradition of historical materialism, to which Marx did in fact appeal once (in the "Holy Family") with an explicit reference to Jacob Böhme in connection with a polemic against the mechanistic materialism of the English seventeenth and the French eighteenth centuries.[4]

Philosophy in Germany lives so thoroughly out of the Protestant spirit that Catholics practically have to become Protestant in order to do philosophy, and Catholic thought has scarcely emerged from the ivory tower of Thomism except in nonphilosophical forms. When one realizes this, the background becomes clear against which Bloch's philosophy (which usually understands Christ very much in an Old Testament context as the prophet of a this-worldly kingdom) has increasingly played a unique mediating function in the traditional realm of philosophy. Hearkening to the divine *Logos* in history through hearing and obedience has estranged Protestant philosophy from nature as much as perceiving the *Logos* in nature with the eyes has estranged Catholic thought from history. This state of affairs can also be easily enough explained sociologically. In contrast with the Catholic and Protestant traditions, both of these ideas come together from the very start in the tradition of the Old Testament prophets: the self-actuated liberation of the human race in the course of history and the restoration of a fallen nature. In the Paris Manuscripts, Bloch finds a formula for rationally disengaging this utopia still entangled in myth: Together with a naturalizing of humanity, socialism promises a humanizing of nature. A nature definitively evolved belongs together with a history definitively produced in the horizon of the future. "Hence, nature does not belong to the past, encompassing us and clouding over us with so much of the brooding, the unfinished, and the cipher about it; instead of something bygone, it is rather a land of the rising sun."

The overtones resonant in this statement refer to a melody played by Schelling. Bloch's basic experience is of the darkness, the open-endedness, the longing proper to the lived moment, proper to the nothingness of the mystic that is hungering for something, a nothingness whose abstract radiance is reflected in the beginning of Hegel's *Logic*. In this primordial hunger, the knot of the world presses toward resolution and, as long as it is unresolved, at each moment casts life back to its beginnings: "Each lived moment would, if it had eyes to see, also be a witness to the beginning of the world which keeps on occurring in it; each moment that has not come to the fore is still in the year zero of the world's beginning." That is a characterization which could have belonged to Schelling's first fragment from the *Ages of the World*, the investigations of "time as a whole." The following statement, too, resonates this way: "What is not, as not-yet, runs straight through whatever has already come to be and beyond; hunger becomes a productive force within the constantly erupting front of an unfinished world. For this reason, the world as process is itself an immense probing in the direction of its satisfactory resolution, that is, toward the realm of its complete satisfaction." And just as "what is unconscious" in Schelling's "System of Transcendental Idealism" receives the double significance of an instinctive subconscious based on the "obscure ground of nature" and a superconscious that has taken wing "from the voluntary gift of a higher nature," so too Bloch separates the unconscious aspect of the night dream from that of the daydream, the no-longer-conscious element ascending out of the past from the not-yet-conscious element pointing toward the future. From this perspective, the romantic pathos of an archaicizing way of treating things misses an entire realm of ciphers and symbols, of mythical elements not only in myth but also in the perception of nature and art, in dreams and visions, in poetry and philosophy. Bloch submits these elements to a "utopian treatment," insofar as within them something not yet made good pushes its essence forward and so allows us to interpret them as emblems of the future.[5] The core of what everywhere appears to the anticipatory consciousness, which integrates even the inverted "archetypes" of Jung and the diluvial "images" of Klages, is the realm of freedom within which humanity sheds its self-estrangement and guides its own history in freedom. Only with the elimination of domination of humans over other humans, precisely in the socialist mode, is this supposed to be brought about, for then the fortune of one no longer arises out of the misfortune of others and only then does the former no longer need to be measured in terms of the latter.

Matter as World Soul and Technology without Violence

However, every dream of a better life would be "restricted to an inner, indeed completely puzzling enclave in isolation" if this anticipation did not encounter a certain potential, above all in history. Bloch leaps past any sociological-historical investigation of objective possibilities promoted dialectically by the social process; instead he immediately refers to their universal substratum within the world process itself—to matter, for "real possibility is nothing other than dialectical matter." This moment of potency, already implied in Aristotle's concept of matter, had been enriched into a pregnant concept in the subterranean streams of Neo-Platonism before Schelling finally adopted the term. Matter, or *natura naturans*, no longer needs any form entelechies; as the one and the whole, it engenders and bears the patterns of its fertility out of itself alone.[6] It is the being-existing-in-possibility in such a way that the history of nature "points toward" the history of humanity and is "dependent on" humanity. The capacity to act and to act otherwise is implanted in the latter, which in exchange with nature releases there a capacity to become and a capacity to become otherwise. The subjective potential reacts to the objective, yet it is not arbitrary but constantly mediated (first by the objective tendencies of social evolution, then by whatever a still open-ended nature makes possible or impossible). What is most genuinely real in this world is still outstanding; it waits, "in the fear of getting stalled and in the hope of getting achieved," for its realization by means of the labor of socialized human beings—the labor of their hands in the literal sense of the words. Bloch gives Schelling's doctrine of the potencies a Marxist interpretation: "The subjective potency converges not only with whatever is in the process of becoming but with the realizing agency in history, and the more so the more humans become the conscious producers of their history. The objective potentiality converges not only with whatever is changeable but with whatever is realizable in history, and the more so the more the independent world outside humans gets to be one increasingly mediated along with them," In a utopianly projected harmony of the unreified object with the manifest subject, and of the unreified subject with the manifest object, this new philosophy believes itself to have deciphered the echo of an ancient identity.

Bloch does not shy away from using the Kantian faculty of judgment as expanded by Schelling's philosophy of nature. Together with the alienation of socialized humans, nature is "lost," and once the shattered project of nature's hidden "subject" has been apprehended it demands to be construed as *natura naturans* and to be brought to its goal by human hands. The "mechanical" mode of treatment, which emerges in the technological manipulation of the forces of nature, does not do justice to nature as something in need of a homecoming. Only when the "teleological" way of treating things perceives them as patterns emanating from itself, do the subjectively purposive human activities no longer hang in a vacuum; then, they find a connection with a purposiveness embedded objectively in nature itself. Bloch resumes Goethe's battle with Newton. Nourished by the deeper heritage of Pythagorean number symbolism, the kabbalist doctrines of signatures, and the Hermetic teachings on physiognomy, alchemy, and astrology, he insists against the sciences on a doctrine of nature as expression, as a sympathetic constellation of patterns. However, only the reference (once again reminiscent of Schelling) to the cognitive mode proper to the experience of natural beauty, a sort of knowledge of nature within works of art, disguises, in a makeshift way, the embarrassing lack of a methodological introduction to the "doctrine of nature as expression." All previous attempts were based on an untenable transfer of the analogy between microcosm and macrocosm, between humans and the universe as a whole.

However, in the course of these considerations Bloch hits upon the noteworthy question of a "technology without violence." Natural scientific theories and their technological application are in fact "estranged from nature." Both of them dispose of nature in accord with the fixed laws of its behavior "for us." The functional correlations fixed in laws do not touch whatever nature may be "in itself," leaving it in a productive ignorance as regards its "essence." Therefore, a technology that must proceed in accord with such laws is lacking any "tie-in" to a favor of nature, to "an old, unspoiled, natural world." Bloch regards its lack of connection with the earth as much in its exaggerated artificiality as in the specific poverty and the specific ugliness of "the bourgeois world of machines." The overworked epithet *bourgeois* comes up in this context because technology not only arose within the framework of capitalist relations of production but has been distorted by it as well. Just as in commerce the abstract relations of exchange values remain extrinsic to use value, so too in the natural sciences abstract laws remain extrinsic to the substratum of nature. This so lightly considered analogy, developed decades before by Lukács in *History and Class Consciousness*, encourages Bloch to expect that under socialism the technological forces of production can shed their abstract contours and be woven into a "co-productivity with nature." The freedom won socio-politically will be furthered in a politics of nature: "Just as Marxism has uncovered in the laboring human the real self-generating subject of history, just as in virtue of socialism it allows this subject to be revealed and actualized completely, so too is it probable that Marxism may penetrate within technology into an unknown subject of natural processes not yet manifest to itself: humans along with nature, and nature along with them, each mutually self-mediating."

According to Marx's original conception, the forces of production (even the technological ones) remain the actual carriers of social wealth; through revolutionizing relations of production that have grown old and confining, they would be merely put into a state of freedom. The irrationality of an order that hinders an objectively possible transition to a higher state of development is charged against these relationships alone. If, by contrast, Bloch calls into question the innocence of the forces of production, whose innocence was guaranteed by Marx's philosophy of history, he obviously sees himself compelled to this view by determinate experiences. Certain indications speak in favor of social developments in the East and the West heading tendentially beyond constant conflict toward a common middle ground. At any rate, both here and there phenomena mount up that suggest a sociological interpretation under the heading of "industrial society." This orientation has misled many in the West into dangerously disregarding divergent trends that still result from different property laws. But technological developments seem *per se* to bring forth an organizational framework that is independent of the relations of production in greater measure than Marxists have ever assumed. Yet even these technologically specified institutions develop at first no less a "power of alienation" than those specific to capitalism. Bloch holds onto utopia by promising a socialist resurrection not only to capitalism but to the technology brought forth by it. The, so to speak, capitalist nature of the technological means employed in socialist countries and of their forms of social organization are thus explained away as merely a sort of cultural lag.

The Extravagance of Utopia and the Melancholy of Fulfillment

This idea should not be confused with the affect associated with it. The latter lets us feel the ressentiment of cultural critique; indeed, it lets us, against our better judgment as it were, feel social romanticism. This is clearly revealed, say, in the polemic against Gropius and Le Corbusier, against the engineering skill of the architects in concrete, against steel mobiles and flat roofs. The curse of abstract technology is shared by the lines of architecture; "the effect is all the more chilling when it has to it no sloppy edges whatsoever, just kitschy lighting effects." In general, Bloch, along with Lukács, goes in for being affronted by modern art not only out of a sense of duty; affinity for classical aesthetics resonates in their applause for "realism." As in Hegel's case, art is construed in accord with the model of the symbolic. In the beautiful illusion is replicated *the* light that things and shapes cast on what they once could have been—luminous matter instead of appearing idea. This aesthetics is related to Adorno's in a significantly complementary way: Art is not supposed to demonstrate its truth in relation to current contradictions.

The aesthetic problem brings us back once again to the political problem—Bloch is a citizen of another republic. [See note 2.] His thought is directed to other addressees, as when he wants to melt a dogmatically and empirically frozen diamat beneath the sun of its utopian origin. His authorship is tied to other conventions, as when he meets his quota of jargon by entering the lists against Heidegger's animalistic–petit-bourgeois phenomenology of experience, belittling Klages as the compleat Tarzan philosopher, and degrading D. H. Lawrence as a sentimental poetizer of the penis. (The aura of vagueness about these slurs is just what is most harrowing about them.) Similar invectives against Jaspers are quite well explained as a defense against the silly flourish that baptizes Bloch as the "Jaspers of the East"—the comparison levies its own verdict against itself. Bloch nonetheless doles out polemic in a coin in which many feuilleton sections here in West Germany could repay him with an appearance of being in the right. He himself does not shun the level on which, in turn, the usual local variety of anti-Communism presents him with his bill. But neither the denunciations in the sphere of day-to-day politics nor the complementary attempts to remove Bloch, the gnostic, to distant theological lands should mislead us in locating the dimension in which his philosophy puts down its political roots: Bloch merely gives a gothic disguise to the intimate relationship of Leninist strategy to violence.

It is not without reason that there lives on in Marxism, along with the, as it were, tolerant element that is expressed in the kingdom of *freedom*, the so to speak *ex cathedra* element as well, which is expressed in the *kingdom* of freedom, in freedom as a kingdom. The paths to it are likewise not liberal; they are the takeover of power in the state; they are discipline, authority, central planning, line of command, orthodoxy. . . . precisely total liberty does not lose itself in frolicking arbitrariness, and in the substanceless despair that lies at its end, but triumphs only in the will to orthodoxy.

This thought might claim to be one with the deep traditions of German philosophy, and yet in the same breath "the aspect of the kingdom," the "essence of order," undergoes a sanctification that, with all due respect, borders on the totalitarian—"order *in every possible field* and sphere, from cleanliness and punctuality to supervision of the masculine and of the masterly, from the ceremonial to the style of building, from the number series to the style of philosophical system." The practical violence of the means outstrips its purpose even in beclouding its theoretical anticipation. Bloch of course knows full well about the "melancholy of fulfillment"; he speaks about the bit of nonarrival even within what does arrive, about the bitter residue in the act of realization. The deed of those doing the realizing cannot be abstracted from what has been realized, because they can only realize themselves step by step in bringing this to realization. The circle presented to the educator by the problem of education returns on the utopian level, but here too a misleading solution to it stands ready in the formula about the increasing mutual self-mediation of humans and nature.

A utopia that apprehends the dialectic of its own realization yet again in a utopian manner is surely not as concrete as it pretends to be. Perhaps the image of the kingdom of freedom owes the rigidification of its features in their "kingdomly aspect" to the extravagant nature of its initial project. This in turn could have its ground in the kind of speculative materialism that removes speculation itself from the realm of materialism. Marx, in a polemic against the philosophy of the Young Hegelians, once grounded the famous statement that one cannot realize philosophy without sublating or eliminating it by saying that Young Hegelian philosophy takes only the critical struggle of philosophy into account, without considering that "*previous* philosophy itself belongs to this world and is its complement, if only an ideal one."[7] From this, Bloch draws the inference that the negation of philosophy refers only to "previous" philosophy and "not to any possible and future philosophy at all." Yet Marx unmistakably asserts the opposite. In the same passage, he goes on to say that Young Hegelian philosophy is uncritical toward itself, inasmuch as it "started from the presuppositions of philosophy and stopped at philosophy's given results . . . though these—their legitimacy assumed—can be obtained only by the negation

of previous philosophy, of *philosophy as philosophy*." Among the presuppositions of philosophy belongs the awareness of its autonomy;
that the philosophizing spirit is capable of grounding itself. Philosophy
that is critical in regard to its presuppositions and has made the transition to critique conceives of itself, on the contrary, as a part of the
very process of criticizing itself, as an expression of the alienation and
at the same time of its overcoming. Only to the extent that it becomes
sublated into practice, which it has to conceive of as the realization
of itself, will philosophy be able to look over its own shoulder and
will knowledge of the sort that speculation always claimed to possess
be possible.

Bloch's mistake in interpretation is more than that; it cancels out
the merely experimental validity of utopia. Hence, the relationship of
philosophical criticism to the sciences remains unclarified as well, which
is equally true within diamat in general. If utopian thought wants to
grasp theoretically the practical necessity of transforming existing conditions from the experience of their contradictions it has to have its
knowledge-orienting interests legitimated scientifically, as a real objective need and as one whose fulfillment is objectively possible. The
hypothetical modesty of utopian thought is to be distinguished from
the awareness of autonomy on the part of speculative thought. The
former holds that the philosophical project is refutable by scientific
analysis of the conditions of possible realization—without ever expecting
a definitive proof of it, since revolutionary practice also transcends
anticipatory theory. In contrast with this, speculative thought believes
it advances philosophy by means of research; it believes that philosophy
can be demonstrated by means of research, but not refuted. Bloch
investigates a third way; he wants to do a utopian variation on the
usual speculation. The guarantee of salvation falls away, but the anticipation of salvation is maintained in its certainty—either this or it
does not work at all. The all-or-nothing point is reached; either the
hope is ultimately fulfilled in accord with the anticipated images of
fulfillment or there is chaos.

If utopia draws the force of its consciousness from the experience
that apparently natural limits have repeatedly been shown to be eli-
minable historically, it has to set up an awareness of limits just as
rigorously with respect to itself. A dialectical analysis that operates
not only with a mere approximation to totalities but out of an anticipatory grasp of these cannot meaningfully be reduced to a differential

analysis, nor can the concept of utopia be reduced to the content of regulative ideas. Yet dialectical analysis has to stay aware of the possibility of such changes, by which, in an unforeseen way, it too could be swallowed up. From a utopia foundering in the process of being realized there could emerge a situation that categorially escapes the utopian prospect. New obstacles, new difficulties, new hardships could enter that, in differing *toto coelo* from anything hitherto, would so little fit the contemporary structure of problems that from the perspective of an ever so utopian awareness they would not be at all envisaged as problematic. The realized utopia would be "otherwise." Of course, this awareness of limits does not cancel out consciousness, nor does it justify a counterenlightenment renunciation of utopia as such. The propaganda against the Jacobin consequences of utopian initiatives and the refurbished sermons against the terrors of morality only heighten the risks against which they render us blind.

Bloch's materialism remains speculative. His dialectic of enlightenment passes beyond dialectic to the doctrine of potency. Metaphorically—and with respect to utopia there always remains a residue of metaphor—Bloch always orients his thought to the development of a generally conjectured pregnancy of the world rather than to breaking the social spell cast by current contradictions. The philosophy of nature becomes the nature of his philosophy.

For the philosophers of what remains of the European tradition, which today occupies the ever narrower space between Anglo-Saxon positivism and Soviet materialism, it remains an irritating fact that a philosophy coming to them from beyond the Elbe allows itself—at the price of having leapt over Kant, and hence of being in some way precritical—to be borne along by the great breath of German Idealism. Thought broadens its sweep; and indeed, it must do so, even when the epoch of its auspices has passed away.

Notes

1. E. Bloch, *Das Prinzip Hoffnung*, two volumes (Frankfurt, 1959).

2. This essay was written before Bloch switched his residence to West Germany.

3. Franz Baader, *Werkausgabe* (1859–1861), Band VII, p. 17.

4. "Among the properties innate in matter, *motion* is the first and most outstanding, not only as *mechanical* and *mathematical* motion, but still more as *drive, vital spirit, tension*, as the *ordeal*—to use the expression of Jacob Böhme—of matter." *Marx-Engels Werke-Ausgabe*, Band 2, p. 135.

5. Compare, for example, the grand interpretation of Bachofen's teaching in *Naturrecht und menschliche Würde* (Frankfurt, 1961), pp. 115 ff.

6. Compare Bloch's *Avicenna und die aristotelische Linke* (Frankfurt, 1963).

7. Marx, *Werke*, Band 1, p. 384.

Karl Löwith: Stoic Retreat from Historical Consciousness (1963)

1

Two important books, *Von Hegel zu Nietzsche* and *Weltgeschichte und Heilsgeschehen*,[1] have gained Löwith the writer publicity worthy of his literary art and of the quality and breadth of his thought; however, they have not been to the advantage of Löwith the philosopher. Two misunderstandings of great consequence have been circulated as widely as the writings themselves. One is that it is as if Löwith had subjected the revolutionary rupture in the thought of the nineteenth century, from Hegel to Nietzsche, to such minute and at the same time marvelously stylized investigation only because he wanted to identify with its historical necessity—to discover himself, so far as possible, as a once more rejuvenated Young Hegelian. The other is that it is as if the same author had, in a convincingly mounted retrospective blend, traced the philosophy of history that arose in the eighteenth century back to its half-tacit, half-forgotten theological presuppositions in biblical salvation history just for the sake of criticizing the secularization of the Judeo-Christian faith as such and of withdrawing by way of these derivatives into some Kierkegaardian primordiality.

Actually, the tendency of both these books was unmistakable. They were linked with the positions that Löwith had clarified during the 1930s in studies on Nietzsche and Burckhardt—and these were elaborations of seminars Löwith had held at Marburg before emigrating. Out of the complementary motifs of these two thinkers taken together Löwith generates the powerful mechanisms with which he hopes to set in motion an ambitious change of scene from modernity to antiquity. He interprets Nietzsche's doctrine of the eternal return of the same as the first attempt (and one that is of prime importance to our own day) to return to the cosmological world perspective of the Greeks at the very apex of a modernity cut off from the world. However, because Nietzsche performed this return dialectically, as a prelude to a philosophy of the future, what can present itself undistortedly only in theory, in the inconspicuous silence of heightened reflection: the world as a whole, as a pitiless cycle of nature, remained for him a troubled project and postulate. Hence, for Löwith the dialogue between Nietzsche, the anti-Christian still indebted to Christian experience, and Burckhardt, with his bourgeois credentials and late-bourgeois resignation, becomes a key, a dialogue from which Löwith liked to cite one passage in particular: He, Nietzsche, was not serene and simple enough; instead of remaining a professor at Basel, he had no other choice than to present himself as a fool and jester of the new eternities. Löwith wants to free Nietzsche's truth from Nietzsche's own horizon, from the transport and rapture of a metaphysics of the will; he reflects this extricated truth in the urban composure of Jacob Burckhardt in order to discover in the easy historical erudition of this scholar so oriented toward antiquity, combined with one half of the still-trapped Nietzsche, a way to steer clear of the cliffs of historical consciousness in general.

The Nietzsche-Burckhardt conversation, in which Löwith's two great scholarly investigations are also set, should really have precluded any doubt about their purposes, which were to employ a reduction of the philosophy of history to its theological presuppositions in order to go back beyond the Judeo-Christian tradition as a whole and to analyze the post-Hegelian critique of Hegel (and of the ontological presuppositions of philosophy) in order to introduce a metacritique of historical consciousness as such—a consciousness that had long been prepared by theology but that only attained a dominant position in the nineteenth century and under atheist auspices. Inasmuch as doubts about this have nevertheless arisen, Löwith has in the meantime explained himself in a manner that cannot be misunderstood in four essays collected under the title *Wissen, Glaube und Skepsis*[2] [Knowledge, Faith, and Skepticism]—essays meant to make plain the incompatibility of philosophical inquiry and Christian faith—and in a series of papers,[3] the most important of which can be reduced to the common denominator of a critique of "historical existence" (or, as we would prefer to put it, historical consciousness). The leitmotif is the repeated appeal to a fragment from the first or second century: "In days to come, on account of the boredom of humans, the cosmos will not be a source of astonishment and will not appear to be a worthy object of prayer. This greatest of all goods in its totality, the best object of contemplation there has ever been, is, or will ever be, will have become endangered. . . ."

It is not by chance that Löwith links up with the Stoics, especially with the Stoic lament over the loss of a self-evident view of the cosmos. Throughout the Roman Empire the *logos* of nature could be apprehended only abstractly and in private; it was no longer visible in the mirror of the polis and immediately present to all who could gaze freely. A composed and absorbed *theorein*, like the ironic quest for truth and the skeptical reservation of judgment, had even then to be forcibly secured in the discipline of the privatized wise man, to be established by means of exercises in ataraxy. This refracted preservation of the classical world view in conflict with a rising Christianity is the ground upon which Löwith would like to gain a footing, for the sake of reestablishing such a world view in a post-Christian context. He would like to restore the Greek apprehension of the cosmos as an eternal whole without beginning or end, to renew the experience of *physis* as the unity and totality of a nature made up of circumscribed entities. As simple as this thesis is, the fears that motivate Löwith to espouse it are just as clear: Through the progressive historicizing of a consciousness that in the end is only "propped up by current history," our gaze seems to be hypnotically captivated by the variables of development, by what is merely current about any happening, by what is in flux and relative. At the same time, consciousness becomes entangled in the passions connected with its needful nature; it allows itself to be claimed by practical necessities and loses the theoretical disinterestedness of a knowledge for the sake of knowledge that is possible only contemplatively. Within this practically and historically restricted horizon of a "world" collapsed to the dimensions of the all-too-human (of world-historically urgent events), the encompassing character of the natural world, of the cosmos as the authentically supporting and conservating order of life, is distorted. The world of nature that both exists of itself and enfolds and undergirds us has been fatefully absorbed into a *world for us*. By this very fact, however, humans (and, in their view, all living species) lose their determinate place in the living totality of the cosmos; the disorientation of the human world can no longer be fitted into the order of heaven and earth.

But how can this grand conservative sentiment be justified from the dispassionate standpoint of a repristinized Stoic world view? How can the mastery of a historically diagnosed menace be grounded in the ahistorical self-understanding of Greek cosmology? The difficulty is patent: Precisely from the eminently practical experience of the risks that appear to be posed by modern consciousness, Löwith wants to get back to an attitude toward the world that is theoretical in the classical sense because it is elevated above practice and free from the restrictions of pragmatic consciousness. Through historical analysis of the rise of modern consciousness as a history of the decline [*Verfalls-geschichte*] of cosmological thought, he wants to forge the path back to the ancient view of the world, because it is elevated above history and free from the restrictions of historicized consciousness. Löwith wants to set the stage for the return of the modern to the ancient, but his reconstruction of the natural view of the world can escape neither the turning wheel of Nietzsche and Burckhardt nor the technical aid of the world theater, whose Christian spell it surely has to break.

2

If one reads Löwith's collected papers all at once and adds to them a few more publications from the most recent period,[4] then one will recognize with admiration, and with a certain astonishment, the sharply defined historical context that spontaneously emerges from the subtle and suggestive interpretations ranging from Anaxagoras to Aristotle, from Augustine to Pascal, from Descartes to Kant, from Kierkegaard to Heidegger. In an unforced manner, the great epochs are shaped into a history of decline: First, there is the biblical overturning of the Greco-Roman concept of the cosmos by Paul and John. This is strengthened by Augustine with the help of philosophical tools. The world which is by nature, stands on its own, passes away, and is formed anew becomes, when placed in the context of salvation, dis-empowered into a transitory creation that occurs for the sake of humans rather than for its own sake. The visible beauty of the cosmos is sacrificed to the hearing of the *logos* of God become invisible. Theory is demoted to curiosity; the presence of *physis* is suspended in favor of ascertaining future salvation. The shrinkage of the world into the world of humans, of independently existing beings into what has been made, of truth into certitude—these are the Christian theological presuppositions which then, from the time of Bacon, Descartes, and Galileo, ground the sciences in a secularized form. This second epoch of the decline of cosmological thought closes with Hegel, who once again justifies logic as ontology and truth as everlasting and constantly present but who is also the first to seriously raise history to the rank of philosophy. The consequences of this point of departure are unfolded in the radical and definitive break of historical thought with the natural view of the world. Historicism, pragmatism, and existentialist philosophy are only derivative world views of this fundamental revolution in the style of thought accomplished philosophically by Marx and Kierkegaard. Philosophy itself falls prey to this revolution—as the dictum has it, there no longer exist any philosophers who have the good conscience required for the contemplation of the universe.

As in any decent history of decline and fall, items are separated into the "not yet" and the "already." On the one hand, the competition between faith and natural thinking that was to be of such great consequence, the autumnal irruption of an awareness of salvation history into the innocence of the wise contemplation of nature, starts with Judaism. On the other hand, right down to our own day, the Mosaic religion of law has an advantage over the Christian appeal to the historical moment of the Redeemer's death in that the continuous regeneration of the Jewish people bears witness to the eternity of the biblical God as a visibly ever-present Reality. The same goes for Christianity itself, which on the one hand fatefully desacralizes the cosmos of the Greeks but on the other hand is to be preferred to the epochs of secularized faith for building a bridge to antiquity; in a theological horizon, the experience of history remained connected and ordered. Even the thought represented by Descartes, Galileo, Vico, and Voltaire and still encompassed within the natural system of the *Geisteswissenschaften* has, despite its distance from its Greek beginnings, not yet crossed the threshold of a post-Hegelian historicizing made possible by Hegel himself.

The more this project (which is inspired by the great breath of Western metaphysics) of a progressive deworlding of the natural world imposes itself on us, the greater will be our wonder and astonishment when we recall the intention it was meant to serve. With each thread of intellectual history that weaves more tightly the fabric of the downfall of ancient consciousness and the rise of modern consciousness, the web becomes more impenetrable; the historical context out of which Löwith would lead us, as out of a context of illusion, must appear the more objective. Löwith reflects on his procedure as follows: "How did we come to this modern aberration, which has succeeded in dissolving the one cosmos of nature into a manifold of historical worlds and the ever-identical nature of the human being into a multiplicity of modes of existence? This question may only be answered by a heightening of historical awareness which, nevertheless, has the purpose of dismantling the construction of historical consciousness."[5] This "nevertheless" hides an unadmitted difficulty. Löwith's own construction is so much under the sway of the logic of historical development that has been obligatory since Hegel that exactly how its singular distinctiveness could be legitimated is unclear. Its distinctiveness would have to consist in this: by means of the claim to have grasped history rationally, to disempower the claim of historical comprehension itself. "The presupposition of all thought in the area of intellectual history, viz. that substantive questions in philosophy may only be handled historically, grows out of a mode of thought that first emerged a hundred and fifty years ago and that consequently can also pass away again." At this particular juncture, Löwith makes use of a figure of thought with which he would like to justify his critical approach in general: Because historical thought itself arose historically, it can also pass away again. But Löwith has to borrow even this form of argumentation from his sharpest opponent; as is well known, in Marxist criticism it served not to regain a horizon of eternal truths but to call into question in principle all doctrines of invariance. Indeed, hope as a principle can only appeal to this argument: that no matter how much existing conditions may want to claim the ontological validity of everlasting reality, in demonstrating their historical origin we have at the same time demonstrated their possible frailty. Even in the contrary case of a critique directed backward this argument does not suspend one from the presuppositions of the historical thought on which it rests, for stated this way it leads to the reestablishment (always thought of from the perspective of the future) of a "beginning" or a "primal stage," whereby the origin itself falls prey to an ideologization. That is to say, one beginning is capable of outdistancing the other;

cosmology outdoes logic, myth outdoes cosmology, magic myth, and so on. For this reason the beginning that is supposed to count as the first is declared to be beyond the continuity of historical development and is legitimated in the end through the sheer aura of an immemorial primordiality. This holds true even when it is thought of as the cyclical movement, without beginning or end and yet limited, of perpetual growth and decay—that is, in the sense of *physis* as it was established within Greek philosophy.

In sober language and without the spectacle of a philosophic etymology, Löwith's "overcoming" [*Überwindung*] of historical consciousness brings us quite close to Heidegger's pretentious "overcoming" [*Verwindung*] of metaphysical thought—a closeness that is surely discomfiting to Löwith. *Physis*, we hear, is emergence into the light; it is the most disclosed and at the same time the most concealed; it is rise and fall at once. Löwith shares with Heidegger the need for a reconstruction of ontology; he, too, constructs a history of the forgetfulness of being with the deworlding of the world. Naturally, the caesuras in the process of decline are not the same in the versions of the two thinkers. Against Heidegger's ontological honoring of the pre-Socratics, Löwith upholds the Greco-Roman unity of cosmological thought right down to Pliny. Löwith sees in the unity of Christian and secularized faith the authentic distortion, whereas Heidegger flirts with eschatological consciousness. In their estimations of Nietzsche, Löwith and Heidegger part ways, though they succumb in like measure to the fascination with which Nietzsche led astray the generation of the First World War—a fascination that now seems strange. To me these differences do not seem nearly so important when one considers that both men literally explain the fate of two thousand years of Western development by the background history of a philosophically and theologically decisive understanding of the world. Both are intent on a return to a rightly understood ontology (or its "repetition"), whether it be a matter of exorcizing or coercing the metaphysical distortion of Being through exalted meditation or of doing the same for the desacralization of the cosmos through skeptical wisdom. In reality the single serious point of difference remains Heidegger's linking of truth (as well as of the true visage of the cosmos and the presence of its *logos*) with the historical world of humans. I have to admit that even Löwith has not been able to persuade me that the fundamentally historical character of the dialectical mediation of nature and the human world, however this dialectics is conceived, can be cogently disputed—least of all by way of a logic of the history of the ontological understanding of the world. But then, Löwith's resources are not exhausted by this either.

3

Just as Löwith mistrusts Nietzsche's turn back to the natural world perspective of the eternal return of the same because it is mediated by the historically connected thought of the will to power, he mistrusts his own enterprise to the extent that it consists of breaking out of the enchanted realm of historical consciousness with incantations he learned from that consciousness. Strictly, for the sake of the immediacy of cosmological intuition he must give up the arts of historical mediation, which he has mastered with too much virtuosity. Consequently, he tries repeatedly to direct a naive gaze toward the world as *physis* by means of a simple affirmation, or, better, to exhibit the cosmos without mediation by means of the ostensive gesture of the expert phenomenologist. Homer's sun shines on us as well; our apprehensions of nature have changed, but nature itself is constantly what it is. The Greeks' uniquely true insight into nature is that nature lets everything living come forth from it and pass away in returning to it.

The word *cosmos* is of course correlative to an experience of the world proper to the Greeks; but who could affirm without any further ado that we no longer live in a cosmos? Doesn't every biologist always presuppose and always reconfirm that the natural world is wonderfully ordered and astonishingly rational, and that it encloses the human being within itself, and that it is only for this reason that he can set himself apart from it?[6]

Once one is committed to this notion of cosmos, only trivial and tautological statements (such as "The world of nature is always itself") suffice to clarify it. All later conceptions are measured against it, as perspectivally foreshortened interpretations are measured against the substance of reality itself. In such passages the argument has, *mutatis mutandis*, an unintended similarity to the "realistic" breakthrough of Nicolai Hartmann, who managed directly to cut off the autistically fragmented reflections of an exhausted epistemology with a fresh "ontological" access to real and ideal being. Löwith invokes both everyday experience in the natural life world (the reliability of day

and night, heaven and earth, spring and autumn) and those mor-
phological and ecological phenomena that have always suggested to
descriptive investigators of nature the teleological image of a har-
monious natural totality. Löwith, who hesitantly gave up his study of
biology in favor of philosophy, reaches in this direct way the dimension
familiar to us from Goethe's intuition of nature and from Romantic
philosophy: Greek *physis* is transformed by sleight of hand into the
figure of nature proper to the New Humanism; the cosmos retains
the physiognomy fashioned by our own cultural tradition.

Of course, we also hear that nature is operating in a natural mode
not only when it permits growth and prosperity but when it destroys,
when it lets the earth quake, the seas toss, and volcanos erupt. It is
all the more risky to declare this nature the totality of what exists as
a whole, to integrate humans into it, pointing out that they are essentially a matter of human growth [*Menschengewächs*]. In my opinion,
an image of man as enfolded within the cosmos—an image revived
in the *Eranos Jahrbuch*—would have to appear risky to the superior
humanistic mind, which is so sensitive to the conversion of Stoic faith
in nature into a biologistic world view. If I am correct, it is from this
vantage that the important essay "Nature and the Humanity of the
Human Being" gets its strategic meaning.

Naturally, Löwith is familiar with the productive efforts of philosophical anthropology to characterize the special status of humans in
nature; he does not confuse the species that walks upright, leads its
life by acting and maintains it in society, speaks and keeps silent,
questions and answers, with plants and animals. However, he insists
that the human being, even in its extremes of suicide and self-ful-
fillment, is contained within the organic circuit of nature. The human
being in its growth is what it is by nature; its openness to the world
does not fundamentally transcend nature. "The transcending that distinguishes humans and their language from animals could still always
be realized within a natural environment that could not be transcended."[7] Accordingly, humanity is exhibited in the formation of the
human being into a "transcending in harmony with nature"; moreover,
it transcends nature only in the direction of immanent reason, the
speechless *logos* of nature itself, whether contemplatively in the wondering persistence of theory or actively in the life of the *polis*. Even
the common life together in the *polis* cannot be in order if it is not
constituted in the manner of the cosmos.

Wherever rigorous guardians shut off the dimension of history from a nature exalted to a totality, the formation of humans into humanness (attained by labor and at once preserved and required by language)—in short, humanness itself—is threatened. Löwith, who is at his most sensitive in this respect, attempts to secure the integration of humans into nature by way of a humanistic transfiguration of nature itself. Politically, this means a return to classical natural law, even though Löwith nowhere has express recourse to it. Classical natural-law theory remains implicit in the occasional references to the political anthropology of the ancient historians, who could narrate their histories without being led astray by the pathos of historicity. Löwith mentions Thucydides's conviction that the struggle for dominance by rulers, rife with change as it is, is rooted in the unchangeable nature of humans and hence must be constantly repeated in the same form. We are reminded of Polybius's teaching that, for the same reason, the cycle in the changing of constitutions, the reversal of victory into defeat and of subservience into domination, is subject to a natural rule. Löwith repeats these opinions as irrefutable insights and thus removes himself from the problematic pressures of contemporary history. In the meantime, the structures and the substances of regimes have changed since Polybius, and even since Machiavelli. The elimination of war has become an objective of diplomatic negotiations, and in many countries the removal of the death penalty has been raised to a constitutional norm. The latter is an example of a change in the organization of domination and the exercise of violence that has effects right down to the deepest anthropological strata; the former is an example of the practical need to change relationships in the future that hitherto have been held to be constant from an anthropological point of view. When not long ago Löwith was asked to contribute to a radio series on the problem of the death penalty, he reacted in a typical fashion. He entitled his contribution "Killing, Murder, and Suicide," and in very few words he explained the difference between killing in a state of war and murdering under the laws that govern bourgeois life. Without any side glance at the death penalty, but also without a glance at the efforts that keep an anxious world in suspense, the efforts (carved out under the mushroom cloud of the atom bomb) to end the state of nature between nations and thus to get beyond the typical distinction between murder and killing, he turned his attention exclusively to the Stoic *topos* of suicide as a sign of the freedom that is proper to the philosophical mastery of life. One can only wonder if it is still wisdom that has to be maintained at the cost of such a restriction of vision.

Just as there is not so much a modern nature as a modern science of nature, Löwith states, so too there is not so much a modern human nature as there are contemporary and antiquated anthropologies. Against this thesis we must consider whether the self-understanding of humans does not pertain essentially to what they naturally *are*; whether what people think of themselves does not determine the way they comport themselves. Is not the nature of the human necessarily mediated by the second nature that has been spelled out in the historically elaborated forms of his labor; in the historically developed and acquired rules of cooperative living, of commanding and obeying; in the historically discovered ways of experiencing, making sense, and gaining mastery, which have been fixed in language and fostered, repressed, or lost, and which have been embodied in the images that diverse societies at different times have had of themselves? We find ourselves in a situation in which the conditions for survival have become exorbitant, in the sense of being incompatible with forms of life that have taken on the bewitching appearance of "quasi-naturalness" by persisting for millennia. In such a situation of analytically definable alternatives between mortal dangers and changes in just such naturelike forms of life, historical experiences of the plasticity of human nature should not get shoved under the cover of the taboos supplied by a doctrine of invariants. It is more in keeping with an attitude of skepticism when we respond to the practical necessity of controlling far-reaching changes by advancing theoretical proposals that stand heuristically by the principle of a broad variability of human needs, capacities, and weaknesses. In contrast, the following thesis reads like a dogma of faith: "Even the distinction between civilization and barbarism reveals under different conditions the same nature of the human, who was no less a human at the start of history than he will be at the end."[8] Even if this proposition could be judged and its truth decided, the question would still be open whether at the level of civilization of advanced industrial society the humanity of the human being can be salvaged only under extreme conditions, whereby substantive changes in the categories of social interaction would have to extend, as far as possible, into the motivational structures and forms of rationality, into constellations of satisfaction and abstinence, into the coloring of the emotions, the mode of sublimation, and the mechanism of the self-

development of the spirit—if the species upon reaching a speculative
end of history is supposed to be "no less human" than it was at the
outset of its civilizing evolution, because human nature could change.

4

Of course, arguments like this belong to a type of thought that permits
itself to be practically engaged by what is needed. However, in relation
to the *unum necessarium*, Löwith would retort, there is only saving truth
[*Heilswahrheit*]: "What does such a profession of faith have to do with
knowledge?"[9] If *knowledge* is understood here in the ambitious sense
of an ontology directed toward being as a whole, Löwith's observation
is correct, for it is difficult to see why a practically challenged historical
consciousness should equate the engaged question about what is practically necessary in the situation as diagnosed with the ontological
question about the world as a whole. It may in fact be doubted "whether
a historical emergency, however great and urgent, can be the essential
motivation behind a philosophical reflection on the nature of being
and of truth."[10] Thus, it does not strike me as altogether satisfactory
when a certain fixation by Löwith on his teacher Heidegger pushes
him to repeatedly single out the author of *Being and Time* as the
extreme instance of a radically historical style of thought; one could
not surrender eternity more resolutely than Heidegger. Nevertheless,
Heidegger thinks of Being from the horizon of time. He does not give
up ontology as such; he refers history back to the structure of historicity.
This exposes him to the already mentioned warning, but at the same
time it shows how little it is he who has brought to completion the
incriminated history of decline that led to the historicization and pragmatization of consciousness. That occurred long ago in the revolutionary
break that took place in the thought of the nineteenth century, the
consequences of which Löwith has recently analyzed once again, with
a clarity that leaves nothing to be desired, in a brilliant introduction
to a selection of texts of the Young Hegelians.[11]

At this threshold, philosophy, which took up its own unavoidable
interest into reflection itself, had utterly renounced the classical claim
and completely withdrawn from ontology into critique. Löwith is a
clear-sighted opponent; in the Left Hegelians he finds even more
rigorous adversaries, and yet a more kindred spirit, than in Heidegger:

The foundational and revolutionary significance of Marx is not confined to his having turned Hegel over from his "head" to his "feet" and transformed metaphysical historicism into historical materialism; it lies rather in that Marx "overcame" philosophy *as such* in that he wanted to "realize" it. This dialectical overcoming was certainly effected in a programmatic fashion by Marx, but it was prepared and seconded by Feuerbach and Stirner, Ruge and Hess, Bauer and Kierkegaard. . . . To be sure, the Left Hegelians still call themselves philosophers, but they are no longer lovers of wisdom and of self-sufficient insight. They no longer believe in philosophical "theoria" as the highest, because the freest, human activity, and in grounding it on the "need for freedom from neediness." The point of departure of the "last philosophers" is the practical need of social and political conditions, in general, of the historical conditions of the time. They do not reflect on the eternal and self-identical reality, but on the changing exigencies of time. For them "spirit" becomes the "spirit of the age" [*Zeitgeist*]. They still do philosophy, but in opposition to pure contemplation and in the practical service of historical movement. For them the "world" becomes the "human world," "worldly wisdom" [*Weltweisheit*] becomes knowlege of the historical "world movement" [*Weltbewegung*], and the truth of their knowledge is confirmed for them, therefore, in the fact of its adequacy to the age.[12]

Further,

On account of this practical-historical tendency, which is unique to it, Marxism is a radical opponent of philosophy and it is at once the most extreme and hence the most doctrinally rich form of radically historical thought. If this dispute between Marxism and philosophy is not always perceived as a dispute between philosophy and nonphilosophy, or is represented as such only for nonphilosophical, practical–political reasons, the reason for this lack of clarity lies in that philosophy for its part has lost its good conscience in relation to itself by giving up both the distinction between practice and theory and the primacy of the latter.[13]

Let us make clear to ourselves once again the context from which Löwith criticizes this historicizing and pragmatizing of philosophic consciousness. From Aristotle to Hegel, theory always excluded from its essential interest what is relative, no matter how rich it might be in its interconnections; what is fleeting, no matter how relevant; and what is contingent, no matter how urgent. By contrast, Young Hegelian critique permitted itself to be practically engaged by just these concerns and committed itself to reflection on its inexpugnable historical stand-point, precisely in experiencing the absolute relevance of what is most relative, temporary, and contingent. Löwith, in turn, criticizes this experience as a dogmatic presupposition by engaging in intellectual history to demonstrate the connection between the Christian belief in creation and the concept of existence as it is increasingly sharpened from Pascal, via Kant, Kierkegaard, and Nietzsche, down to Heidegger and Sartre. If the world (which by nature is everlastingly what it is) is no longer conceived as a cosmos but instead as a transitory creation out of nothing, then the existence of every entity becomes certain only through faith in a factual creation of a factual world, and in the measure that this faith itself falls victim to secularization it becomes the blindest and most problematic matter of fact. "Existence," then, asserts both the urgency and the problematic character of the factual; it means the unmastered relevance of something that is relative, that can no longer be justified in terms of its relation to the Absolute, though it still keeps the need for justification alive as before. From this modern philosophy draws its motivation for a reflection that is supposed to furnish an ultimate grounding and post-Hegelian critique gets its impulse for the claim to realize practically what is too much for the power of reflection alone. Both, Löwith argues, derive their motifs—unbeknownst to them, and hence dogmatically—from re-pressed Christian doubt about the independence of nature, from mis-givings about the reliability of a world not founded on itself. However things might stand on this point as regards the history of ideas, the argument can work only under Löwith's own presuppositions, which are themselves quite dogmatic: first, that history is determined and changed essentially according to the dominant ontological understand-ing of the world; second, that it transpires in accord with the Romantic model, as a decline from its true beginning to a progressively self-destructive end; and third, that, by reason of sheer reflection on the post-Greek understanding of the world, historical tradition as such can be delivered of its lack of substance and history as a whole can be delivered of its contingency.

On the other hand, might not the demonstrated link between the Christian belief in creation and the critical self-understanding of a practically engaged historical consciousness be maintained in the op-posite way? That is, might not secularization in the sense of the de-mythologization of the tenets of faith bring out the moment of truth in myth? If the natural world in which the human race sustains and leads its life is contingent as a whole and does not speechlessly harbor its *logos* within itself, then history is in fact the process of a creation "after the fact"; on the basis of nature, within the natural world and beyond it, it is the formation of the human world by the hands of humans themselves. The myth of creation deciphered in this way would then not even be incompatible with pagan naturalism. The human race, as a component of nature, would have to be thought of as no less contingent than nature itself, and history would have to be conceived as natural history. History would lose its contingency to the extent that a progressive rationalization could be retrieved from the aimless growth of technical mastery over a reified nature and society—in a self-critical way, through the rational communication of humans about the practical mastery of their fates. I suggest the shadowy outlines of this utopian vision only in order to demonstrate that in relation to it the reference to "theological presuppositions" loses its force. Secularization is then admittedly the progressive critical appropriation of traditions from which alone we can obtain the *logos* of a humanity that is to be realized through the historical mediation of nature with the human world—from these traditions alone, if we are to take with full seriousness the contingency of the world as a whole and thus the necessity for begetting the *logos* through the world-historical labor of reproducing human life. Perhaps there is inherent in the very nature of our self-preservation a kind of *logos spermatikos*, or at any rate the immoderate claim that the life of the human race can only be sustained in the long run as humane. If there is something everlasting in history, then it is at most a knowledge of this anthropological lack of moderation (or measure), a knowledge of the basic unalterability of the luxurious element in human beings, whose nature is civilization. Such knowledge springs from the most primitive and most naked, the most sublime and most adventurous experiences, from everyday practice and from extraordinary moments; together with the other traces of historically sedimented experiences of the species, it has entered into myths, religions, philosophies, into the shapes of the objective spirit. About it we know in the abstract only that it is not knowable in the abstract.

The power of historical tradition may follow as a consequence from this; then we cannot get behind it—even when we are trying precisely to free ourselves, in the clarity of historical self-reflection, from the irrationality of sheerly traditional validity (indeed, from history as natural history). In contrast with this, Löwith ironically agrees with the Young Hegelian critique of religion that the post-Christian epochs simply cancel out Christianity, as if we could jump beyond the tradition of thought concerning salvation history and the rational claim of its secularized motifs in one leap and thereby overcome the hermeneutical basis of our self-understanding by way of simple negation. Indeed, Löwith's critique of the consciousness of historical dialectic as developed by the Young Hegelians proves also to be itself a radicalization of the Young Hegelian critique of religion,[14] and his apologia for the natural world view would amount to Feuerbach's anthropology thought through again in cosmological terms—if only Feuerbach had thought philosophically.

5

Beyond the hesitations that inevitably set in when one is confronting a superior mind, a critical discussion with Löwith runs up against a specific difficulty. Even before an argument is drawn out to its conclusion, one is irritated by an uneasy thought: Hasn't Löwith himself already analyzed it and formulated it in a far better way? His critics stand on ground already prepared by him. I would like to mention one example of this. The fixation on the classical concept of philosophy and on the cosmological world view of antiquity, Löwith once remarked, seems to our historical consciousness an impossible backtracking to a Greek world of the past in which there once were slaves and free men, the vulgar and the philosophers. In the course of my study of Löwith I have learned that in such cases it is more appropriate to take upon oneself the reproach of vulgarity and, without any elegance and against the rules, nod assent to his rhetorical questions. Like scarcely any other thinker, Löwith has tracked down the art of historical consciousness and its points of finesse (of course, only for the purpose of disempowering it; he has learned to wield it in the way one masters a skill to outplay an opponent rather than to play the game). He is so exactly familiar with the positions of a historical consciousness called upon for practical purposes that one has to be on the lookout against launching a metacritique with arguments long since anticipated. Thus, the Stoic retreat from historical consciousness, the return to antiquity that is just as stubborn as it is unmediated, is all the more astonishing.

Regression lives from unconscious anxieties and not from critical familiarity with the negated stage. For this reason it seemed unfair to me to pin down his hostility to modernity and hold it responsible for a reaction that one cannot otherwise explain. Löwith's definite elective affinity with Burckhardt may indicate a limited critical horizon amounting to a rejection of a present in which "there are no longer any philosophers" (a suggestion, perhaps, of a humanistically cultivated contempt for the extravagant nineteenth century and of a spiritual-aristocratic fear of the violent twentieth century), but another suggestion strikes me as more legitimate. As I was reading the artful autobiography of the scholar Löwith, his inaugural address before the Heidelberg Academy of Sciences,[15] I was fascinated by the quiet logic of this philosophical career. How was it possible that a destiny so outwardly driven about by political catastrophes—the fate of one who emigrated via Rome to Tokyo, from the East to the West, and from the United States to Germany—could inwardly have made possible not only the identity of the person, not only the continuity of doing philosophy at all; that in such a shell early seeds eventually bore the fruit of developed thought in an almost cyclically maturing evolution? Even if one considers the tendency to self-stylization that is all the more tempting for a great writer, this striking and deeply moving lack of symmetry still requires a stronger motivation, a motive integral to the life history itself— perhaps the privatized turn away from the political world that is expressed so inimitably and classically in the statement that "the unrest within the *Räterepublik* of Munich drove me to Freiburg, where I enjoyed the rigorous phenomenological schooling with E. Husserl."

In this turning away, Löwith cannot perceive the challenges of situations, and he is not permitted to acknowledge them as such. He does not realize that distancing oneself from *pragmata* (objects of practical concern) in pure contemplation is no longer objectively as possible as it was in the days of, and under the circumstances of, Heraclitus or even Aristotle. Reflection may have been able to detach itself from that immediate action in a confined and surveyable environment, so that action in turn might be determined by good deliberation if not by reflection itself. Today, action, even on the level of everyday life, is mediated by a technology that has expanded into a practical force and is itself guided scientifically; action has lost its relative ineffectuality, and for that reason it challenges philosophical consciousness practically; it forces it to reflect on current history. To be sure, a hundred years of engaged thinking have made terrifyingly clear the dialectic of engagement, but this does not give any dispensation from historical consciousness.

Löwith ignores the practical consequences of the sciences as they are applied to technology. He is content to locate the presuppositions of their philosophical self-understanding in a context of delusion brought about by the pragmatization and historicization of the natural understanding of the world, because in principle he cannot acknowledge that the relationship between science and philosophy has been reversed; that philosophy has to pose itself the practical tasks set by the objective consequences of a technology that has been transformed by science and has become socially effective, or it has to cease being philosophy.

The single outcome of modern science in which Löwith shows a certain interest is the penetration into outer space. This appears exorbitant to Löwith, not only in the literal sense of the word but also because on account of it the Earth's place at the center of the natural world view is displaced objectively. But is not this rather a question of something merely becoming manifest at this stage—a transformation that has been relentlessly underway ever since humans sustained their lives by the labor of their own hands? Marx once objected that Feuerbach "does not see that the world surrounding him is not something directly given and the same from all eternity but the product of industry and of the state of society in the sense that it is a historical product, the result of the activity of a whole succession of generations, each standing on the shoulders of the preceding one, developing further its industry and commerce, and modifying its social order according to changed needs."

Notes

1. *Von Hegel zu Nietzsche* (Stuttgart, 1958); *Weltgeschichte und Heilgeschehen*, fourth edition (Stuttgart, 1961). [Translator's note: These books have been translated into English as *From Hegel to Nietzsche* (New York, 1964) and *Meaning in History* (Chicago, 1949).]

2. *Wissen, Glaube und Skepsis*, second edition (Göttingen, 1958).

3. *Gesammelte Abhandlungen* (Stuttgart, 1960).

4. *Die Weltbegriff der neuzeitlichen Philosophie. Sitzungsberichte der Heidelberger Akademie der Wissenschaften* (Heidelberg, 1960); "Der philosophische Begriff des Besten und Bösen," *Studien aus dem C. G. Jung-Institut* 13: 211-236; "Nietzsches anti-christliche Bergpredigt," *Heidelberg Jahrbuch* 6 (1962): 39 ff.

Stoic Retreat from Historical Consciousness

5. *Abhandlungen*, p. 164.

6. *Wissen, Glaube und Skepsis*, p. 76.

7. *Abhandlungen*, p. 205.

8. Ibid., p. 160.

9. *Wissen, Glaube und Skepsis*, p. 17.

10. *Abhandlungen*, pp. 176 ff.

11. *Die Hegelsche Linke*, (Stuttgart, 1962), pp. 7–38.

12. Ibid., pp. 9 ff.

13. Ibid., p. 37.

14. Characteristic of this tendency is the study "Hegels Aufhebung der christlichen Religion," in *Einsichten. Festschrift für Gerhard Krüger* (Frankfurt, 1962).

15. See *Jahreshefte der Heidelberg Akad. d. Wiss.*, 1958–59, pp. 23 ff.

Theodor Adorno: The Primal History of Subjectivity— Self-Affirmation Gone Wild (1969)

When we were last together a few weeks ago, Adorno told me this story about Charlie Chaplin: At a party in Hollywood for the producer of "The Best Years of Our Lives" there was a man who had lost both his hands in the war. Adorno, the only one unaware of this, extended his hand to the celebrated hero but drew back when he felt the metal claws of the prosthesis. Chaplin, reacting with lightning speed, translated into pantomime Adorno's physical horror and his hopeless attempts to cover it up. The story about Chaplin is also about Adorno.

Adorno had called coldness the principle of bourgeois subjectivity without which Auschwitz would not have been possible. He had deciphered in even the most unsuspect normality a vitality grown cold. This sensitivity developed to the point of virtuosity does not (as Bloch had supposed) evince the malicious gaze of the experienced misanthrope, but instead a bit of unrelinquished, constantly arousable, and repeatedly disconcerted naiveté. In the midst of the sociability, which was surely put on for a look at the lifeless body part, the coldness of the metal had caught Adorno completely off guard. What the speechless mimesis of the great clown had made possible for that fleeting moment—the release of tension on the part of the quivering Adorno, trying to regain his composure—may have remained a motif of Adorno's language and of his enchanting analyses.

In Adorno's last philosophical work, *Negative Dialectics*, there is a difficult statement that draws together in one breath the central idea of the "dialectic of enlightenment":

That reason is something different from nature and yet a moment within it—this is its prehistory, which has become part of its immanent determination. As the psychic force branching out for the purposes of self-preservation, it is natural; however, once it has been split off and contrasted with nature, it also becomes the other of nature. Reason, projecting ephemerally out of nature, is identical and nonidentical with nature, dialectical in accord with its own concept. Yet the more unrestrainedly reason is made into an absolute over against nature within that dialectic and becomes oblivious of itself in this, the more it regresses, as self-assertion gone wild, into nature; only as nature's reflection would it be supernature.

Adorno had used the *Odyssey* to secure the almost lost traces of a primal history of subjectivity. The episodes in the wanderings of the one beaten in a double sense reveal the crises that the self, in the process of forming its own identity, experiences in itself and within itself. The cunning Odysseus escapes animistic charms and mythological forces; he evades ritually prescribed sacrifices by apparently subjecting himself to them. The intelligent deception of those institutions that uphold the connection between an overpowering nature and a mimetic, self-adapting, still diffuse self is the original Enlightenment. With this act a permanently identical I is formed and power is gained over a desouled nature. The I acquires its inner organizational form in the measure that, in order to coerce external nature, it coerces the amorphous element in itself, its inner nature. The triumphant self-consciousness of the Enlightenment prides itself on this relationship of autonomy and mastery of nature; Adorno calls into question its undialectical self-certitude.

If the subjection of outer nature is successful only in the measure of the repression of inner nature, mounting technological mastery strikes back at the subjectivity that gets shaped in these conquests. The primordial constitution of an I permanently identifying with itself already results, according to Adorno's surmise, from the dissolution of that fluid, sympathetic, and at the same time murderous connection with nature which the sacrifice of the self called for in ritual promised to maintain. The history of civilization arises, then, from an act of violence, which humans and nature undergo in the same measure. The triumphal procession of the instrumental spirit is a history of the introversion of the sacrifice (that is to say, of the renunciation) no less than it is a history of the unfolding of the forces of production. In the metaphor of the mastery of nature, this coupling of technological control and institutionalized domination still resounds: Mastery of nature is chained to the introjected violence of humans over humans, to the violence of the subject exercised upon its own nature. Thus, even the trust Marx placed in the unfolding of the forces of production as such is precipitous. The sphere of freedom of mounting technological control can no longer be deployed for the revolutionizing of forms of social interchange if, among other things, the subject is truncated by the very instrumental spirit that has created the potential for liberation. The irrationality of an Enlightenment that does not reflect on itself consists in this: "With the denial of nature within human beings, not only the *telos* of the outward mastery of nature, but the *telos* of one's own life becomes confused and untransparent."

In the positivist common consciousness we find mirrored today the lack of will and the incapacity to perceive the dimension in which subjectivity is transformed historically; it is as if the subjects in the caves at Altamira and in the lunar capsules were the same. The specific speechlessness of those who for the sake of rendering palpable a gigantic, outwardly oriented enterprise finally set foot on the moon, and the equally speechless echo of the spectators, could have indicated that what Hegel once called the experience of consciousness has been silenced. Astronauts, and we along with them, do not belong in the series of Odysseus's successors. His quasi-natural destiny goes on, of course, as long as the reproduction of life does not break the spell of sheer self-assertion, especially where self-assertion luxuriates. The new transcendence of a scientific-technological progress isolated from communicable needs is "self-assertion gone wild."

If the diagnosis of the age expressed by Adorno and Horkheimer in the dialectic of the enlightenment is correct, a question arises concerning the privilege of the experience to which the authors must lay claim in relation to the withered contemporary subjectivity. In his introduction to the *Minima Moralia*, which may be construed without irony as a doctrine concerning the right way to live, Adorno tried to respond. Individual experience is necessarily based on the old subject, which, historically, has already been condemned—"which is still for itself, but no longer in itself." If we wish (following Hegel) to treat what is disappearing as essential, then the bourgeois subject, apprehended in the process of disappearance, is the essence that experiences its frayed substance today in suffering under an overwhelming objectivity of social compulsion.

In psychological terms, with a view to Adorno's person, this outcome is convincing. The incomparably brilliant geniality of Adorno has constantly evinced as well something of the awkward and fragile position of a subject still for itself but no longer in itself. Adorno never accepted the alternatives of remaining childlike or growing up; he wanted neither to put up with infantilism nor to pay the cost of a rigid defense against regression, even were it to be "in the service of the I." In him there remained vivid a stratum of earlier experiences and attitudes. This sounding board reacted hypersensitively to a resistant reality, revealing the harsh, cutting, wounding dimensions of reality itself. This primary complex was occasionally released encapsulated into his behavior, but it was consistently in free communication with his thought—opened, as it were, to his intellect. The vulnerability of the senses and the unshockability of a thought free from anxiety belonged together. This gift, which was not simply an endowment, exacted its tribute in spite of everything.

Adorno was not defenseless in the sense of having been afflicted by an especially bitter fate. (This is not said lightly, in view of his very real exile and emigration in flight from anti-Semitism; and it is true that the uncurtailed primal element in him was able to flourish only inside the pacified realm preserved for him first by his mother and his aunt and later by Gretel, his wife and collaborator.) Rather, Adorno was defenseless for an altogether different reason: In the presence of "Teddy" one could play out in an uncircumspect way the role of the "proper" adult, because he was never in a position to appropriate for himself that role's strategies of immunization and adaptation. In every institutional setting he was an "alien," and not as if he intended to be. To his university colleagues this out-of-the-ordinary man was not exactly uncanny, even if he was considered suspect. However, academic philosophy (if the term suffices in this context) never really acknowledged this unusual intellectual. Even in the sphere of the literary public, which he influenced as hardly anyone else had for a decade and a half, Adorno did not get one of the official prizes, so his joy was disproportionately great when the German Association for Sociology made him its president. Adorno was defenseless in the unqualifiedly adult situations in which the routinized types exploited his weaknesses because they either did not realize or did not want to perceive that Adorno's specific weaknesses were profoundly connected with his eminent qualities. Even among his students there were such routinized types.

In more recent times Adorno bore many other things, even insults that might have been defused with a couple of sentences. I mention only the charge that Adorno's edition of Benjamin had suppressed Benjamin the materialist who sided with the Marxist party. This objection is based especially on the fact that at one time Adorno had criticized and rejected a three-part work by Benjamin about Baudelaire. Benjamin's revised version of the middle section was published in the *Zeitschrift für Sozialforschung* in 1940 and later included in the two-volume edition of his selected writings, and the original version of "Baudelaire" is coming out this fall. Now, the letters exchanged between Benjamin and Adorno in November and December of 1938 confirm to any unbiased reader that—as Benjamin himself would never have disputed—in this debate, too, Adorno was the theoretically more reflective party and the Marxist who was more erudite and more firmly fixed in the saddle. It is precisely under Marxist presuppositions that his argument is compelling. However else one may want to evaluate Adorno's arguments, the accusation of an anti-Marxist falsification of Benjamin is oversimplified and malicious agitation. According to Gershom Scholem, Benjamin had been especially close to Adorno; Adorno communicated with him, learned from him, and stimulated him in return. With his Benjamin edition and his Benjamin interpretations, and still more with the relentless recourse to Benjaminian motifs in his own writings, Adorno was the first to make the thought of his friend an unfalsified and irrevocable component of German discussion. That is why the ridiculous polemic of those who came to know Benjamin through Adorno hit him so hard.

One of Adorno's students called into the master's open grave, "He practiced an irresistible critique of the bourgeois individual, and yet he was himself caught within its ruins." That is quite true. To respond that "whatever is capable of falling down ought to be knocked down" and to say that Adorno should have had the power to strip away the last layer of his "radicalized bourgeois character" and go before the parade of activists carrying a flag demonstrates not only political and psychological foolhardiness but also a lack of philosophical understanding. The figure of the bourgeois individual, now relegated to the historical past, could only be left behind, voluntarily and with good conscience and not merely sadness, if from the dissolution of the old subject a new subject had already emerged. Now, Adorno never pretended to tell stories about a "new subject," but one thing was certain for him: The freedom that would be the polemical counterimage to suffering under social compulsions would have not only to eliminate the repressivity of the I principle but also to preserve its resistance against melting into the amorphous character of one's own nature or that of the collectivity. Adorno had shown, in a text that, God knows, meets the usual standards of academic philosophy, that the two belong together. In it he unfolded the aporias of the Kantian concept of the intelligible character, and he specified "freedom" in the following manner:

On the Kantian model, subjects are free to the extent that, as they are conscious of themselves, they are identical with themselves; and within such an identity they are at once unfree to the extent that they are subject to its compulsion and perpetuate it. As nonidentical, as diffuse nature, they are unfree; and yet as such they are free, because in the impulses that overwhelm them they are rid as well of the compulsive character proper to identity. This aporia is based on the fact that the truth behind the compulsion proper to identity would not simply be something altogether different from it, but would be mediated through it.

This statement makes plain the right that the untrue bourgeois subjectivity still retains in the process of disappearing in relation to its false negation. Adorno realized this and consequently never leaped over his shadows.

In the *Negative Dialectic*, which has become his philosophical testament, Adorno took up again the impetus the *Dialectic of Enlightenment* had carried: to save the dimension of nonidentity that the spirit seeking identity must cut away from the object.

The concept of the nonidentical is foreshadowed in Adorno's construal of Odysseus, in which he took aim at the prehistorically amorphous self that falls prey to the disciplining of an I capable of self-identical and hence identity-seeking thought. Now, however, the nonidentical stands for all "the truth that is hit upon by concepts, beyond their abstract scope." "The utopia of knowledge would be to open up what is nonconceptual by means of concepts, without making it identical with them." In this way the dialectic of the universal and the particular once unfolded by Hegel is taken up again. It has been gleaned from the model of communication in everyday language and can be made plausible in relation to it.

That we can never describe concrete objects completely in explicit discourse is a trivial insight. In making a statement about a particular (a thing, an event, or a person), we always apprehend it in view of a universal determination. The significance of the particular object can never be "exhausted" by progressively subsuming it under such generalities. However, as soon as subjects speak with one another and not just about objectified states of affairs, they counter one another with the claim to be recognized as irreplaceable individuals in their absolute determinateness. This recognition requires the paradoxical achievement of grasping—with the aid of what are in principle universal determinations and by means of these, as it were—the full concreteness of that which is precisely not identical with these generalities. Adorno turns this moment of the nonidentical within inevitable acts of identification against the necessity proper to formal logic, which has to determine the relationship of universal and particular in an undialectical way.

In this respect, Adorno only revives Hegel's critique of the limitations of thought within the faculty of judgment [Verstandesdenkens], without which thought would, of course, be impossible in principle. But Adorno turns this critique once again upon Hegel himself. Hegel's dialectic, too, is proved to be ultimately indifferent to the unique weight of the individuated singular entity. That is to say, Hegel does not grasp totality conceptually as a nexus of compulsion—for example, that of a society that mediates the particular, the individuals interacting with one another, through the universal, by means of the categories of social labor and political domination and its legitimation. Consequently, he does not see that the reconstructive power of dialectic can only disclose the kinds of relationships resulting from repression of communication free from compulsion—namely, coercive relationships of systematically distorted communication, under which individuals do not know one another as an objective context renders them. In Adorno's expression, society is just as much an embodiment of subjects as it is their negation; if it were no longer so, then the nexus of coercion whose dialectic is inwardly empowered to release it would have fallen away. In this sense, for Adorno the totality that dialectical thought tries to decode counts as "the untrue," although then Hegel's category of untruth can only be thought ironically, against Hegel himself.

The key term of *Negative Dialectics* is the "primacy of the objective" [*Vorrang des Objektiven*]. Adorno connects a fourfold meaning with this. First of all, objectivity denotes the coercive character of a world-historical complex that stands under the causality of fate, can be interrupted by self-reflection, and is contingent as a whole. Next, the primacy of the objective means suffering from that which weighs upon subjects. Knowledge of the objective context thus arises out of an interest in warding off suffering. Further, the phrase means the priority of nature in relation to all subjectivity it establishes outside itself. The pure I, in Kantian terms, is mediated by the empirical I. Finally, this materialist primacy of the objective is incompatible with any absolutist claims to knowledge. Self-reflection, and precisely self-reflection, is a finite power, for it itself pertains to the objective context that penetrates it. This inherent fallibility leads Adorno to plead for an "addition of leniency": "Even the most critical person would be utterly different in a condition of freedom such as he wishes to see. A just world would probably be unbearable for every citizen of a false world; he would be too damaged for it. That should stir a pinch of tolerance in the midst of resistance into the consciousness of the intellectual who has no sympathy for the world spirit."

Even the faculty of knowledge is not elevated above the frail and damaged state of the subject. If this is the way things are, however, the question how critical thought can be justified recurs. Our psychological response does not meet this question; it demands that the reasons for the right of criticism be made explicit.

Adorno has stubbornly refused to give an affirmative answer. He has even contested the view that reference to the negation of experienced suffering provides such grounds for the right of critique. This reference, doubtless the most extreme, may have no implications in the sense of a determinate negation, and yet Adorno is repeatedly forced by systematic considerations to take seriously the idea of reconciliation. This Adorno cannot escape. As soon as suffering is sublimated beyond immediate physical pain, it can only be negated if at the same time we express whatever is being repressed under the objectivity of societal coercion. Adorno once did this, tying in with Eichendorff's saying about "the beautifully alien" that rises above the sentimental suffering of alienation and above Romanticism: "The reconciled state would not annex the alien with a philosophical imperialism, but would find its happiness in the fact that the alien remained distinct and remote within the preserved proximity, beyond being either heterogeneous or one's own." Whoever meditates on this assertion will become aware that the condition described, although never real, is still most intimate and familiar to us. It has the structure of a life together in communication that is free from coercion. We necessarily anticipate such a reality, at least formally, each time we want to speak what is true. The idea of truth, already implicit in the first sentence spoken, can be shaped only on the model of the idealized agreement aimed for in communication free from domination. To this extent, the truth of propositions is bound up with the intention of leading a genuine life. Critique lays claim to no more than what is implied in everyday discourse, but also to no less. Adorno, too, has to assume no more and no less than this formal anticipation of just living when, with Hegel, he criticizes the identity-seeking thought of the faculty of judgment [*Verstand*], and then in turn the compulsion to identity in Hegel's idealist reason. Adorno might just as well have not assented to this consequence and insisted that the metaphor of reconciliation is the only one that can be spoken, and only because it satisfies the prohibition of graven images and, as it were, cancels itself out. The wholly other may only be indicated by indeterminate negation, not known.

This lack of consistency, which exposes Adorno's philosophy to an objection that can be avoided, has a deep underlying motive. If the idea of reconciliation were to "evaporate" into the idea of maturity, of a life together in communication free from coercion, and if it could be unfolded in a not-yet-determined logic of ordinary language, then this reconciliation would not be universal. [Compare my essay on a theory of linguistic communication in J. Habermas and N. Luhmann, *Theorie der Gesellschaft oder Sozialtechnologie?* (Frankfurt am Main, 1971).] It would not entail the demand that nature open up its eyes, that in the condition of reconciliation we talk with animals, plants, and rocks. Marx also fastened on this idea in the name of a humanizing of nature. Like him, Adorno (and also Benjamin, Horkheimer, Marcuse, and, of course, Bloch) entertained doubts that the emancipation of humanity is possible without the resurrection of nature. Could humans talk with one another without anxiety and repression unless at the same time they interacted with the nature around them as they would with brothers and sisters? The "dialectic of the enlightenment" remains profoundly undecided as to whether with the first act of violent self-assertion (which meant both the technological control of external nature and the repression of one's own nature) a sympathetic bond has been torn asunder that has to be reestablished through reconciliation, or whether universal reconciliation is not a rather extravagant idea.

Perhaps one can say that in a certain measure we "repress" nature in the methodical attitude of science and technology, because we only let it "have a say" in relation to our own imperatives instead of apprehending it and dealing with it from its own point of view. The pain from this has been buried over by a Judeo-Christian tradition for thousands of years, even if it is not without traces in this tradition's apocryphal background. Uninhibited, we subdue the earth, and now the entire universe is bereft of mystery. In contrast, the "dialectic of enlightenment" makes it clear that we ought to recall the reluctantly repressed sorrow over what we have perpetrated on technologically dominated nature in order to become aware of the repression of our own nature (that is, the deformations of subjectivity). Clearly, however, in order to eliminate avoidable social repression, we cannot refuse the exploitation of nature that is necessary for survival. The concept of a categorially different science and technology is as empty as the idea of a universal reconciliation is without basis. The latter has its ground instead in the need for consolation and confidence in the face of death, which the most insistent critique cannot fulfill. Without theology this pain is inconsolable, although even it should not be indifferent to the possibility of a society whose reproduction would no longer require the exploitation of our repressed anxieties.

Adorno, undeviating atheist that he was, nevertheless hesitated to moderate the idea of reconciliation to that of autonomy and responsibility. He was afraid to cloud the light of the Enlightenment, since "there is no light shining on human beings and things in which transcendence is not reflected."

With this might be connected the fact that Adorno, for whom theoretic rigor was second nature, mistrusted the claims of rigorous theory. He intentionally contented himself with "models." A young critic, still sure of his Hegel, once told him that the theory that apprehended the totality of society as untrue would actually be a theory of the impossibility of theory. The material content of the theory of society would then also be relatively meager, a reprise of the Marxist doctrine. After Adorno's opening talk to the sixteenth German Congress for

Sociology on "Late Capitalism or Industrial Society" one could not maintain this in the same fashion; however, the point remains.

Adorno was convinced that the principle of identity attained universal dominance in the measure that bourgeois society was subjected to the organizing principle of exchange. "In exchange [bourgeois society] finds its social model; through it nonidentical individual natures and achievements become commensurable, identical. The exploitation of the principle (of exchange) relates the whole world to what is identical, toward a totality." Exchange actuates the abstractive operation in a way that is tangibly real. In this "primordial affinity" between identity-seeking thought and the principle of exchange Adorno saw the link between the critique of the instrumental spirit and the theory of bourgeois society. This link was sufficient for him to bring in just a little too precipitously the analyses handed down from Marx. Adorno was not bothered with political economy. Albrecht Wellmer, in his recently published *Critical Theory of Society and Positivism*, has drawn attention to the danger that arises when the dialectic of enlightenment is misunderstood as a generalization in the field of philosophy of history of the critique of political economy and tacitly substituted for it. Then, that is to say, the critique of the instrumental spirit can serve as the key to a critique of ideology, to a depth hermeneutics that starts from arbitrary objectifications of the damaged life, that is self-sufficient and no longer in need of an empirical development of social theory. Of course, Adorno never let himself fall into this misunderstanding, but the activism of some of his students leads one to suppose that the decodifying of the objective spirit by ideology critique, to which Adorno had turned all his energy in such a remarkable way, can be easily confused with a theory of late-capitalist society. That praxis miscarries may not be attributed to the historical moment alone. The added circumstance that the impatient practitioners have no correct notion of the imperfection of theory may also contribute to this impasse. They do not realize all that they are incapable of knowing in the present state of affairs.

In this situation Adorno's aid was indispensable. It has been taken away from us by his death. There is no substitute for it, however slight.

Arnold Gehlen: Imitation Substantiality (1970)

1

For more than a decade Gehlen has been at work on his "Ethics."[1] The most consistent proponent of a counterenlightenment institutionalism, he has produced a bulk of work. *Urmensch und Spätkultur* set the tenor; one could foresee the object against which the moral-philosophical implications of his anthropology would be directed. Given the material that the cultural revolutions of recent years seemed to furnish especially for a Gehlenian ethics, one could even be filled with apprehension. What could not be foreseen was the satyr play which the author has provided us.

Gehlen parallels our age with that of Hellenism, or at least with the picture of it we have contrived. For some time Gehlen flirted with the role of the Stoic, but this costume no longer suits him. In his new book he presents Antisthenes and Zenon as the precursors and representatives of an apolitical Attic cosmopolitan culture that undermined the ethos of the state. They offer a prelude to the eighteenth century, in which once again the intellectuals, in the name of a defamation of authority, set about grasping authority indirectly. The first two chapters are, for the most part, written in the style of the humanistic tradition; the *topoi* of the ancients are presented as the pillars of wisdom of a contemplative life experience.

Gehlen's next three chapters unravel the theoretical intent of the book. In the style of an anthropological treatise, which is familiar to us from earlier publications, they give an overview of the biological roots of moral behavior. With the sixth chapter, however, criticism of contemporary culture shifts into the foreground and shunts off a course of thought that is repeated at ever briefer intervals. As a counterpart to modish self-incinerations, Gehlen makes use of the gesture of self-stoning. The hatred for humanitarianism (which Gehlen does not put in quotation marks, although it belongs to the Nietzschean jargon that passed over into the Nazi vocabulary) exercises a painful influence on the distinction-making capacity of an evidently highly differentiated mind. Venerable proverbs about life and theoretically interesting assumptions are mixed in with the standard political fare of an out-of-step intellectual of the Right who is no longer up to the biographical aporias of his role. In order to conclude this chapter as painlessly as possible, I shall confine myself to reproducing a few of the fruits of my reading:

The collective guilt of the Nazis and their victims: "After the year 1933 the integrity of the institution known as 'the German Reich' was not only injured; the Reich was destroyed from within and without by the National Socialists as well as by their opponents. Consequently, those who actively cooperated in this process cannot be exonerated even though they lacked an awareness of injustice or acted in the awareness of a more sublime, perhaps even humanitarian justice." (p. 99)

The greatness of the nation and German tragedy: "It is the most significant achievement of a nation simply to maintain itself as a duly constituted unity, and such a fortune has not fallen to the Germans. Self-preservation includes the spiritual affirmation and profession of a nation to itself before the whole world as well as security in the political sense, and this consists of the power of a people to make physical and moral attacks upon itself impossible." (p. 103) "The two or three nations in which something like this proceeds today will be free, i.e., they will determine their very fate." (p. 115)

The morality of the victors or reeducation: "Napoleon, who covered all Europe with graves, tears, ashes, and worldwide fame, will never be forgotten, but Prussia will be stricken from history. Those who are conclusively defeated have to pay a high price; they are prescribed the diet of moral invalids, a diminished consciousness, administered from now on by editors." (p. 120) "The concept (of the spiritual integrity of the group) comprises naturally the traditions and cultural heritage of an association as well as its honor, and to violently cut off a nation from its history or to dishonor it comes to the same as to murder it.

Recently some Americans seem to apprehend this and doubt their right to impose their political ideology on others." (p. 185)

What does the incapacity for enmity mean, and to what does it lead? "In human beings who render themselves incapable of enmity and only want to gain what they earn for themselves, namely forbearance, there remains something akin to a tiny diabolical seed that spells enjoyment at the annihilation of the defenseless, the theme of a genuine horror movie. Here one cannot wonder enough about the cleverness of *tyche* (fate), which metes out to the totally exhausted and defeated continent the chance of sheer physical survival—to be sure, a role that one enacts zealously by clearing away with anxious eagerness what is spiritually sustaining; but fate also leaves the outcome undecided. For the others have the power, and whoever wants to exercise the ethos of power—which we are trying to convince ourselves does not exist— needs an opposition that carefully keeps within striking distance. The latter, however, cannot play the right to existence as their single card without lowering themselves to the level of the natural realm—but at that point it is turned, as it ever is, into the right of the stronger. When that arises, the sacrificed ones can wonder whether they have not taken pleasure in the destruction of the defenseless." (pp. 145 ff.)

Disgust, and exemplar: "Since sharp distinctions (especially spiritual ones) *eo ipso* create a distance, and one does not want this, what can be expressed becomes vague at the margin, and one has to converse in vague ideas: democratization, repressive structures, reform of higher education, etc." (p. 47) "Soon one will no longer understand how the aged Clemenceau could say, 'From time to time one has to bend over the abyss in order to breathe in the breath of death, and then everything reaches equilibrium again.' " (p. 77)

Demonization, or shooting from the hip ethically: "Demonic is one who erects the kingdom of lies and forces other people to live in it. Then the kingdom of the inverted world is set up, and the Antichrist wears the mask of the redeemer as in Signorello's fresco in Orvieto. The devil is not the murderer: he is *diabolos*, the slanderer; he is God in whom the lie is not cowardice, as it is in human beings, but domination."[2]

2

In what follows I intend to confine myself to the theoretical starting points for an anthropological ethics. Gehlen distinguishes (p. 47) the following:

1. the ethos developed out of reciprocity,

2. numerous instinctual regulations that can be rendered in behavioristic terms, including the ethics of satisfaction and of happiness (eudaimonism),

3. ethical behavior rooted in the family, together with derivative extensions down to humanitarianism, and

4. the ethos of institutions, including the state.

Gehlen affirms that these four ethical programs have independent biological roots. Competing regulations for action are brought into balance in day-to-day behavioral routines. As soon as a value system lays claim to dominant validity in a lasting way, it becomes incompatible with the rest of the value systems. Then there arise conflicts that are insoluble in principle, not only between groups and individuals but also in the breast of the individual. Moreover, the stylization and one-sided prevalence of a pure morality always allow a discharge of aggression justified in the name of this morality.

The application of these theses to the present situation leads Gehlen to the assertion that the ethos of institutions is being suppressed by a generalized family morality. The "humanitarianism" spread aggressively by a stratum of intellectuals violates the biologically grounded metaethical equilibrium of equiprimordial value systems and destroys the anthropological health of the human race, as is demonstrated by the deformations of subjectivism. Out of this prognosis results an action-oriented "marking off of the enemy." There is a need to stand up to the carrier stratum of humanitarianism, the irresponsible intellectuals. Since the latter exercise their power indirectly (that is, over the mass media), they may be forbidden to exercise their trade only by means of censorship:

The word *responsibility* has a clear meaning only where someone is held publicly accountable and knows this. This occurs with the politician in relation to success, with the manufacturer in the marketplace, with the official in the criticism of superiors, with the worker in the checking of performance, etc. Wherever such supervision is not to be found or is expressly forbidden, as is the case in Article 5 of the basic law (freedom of the press) with respect to censorship, one is released from responsibility and can wholeheartedly look after the morality of others. (p. 151)

Whoever allows himself such far-reaching conclusions has to be very sure of his theoretical assumptions. And yet it may be that the central argument used to support the derivation of so-called humanitarianism from the ethos of kinship and the grounding of the opposition between universalism and the ethics of the state is not convincing. Gehlen unfolds the following train of thought: "Familial ethics" arose within the large family. It institutionalizes values of peaceful living together—reciprocal recognition, individual care, considerateness, and solidarity. "Humanitarianism" is due to an expansion of the area of application of this ethics from the obvious scope of interaction of the large family to abstract humanity. By contrast, the "ethos of the state," which is crystallized around values of service, fulfilling obligations, and readiness to make sacrifices, can be traced back to another root. Gehlen grounds the heterogeneity of the two value systems phenomenologically (in terms of the opposition between private and public, pacifist and warlike virtues) as well as historically-sociologically (in terms of the often-documented conflict between loyalty to family and loyalty to state).

Both suggestions are misleading. Gehlen garners the phenomenological distinction by treating the familial ethos as an internal morality and screening out the pertinent regulation of external relations, whereas he describes the ethics of the state only under the external aspect of self-assertion against potential enemies. Even if we prescind for a moment from the fact that the familial "ethos of peacableness and lack of danger in neighborly relationships" was constantly joined to the sturdy exercise of patriarchal power, it remains true that ethos covers only the internal aspect of a morality of small ethnocentric groups that purchases the latency of conflicts within the group by displacing aggression toward outside groups. An ongoing and easily provoked readiness for conflict, with polemical external relationships, is the reverse side of ethnocentric group solidarity. Gehlen (p. 169) cites Bergson in agreement: "The primordial and basic moral structure of human beings is fashioned for simple and closed societies, namely, of the sort that require that the group be closely united; but between different groups a virtual enmity reigns; one has always to be prepared to attack or defend oneself." However, if this is the case, then the value standard crystallized around honor, discipline, spirit of sacrifice, and readiness to take risks is as much a component of the familial ethos as it is of the ethos of state—both call for pacifist virtues within and polemical virtues toward the outside. The morality of the family is even more remote from a universalist ethics than is the morality of the state.

With the attainment of the stage of higher civilization, the hitherto dominant principle of organization, namely the differentiation of society according to kinship status, is dissolved by another: The kinship system is mediated by state-centered domination and socio-economic classes. Traces of this transition to high civilization, which revolutionized the human race's living conditions a second time (after the establishment of agricultural civilizations), have never completely disappeared in the phases of high civilizational development. What is reflected in the repeatedly actuated struggle between family loyalties and state-oriented value systems is not a biologically grounded antagonism but rather a historical conflict that goes back to the repression and relativization of the morality of small groups (first observable in regard to the primary roles within the family) by the more abstract morality of politically organized large groups (in Europe, the polis, the state, and the nation). The two competing value systems indicate world-historical stages of moral consciousness, which are marked by the differentiation of a pacifist internal aspect and a polemical external aspect.[3]

Piaget, linking up with Durkheim and in a certain agreement with Freud, has conceived the ontogenetic development of moral consciousness as a progressive universalization and internalization of value systems. From these viewpoints the ethics of the state is also the "more developed" form in relation to the familial ethos. It is "more abstract," because the realm of application of the internal morality is expanded beyond the limits of kinship systems toward the sphere of interaction of the large group: It is no longer the relative in a nuclear family, an extended family, or a tribe that is the morally obligatory reference person that is relevant, but the citizen of the state. And the ethics of the state is also "more abstract" in the wider sense of a higher degree of internalization of binding norms: Following the norm has in far greater measure to be independent of the control of external stimuli if the morally relevant action can no longer be played out "under the eyes" of sanctioning authorities—that is to say, of perceptibly present members of the small group.

Gehlen, of course, makes use of the category of the "expansion" of moral systems. In this way he derives "humanitarianism" from an expanded familial ethics. However, in doing so he does not have in mind a mechanism for engendering more abstract moralities in social systems with growing complexity. In the framework of his doctrine of anthropological constants, "expansion" amounts to an overextension and overstraining of a system of norms set up on the basis of the nearsightedness of small groups—a process, therefore, that is dysfunctional for biological equilibrium. This prejudgment keeps Gehlen from seeing that the ethics of the state, as well as that of "humanitarianism," has arisen from the expansion of familial ethics.

"Humanitarianism" is the agitation formula for universalist morality. What is it all about?

Not only does moral consciousness develop ontogenetically beyond the still externally supported level of the ethics of puberty toward a more abstract form; there is also a parallel to this in world history with the transition to modernity. In the course of this process—which was first achieved through the success of the capitalist mode of production within the framework of one (namely, our) high civilization— competition arose for the ethics of the state. Max Weber investigated this new universalist morality in the guise of the "Protestant ethic." Characteristically, Gehlen does not mention this type of morality. Kant conceptualized this morality. Every binding norm is distinguished by having to be binding for every person in the same measure; the hitherto maintained difference between internal and external morality is now overcome. Universalist morality is simultaneously qualified by an extreme degree of internalization. Monitoring whether norms are observed is sundered from external sanctions and brought completely within; Kant replaces the monotheistically supported authority of conscience with practical reason, which gives itself its laws in accord with a universalistic principle. The bourgeois concept of autonomy breaks out of the limits of an already abstract but still particular morality of the citizen of the state. It is the central notion of the European Enlightenment—for Gehlen, the core of "humanitarianism."

3

The logic of the development of modern consciousness is disclosed in relation to this point, tentatively associated with the name of Kant. As long as universalization and internalization are not yet complete, a global interpretation of nature and society is needed that at once delimits the scope of validity of the system of norms and establishes and justifies the controlling authorities that externally support and sanction conduct. These two functions become superfluous as soon as morality has become universalistic and requires complete internalization in accord with its very concept. Along with these two functions, the world pictures that ground morality become unnecessary as well; the system of norms is now reduced to the "legislation of reason."

In this way the following problem is posed. On the one hand, along with the interpretations of the world underpinning systems of morality we lose the very possibility of ontologizing single distinctive norms; ethics necessarily becomes formal. On the other hand, this principle of formalism, which now requires only the universal form for the validity of norms, becomes problematic; when norms are no longer moored in the world by an ontological interpretation but in the acting subject alone, they lose their binding character. Universally binding character can no longer be predicated on the arbitrary individual positings of a multitude of absolute individuals. Ethics necessarily becomes subjectivistic. In order to evade this dilemma, Kant ontologizes the ego (inasmuch as he distinguishes the "intelligible" ego from the empirical ego). This solution, repeatedly criticized since Schiller and Schelling, conceals the aporias of a fully conceptualized universalistic morality.

The "highest" level of moral consciousness connects the universal validity of morality with an extreme individualizing of the agents. The remainder of ontological thought still hidden within transcendental philosophy furnishes Kant with the motive for unifying both moments in a kind of subject that is a subject and yet is elevated above the empirical manifold of subjects. This transcendental superego is supposed to secure universality and individuation simultaneously—that is, the transcendence of the lawgiving of the moral ego in relation to the empirical and at the same time the independence of this ego from any external force. But even the inwardly erected force of the abstract universal remains alien to the individual, for, as Hegel saw, internalization alone—the blind spot of bourgeois ethics and of Kantian moral philosophy—cannot achieve individuation (namely, reconciliation of the universal with the particular). Internalization does justice to the moment of independence from external force; however, if the inward authority is supposed to operate not blindly (i.e. in an authoritarian manner) but rationally, then it should not be equipped with the quasi-ontological dignity of an intelligible lawgiver set above the factual communication of acting subjects. Those two moments that have to be brought into harmony in universalist morality—the individuality of the single person and the universal validity of norms—require mediation through discourse, that is, through a public process of formation of will that is bound to the principle of unrestricted communication and consensus free from domination. The absolutization of the generalized but communicationless privatism of bourgeois subjectivity, which lies at the basis of Kant's transcendental philosophical grounding of morality, makes possible for the last time a "world picture" justifying morality—although it is no longer permitted to perceive itself as a world picture and so has stripped away the form of ontology. When this last hypostatizing of a "foreign territory within" (Freud) is seen through and universalistic morality can no longer be established in relation to the paradoxical determinations of an intelligible ego,[4] the structure of possible speech, the form of the intersubjectivity of possible agreement, becomes knowable as the single principle of morality. The world-historical process of universalization and simultaneous internalization of norms of action (i.e., of the rules and metarules of interaction conducted in ordinary language) breaks out of not only local myths and high religions, but ultimately the concept of pure practical reason as well. The absolute freeing from external coercion contained in the notion of autonomy, and the unrestricted and equal validity of norms demanded by the categorical imperative, are determinations taken from the ethics built into the structure of possible speech.

On the one hand, after the destruction of the final world picture grounding morality we have to learn that an absolute justification of norms of action is impossible; all norms are fundamentally up for discussion. On the other hand, we realize that all discussions, even scientific ones, take place under empirical conditions; every empirically achieved consensus therefore is basically under suspicion of bringing to expression the coercion of a privileged opinion. A rational process of formation of will has to be linked with the communication of the participants, but the claim to a rational decision about practical questions can only be joined to communication through ordinary language when the latter is bound to the principles of unlimited access and freedom from coercion. The determinations of the intelligible ego thus recur as idealizations of the speech situation in which practical questions are argued. These idealizations are of course already implied in all speech, no matter how distorted, for with each communication (even in attempts to deceive) we are claiming to be able to discriminate true from false assertions. However, in the final analysis the idea of truth requires recourse to an agreement that, if it is to be capable of holding as an *index veri et falsi*, has to be conceived as if it were achieved under the ideal conditions of an unrestricted discussion free from coercion.[5]

The status of this unavoidable anticipatory grasp of an ideal speech situation is unique. The conditions of empirical speech are not identical with the ideal speech situation, yet it is pertinent to the structure of any possible speech that we anticipate this identification and counter-factually act as if the anticipatory grasp were not a sheer fiction — as an anticipation it is precisely real as well. What Gehlen (along with Schelsky) calls the ethos of reciprocity is grounded in this structure of possible discourse. Universalist morality that has become aware of itself explicitly lays claim to the basic norms of speech that already hold, inasmuch as it bases a requirement of legitimation on the ideal speech situation and declares rational only those norms of conduct that are capable of (repeated) justification within an unrestricted discussion that is free from coercion.[6]

The ethos of reciprocity, which is, as it were, implied by the fundamental symmetries of possible speech situations, is (if one wishes to pursue the logic of the development of moral consciousness sketched above) the unique root of ethics in general, and it is certainly in no way a biological root. If labor and interaction are equiprimordial, the life of the human race depends in equal measure on the material conditions of production and the ethical conditions of social organization. Because socialization is achieved in the medium of communication through ordinary language, the identity of the individual has to be established outside his organic system, in the symbolic relationships of interacting individuals within the community of communication. The profound vulnerability that makes necessary an ethical regulation of behavior as a counterpoise is rooted not in the biological weaknesses of humans, in the newborn infant's lack of organic faculties, and in the risks of a proportionally overlengthy rearing period, but in the cultural systems that are constructed as compensation.

The fundamental problem of ethics is guaranteeing mutual consideration and respect in a way that is effective in actual conduct. That is the true heart of the ethics of compassion. But compassion in the sense of sensitivity to the vulnerability of other persons is a basic motive of ethics only to the degree that it is related to the specific vulnerability of ego identity as such, and hence to the chronically fragile and, so to speak, constitutionally endangered integrity of the person (and only indirectly to the vulnerable integrity of the body). Because on the socio-cultural level the internal-external relationship is established not organically but symbolically, in the framework of forms of intersubjectivity constituted through ordinary language, the ethical achievements of a system of institutions is gauged first of all in terms of the extent to which it solves the problem of identity formation as well as that of avoiding and defending against threats to identity. This can take place at all levels of the "repressivity" lodged within the system of institutions. The degree of repressivity changes, I assume, with the condition of the forces of production and the organization of the system of domination. It is expressed in the systematic restriction and distortion of habitual communication. Repressive societies require legitimations of domination secured a priori with relatively dense hindrances to communication, whereas more liberal societies can leave a relatively large portion of the legitimation of domination to public discussion. The less repressivity is secured through systematically distorted communication, the more a universalist morality (and hence the chances for progressive individuation) spreads. If these empirical assumptions are correct, there is a connection between the degree of repression of institutions and the forms of intersubjectivity, on the one hand, and the systematic distortion or scope for tolerance found in communication and the stages of moral consciousness, on the other hand. Upon this connection depend, in turn, the symbolic organization of the ego that the individual acquires in processes of socialization and the strength of the ego identity that allows him to affirm his integrity against disturbances, burdens, and injuries. Thus, the unfolding of moral consciousness corresponds to a vulnerability of the identity that increases with the degree of individuation. That is, the reflexivity of the person grows only in proportion to its simultaneous externalization. The person is pushed ever further into an ever-denser network of reciprocal defenselessnesses and exposed needs for protection. Being human may be understood as the effort not to let this imperceptible network be rent asunder. Being human is the fearlessness ultimately left to us once we have had the insight that only the perilous means of an ever-so-fragile communication can resist the dangers of a universal fragility. *Contra Deum nisi Deus ipse.*

Gehlen, in contrast, recommends the paradox of an intentional re-trogression in humanity—the return to the ethos of the great and untransparent institutions. In a time when one could still muster illusions about such recommendations, one labeled this "revolution from the Right."

4

Up to this point, my argument has headed in the direction of dem-onstrating the unity of moral consciousness. The ethics of family and the ethics of the state do not go back to different roots; they may be apprehended as stages in the socio-cultural development of moral consciousness. The form of universalistic morality devalued to "hu-manitarianism" stands at the end of a process of universalization and internalization. The inner logic of this process finally makes the ethos of reciprocity that is built into the symmetry of relations proper to the ideal speech situation stand out as the foundation of morality in general. It has no biological root. All ethics depend instead on the morality immanent within discourse.

What is the status, however, of value systems (such as hedonism) that appeal to natural drives, no matter how residual? The life of the human race is organized in forms of intersubjectivity pertaining to communication through ordinary language. *Per se*, these are moral and immoral. The drive potentials transmitted through natural history are also taken up into this socio-cultural form of life—especially the basic drives of aggression and sexuality that have become objectified in a way that is dysfunctional in relation to the imperatives of self-preservation. Gehlen speaks of a number of instinctive regulations that are apprehensible by behavioral psychology as the roots of ethics, e.g., that of well-being and happiness (hedonism). Perhaps some instinctual remainders, such as those concern stimuli released by the image of the little child or libidinous drives in general, can be transposed more easily into the form of socially permissible motivations, and perhaps they correspond better with the ethics of speech than, for example, destructive drives; however, they are still not therefore roots of ethics. Whatever their affinity with the fundamental symmetries of possible communication through ordinary language, what is ethically relevant is not the natural-historical potential as such but the form of the symbolic structure it receives. This anthropological differentiation has been fixed in the Kantian distinction between duty and inclination.

Gehlen first introduces eudaimonism (better: hedonism, the doctrine that raises pleasure and private well-being to the status of ethical norm) as a biologically rooted ethics, for the sake of then construing "social eudaimonism" as its degenerate form:

It may be difficult for us to accept that the doctrine of the process of happiness can issue in an ethics, but without this insight one would not at all be able to understand the meaning of the word "social," which intends just this accessibility for all to vital material goods as an ethical postulate. (p. 62)

The union of humanitarianism and eudaimonism was projected by the intellectuals of the age of the Enlightenment, and still it could only become a massive, embodied, taken-for-granted issue when the industrialization of Western Europe and America had raised high the standard of living and when an all-encompassing world commerce (embracing the technology of news reporting as well) brought out the palpable contrast with the large number of those still needy, helping whom both humanity and the interest in selling commodities recommended to the same extent. In no earlier constellation would this ethos have been capable of living. (p. 84)

In the present context, what is of interest here is not the quotable cry of alarm with which Gehlen advances the complaint of bourgeois self-hatred in the face of a victorious "social eudaimonism." This began, if I am not mistaken, with Ferguson and Montesquieu, and was promoted in grand style by Hegel and Tocqueville, but since Ortega, Carl Schmitt, and the neo-Romantics of the Right it has not produced any novel nuances. The grievance has become a litany. Private well-being corrupts the readiness to take risks; the primacy of the social corrupts the politics of the great individuals; the social interest corrupts the substance of the state. From his reading of the magazine Der Spiegel, Gehlen adduces a few more touching instances of decadence, such as the scandalous instance that "Starfighter crashes as well as traffic accidents are discussed only as questions of guilt"; in such cases one has in fact to fear that "for us the personal is more plausible than the nation." (p. 157) The antifeminist extras are also quite refreshing.

Now, the phenomenon of the depoliticization of the masses within the bureaucratic welfare state can hardly be denied. What are interesting from a systematic point of view are the difficulties Gehlen has in analyzing this entire complex.

Socialism has established the insight that the emancipation of the oppressed and the suffering promised by rational natural law and the bourgeois revolution cannot be realized without the economic liberation of those who are miserable and heavily burdened. The pertinent economic definition of unfreedom as exploitation has nevertheless brought about a false connection between the poverty of the masses and their political oppression. That is, if the definition of unfreedom that is applicable under the specific conditions of liberal capitalism is maintained under the changed conditions of capitalism governed by an interventionist state (as is also the case in industrially developed socialist countries), the exploitation can be corrected even while the unfreedom is preserved, but the unfreedom will not become indentifiable. Instead, the government is legitimated by the fact that the elimination of hunger already represents the realizing of freedom. The overcoming of mass poverty is equated with the emancipation of the masses.

Marx certainly did not think there could be economic relief without liberation from economically institutionalized domination. However, the satisfaction of hunger, to the extent that it can be a moral exigency as a condition of freedom, is not itself—like the establishment of freedom—a political-moral category. Ernst Bloch made this distinction for the first time with all the clarity that is to be desired for the Marxist tradition: Once the miserable and heavy laden were also the oppressed and the suffering, but in our day those unburdened and set free from misery are not *eo ipso* already the upright and reconciled as well.[7] This is not welfare cynicism but the salvaging of a distinction distorted by "social eudaimonism."[8] This distortion may have been the more easily established historically when the bourgeois concept of Enlightenment was directed against the kinds of dependencies proper to an epoch in which the immediate feudal unity of subjection, poverty, domination, and possession was a constitutional principle. Gehlen can renew the despicable category of "humanitarianism" only because he does not make that distinction. He lays the new welfare privatism uncovered by contemporary criticism—which Adorno would regard no less critically—to the account of universalistic morality, although it can only come about in virtue of the neutralization and depoliticization of that morality. Gehlen casts both of them into the same dustbin of "subjectivism" in which he collects everything that shakes faith in institutions.

5

The appearances of the anarchistic underground cultures and counter-cultures might have been presented as a test case of the subjectivism thesis. As is becoming ever more clear, these are really the institutional core of the more elusive protest movement. It is astonishing that Gehlen completely ignores these phenomena.

The more recent cultural anarchism seems to be characterized by the way its representatives distinguish quite clearly between the privatized goal of a secure standard of living and the genuinely political goal of emancipation. They rely, in a deliberately parasitical way, on the experiences of private welfare specific to certain social strata, from which they are able to distance themselves because such welfare in principle remains available. They exaggerate the powers of spontaneity and immediate interaction and make drug-supported experiments with forms of, if not the good, then surely the better life. The elimination of deeply based norms is probed, and the conditions of a social intercourse free from repression are tested in the medium of ongoing communication. Gehlen could have posed the question whether these subcultural forms of life do not provide a model for the ethics built into the structure of possible speech, an ethics in which the unfolding of moral consciousness putatively reaches its term. He might have added the question whether this example does not document most clearly his subjectivism thesis—the thesis that a realized ethics of reciprocity that destroys rigid institutions has to end in self-destructive irrationality. He could pick up *Acid* and point to some unique phenomena that justify Leslie Fiedler's talk about the new irrationalism.[9]

These appearances do speak for an at first sight contradictory devaluing of the principle of rational discourse precisely in groups that—for the first time, apparently—radically liquefy in ongoing communication all the norms of conduct, and they culminate, as Fiedler observes quite correctly, in the idealization of a state of nature that undermines the organizational form of socio-cultural life with the demand "to take the risk of the final leap in evolution and to completely abolish adulthood, at least in the realm of the sexual."[10] If the new form of life is supposed to get behind the unfolding of moral consciousness as such, however, then only an empty shell of communication in ordinary language can remain behind—a shell that has been robbed of the moral infrastructure of discourse and is only capable of using some expressions from a private language. Were one to think out to its end the impulse behind such a life form, one would see that it must think itself capable of the paradoxical achievement of an intentional return to the level of prelinguistic symbol organization. Its productivity would consist in the artificial engendering of paleosymbols (Arieti). That sympathy with insanity then takes the place of love of wisdom is not without a certain consistency.

In carrying through the construction to this point I am attempting to answer the question hypothetically imputed to Gehlen. Cultural anarchism teaches us about an unforeseen possibility. It frees the moral-political category of liberation and individuated life from being matted together with the categories of gratification and an administratively unburdened life; yet it merely substitutes for the old privatism a new one, which Fiedler calls the turn from the *polis* to the *thiasos*. The subcultural counterworlds are also cut off from the serious situation of public communication; they confirm a depoliticization that corresponds in a subterranean way with that of the dominant welfare privatism. The violence of cultural anarchy is just not capable of a rational transformation of norms; it can only introduce an erosion of norms, which simply because they are norms, fall prey to slogans about elimination. The result is apolitical and capable of being generalized only in the form of new fads, for the mode of decision remains unaffected by it. For these reasons I do not think it improbable that some of the countercultures—even if they become widespread—will, without great resistance, be restylized into subjectivistic leisure cultures and be absorbed by way of the division of labor into the existing system. Furthermore, the gray zones of a new social pathology, which evade the old definitions of illness and criminality, will cause an increase in the supervision of the social state. They could soon belong to the culturally taken for granted realities of the coming megalopolis.

A political reaction would then have to enter in only if the subculturally supported attitudes should endanger, by removal of motivation, the minimum of a readiness to obey and of a work ethic needed for the system. At that point, the new subjectivism could be interpreted as massively effective in the sense of Gehlen's ethics of institutions and could serve the purpose of legitimating the restriction of formal democracy that he is already urging. Gehlen disguises his recommendation in euphemistic references to the merits of Stalinism:

Similarly (to the universalistic culture of the intellectuals), the culture of the mass media today spreads the liberal-humanitarian mentality among business people, students, soldiers, etc.—a mentality against which the states of the Eastern bloc are putting up a defense. (p. 29)

. . . it was decisive when the Russians, in August 1968, excluded this kind of freedom in Czechoslovakia, namely a co-regime set up by the culture itself quite remote from the scarcely comprehensible Chinese resolve to transform intellectuals periodically into farm workers.

The drastic renunciation of this kind of freedom by the Soviets in August 1968 was an event of the first rank, and it initiated a trauma. (p. 154)

By whose tanks are we actually supposed to be traumatized?

Once upon a time in our country we experienced the effects of the politics of primordiality imitated in a technologically developed civilization. Can Gehlen deceive himself about the consequences the politics of an artificially revived substantiality of institutions possessing the means of violence would have in our technically more advanced civilization? An institutionalism developed within the triangle of Carl Schmitt, Konrad Lorenz, and Arnold Gehlen could easily receive the measure of widespread credibility that satisfies collective prejudices in order to release and direct virulent aggression against internal enemies, should external ones be lacking. For this reason, I contend that it is fitting, even in times of relative liberality, to take seriously the unhappy consciousness of the intellectuals of the Right, in order— with the aid of the one means that only the Left intellectuals have at their disposal (despite Gehlen's visions of conspiracy)—to trace that consciousness back to its thoroughly historical roots, precisely through analysis.

Notes

1. A. Gehlen, *Moral und Hypermoral* (Frankfurt, 1969).

2. The diabolical is not called by name, since it belongs to a sympathetic world picture. What is meant are the great figures of the Enlightenment and intellectuals from Lessing and Lichtenberg to Benjamin and Brecht, from Kant to Popper and Adorno. However, Gehlen's devil remains adamantly anonymous. At any rate, Marx is cited once—from a book published in 1919 by Hugo Ball.

3. In addition, it does not make sense, even according to Gehlen's own presuppositions, to affirm two different roots. The family is just as much an institution in his sense as the state.

130

Arnold Gehlen

Why should the value systems of domination organized by the state be instances of an ethos of institutions and not those of the familial ethos? Here at least the linguistic usage is unclear.

4. Compare Adorno, "Freiheit zur Metakritik der praktischen Vernunft," in *Negative Dialektik* (Frankfurt, 1967), pp. 209 ff., especially pp. 277 ff.

5. Compare my "Vorbereitenden Bemerkungen zu einer Theorie der kommunikativen Kompetenz," in Habermas and Luhmann, *Theorie der Gesellschaft oder Sozialtechnologie?* (Frankfurt, 1971).

6. Compare the interesting suggestion for the grounding of pure practical philosophy by P. Lorenzen, "Szientismus versus Dialektik," in *Hermeneutik und Dialektik*, Band I, R. Bubner, K. Cramer, and R. Wiehl, eds. (Tübingen, 1970), pp. 57–72, and O. Schwemmer, *Philosophie der Praxis* (Frankfurt, 1971).

7. Ernst Bloch, *Naturrecht und menschliche Würde* (Frankfurt, 1961).

8. From other perspectives, Hannah Arendt insists on the same distinction, above all in *Vita Activa* (Munich, 1957).

9. Leslie A. Fiedler, "Die neuen Mutanten," in *Acid*, Brinkmann, Rygulla, eds. (Darmstadt, 1969).

10. Ibid.

Walter Benjamin:
Consciousness Raising or
Rescuing Critique (1972)

Benjamin is relevant even in the trivial sense: In relation to him there is today a division of opinion. The battle lines drawn in the brief period since the appearance of his collected works[1] and their almost eruptive influence in Germany were presaged in his biography. The constellation of Scholem, Adorno, and Brecht, a youthful dependence on the school reformer Gustav Wyneken, and later closer relations with the surrealists were decisive for Benjamin's life history. Scholem, his most intimate friend and mentor, is today represented by Scholem the unpolemical, sovereign, and totally inflexible advocate of the dimension in Benjamin that was captivated with the traditions of Jewish mysticism.[2] Adorno, Benjamin's heir, partner, and forerunner all in one person, not only introduced the first wave of the posthumous reception of Benjamin but also put his lasting imprint on it.[3] After the death of Peter Szondi[4] (who doubtless would have stood here today in my place), Adorno's place was taken mainly by Benjamin's editors, Tiedemann and Schweppenhäuser.[5] Brecht, who must have served as a kind of reality principle for Benjamin, brought Benjamin around to breaking with his esotericism of style and thought. In Brecht's wake, the Marxist theoreticians of art H. Brenner, H. Lethen, and M. Scharang[6] put Benjamin's late work into the perspective of the class struggle. Wyneken, whom Benjamin (who was active in the Free School Community) repudiated as a model while still a student,[7] signalizes ties and impulses that continue on; the youthful conservative in Benjamin has found an intelligent and valiant apologist in Hannah Arendt,[8] who would protect the suggestible, vulnerable aesthete, collector, and private scholar against the ideological claims of his Marxist and Zionist friends. Finally, Benjamin's proximity to surrealism has again been brought to our attention with the second wave of the Benjamin reception that took its impetus from the student revolt; the works by Bohrer and Bürger, among others, document this.[9]

Between these fronts there is emerging a Benjamin philology that relates to its subject in a scholarly fashion and respectably gives notice to the incautious that this is no longer an unexplored terrain.[10] In relation to the factional disputes that have nearly splintered the image of Benjamin, this academic treatment furnishes a corrective, if anything, but surely not an alternative. Moreover, the competing interpretations have not been simply tacked on. It was not mere mysterymongering that led Benjamin, as Adorno reports, to keep his friends apart from one another. Only as a surrealistic scene could one imagine, say, Scholem, Adorno, and Brecht sitting around a table for a peaceful symposium, with Breton and Aragon crouching nearby, while Wyneken stands by the door, all gathered for a debate on Bloch's *Spirit of Utopia* or even Klages's *Mind as Adversary of the Soul*. Benjamin's intellectual existence had so much of the surreal about it that one should not confront it with facile demands for consistency. Benjamin brought together motifs that ordinarily run at cross purposes, but he did not actually unite them, and had he united them he would have done so in as many unities as there are moments in which the interested gaze of succeeding interpreters breaks through the crust and penetrates to where the stones still have life in them. Benjamin belongs to those authors on whom it is not possible to gain a purchase, whose work is destined for disparate effective histories; we encounter these authors only in the sudden flash of "relevance" with which a thought achieves dominance for brief seconds of history. Benjamin was accustomed to explaining the nature of relevance in terms of a Talmudic legend according to which "the angels—new ones each moment in countless hosts—are created so that, after they have sung their hymn before God, they cease to exist and pass away into nothingness." (*GS* II p. 246)

I would like to start from a statement Benjamin once turned against the procedure of cultural history: "It [cultural history] increases the burden of treasures that is piled on the back of humanity. But it does not bestow upon us the power to shake it off, so as to put it at our disposal." (F, p. 36) Benjamin sees the task of criticism precisely in this. He deals with the documents of culture (which are at the same time those of barbarism) not from the historicist viewpoint of stored-up cultural goods but from the critical viewpoint (as he so obstinately expresses it) of the decline of culture into "goods that can become an object of possession for humanity." (F, p. 35) Benjamin says nothing, of course, about the "overcoming of culture" [Aufhebung der Kultur].

1

Herbert Marcuse speaks of the overcoming of culture in a 1937 essay, "The Affirmative Character of Culture."[11] As regards classical bourgeois art, he criticizes the two-sidedness of a world of beautiful illusion that has been established autonomously, beyond the struggle of bourgeois competition and social labor. This autonomy is illusory because art permits the claims to happiness by individuals to hold good only in the realm of fiction and casts a veil over the unhappiness of day-to-day reality. At the same time there is something true about the autonomy of art because the ideal of the beautiful also brings to expression the longing for a happier life, for the humanity, friendliness, and solidarity withheld from the everyday, and hence it transcends the status quo: "Affirmative culture was the historical form in which were preserved those human wants which surpassed the material reproduction of existence. To that extent, what is true of the form of social reality to which it belonged holds for it as well: Right is on its side. Certainly, it exonerated 'external relationships' from responsibility for the 'vocation of humanity,' thus stabilizing their injustice. But it also held up to them the image of a better order as a task." (Negations, p. 120) In relation to this art, Marcuse makes good the claim of ideology critique to take at its word the truth that is articulated in bourgeois ideals but has been reserved to the sphere of the beautiful illusion — that is, to overcome art as a sphere split off from reality.

If the beautiful illusion is the medium in which bourgeois society actually expresses its own ideals but at the same time hides the fact that they are held in suspense, then the practice of ideology critique on art leads to the demands that autonomous art be overcome and that culture in general be reintegrated into the material processes of life. The revolutionizing of bourgeois conditions of life amounts to the overcoming of culture: "To the extent that culture has transmuted fulfillable, but factually unfulfilled, longings and instincts, it will lose its object. . . . Beauty will find a new embodiment when it no longer is represented as real illusion but, instead, expresses reality and joy in reality." (*Negations*, pp. 130 ff.)

In the face of the mass art of fascism, Marcuse could not have been deceived about the possibility of a false overcoming of culture. Against it he held up another kind of politicization of art, which thirty years later seemed to assume concrete shape for a moment in the flower-garlanded barricades of the Paris students. In his *Essay on Liberation*[12] Marcuse interpreted the surrealist praxis of the youth revolt as the overcoming of art with which art passes over into life.

A year before Marcuse's essay on the affirmative character of culture, Benjamin's treatise *The Work of Art in the Age of its Technological Reproducibility* (*I*, pp. 219–251) had appeared in the same journal, *Zeitschrift für Sozialforschung*. It seems as if Marcuse only recast Benjamin's more subtle observations in terms of the critique of ideology. The theme is once again the overcoming of autonomous art. The profane cult of beauty first developed in the Renaissance and remained valid for 300 years. (*I*, p. 224) In the measure that art becomes dissociated from its cultic basis, the illusion of its autonomy disappears. (*I*, p. 230) Benjamin grounds his thesis that "art has escaped from the realm of 'beautiful illusion' " by pointing to the altered status of the work of art and to its altered mode of reception.

With the destruction of the aura, the innermost symbolic structure of the work of art is shifted in such a way that the sphere removed from the material processes of life and counterbalancing them falls apart. The work of art withdraws its ambivalent claim to superior authenticity and inviolability. It sacrifices both historical witness and cultic trappings to the art spectator. Already in 1927 Benjamin noted that "what we used to call art only starts 2 meters away from the body." (*GS* II, p. 622) The trivialized work of art gains its value for exhibition at the cost of its cultural value.[13]

To the altered structure of the work of art corresponds a changed organization of the perception and reception of art. As autonomous, art is set up for individual enjoyment; after the loss of its aura it is geared to reception by the masses. Benjamin contrasts the contemplation of the isolated, art-viewing individual with the diffusion of art within a collective, stimulated by its appeal. "In the degeneration of the bourgeoisie, meditation became a school for asocial behavior; it was countered by diversion as a variety of social behavior." (*I*, p. 238)

Moreover, in this collective reception Benjamin sees an enjoyment of art that is at once instructive and critical.

I believe I can distill from these not completely consistent utterances the notion of a mode of reception that Benjamin acquired from the reactions of a relaxed, and yet mentally alert, film-viewing public:

Let us compare the screen on which a film unfolds with the canvas of a painting. The painting invites the viewer to contemplation; before it the viewer can abandon himself to his own flow of associations. Before the movie frame, he cannot do so. . . . In fact, when a person views these constantly changing (film) images, his stream of associations is immediately disrupted. This constitutes the shock effect of the film, which like all shock effects needs to be parried by a heightened presence of mind. Because of its technical structure, the film has liberated the physical shock effect from the moral cushioning in which Dadaism had, as it were, held it. (*I*, p. 238)

In a succession of discrete shocks, the art work deprived of its aura releases experiences that used to be enclosed within an esoteric style. In the mentally alert elaboration of this shock Benjamin notices the exoteric dissolution of a cultic spell that bourgeois culture inflicts on the solitary spectator in virtue of its affirmative character.

Benjamin conceives the functional transformation of art, which takes place the moment the work of art is freed "from its parasitic dependence on ritual," as the politicizing of art. "Instead of being based on ritual, it begins to be based on another practice—politics." (*I*, p. 224) In the claim of fascist mass art to be political, Benjamin, like Marcuse, sees the risk in the overcoming of autonomous art. Nazi propaganda art carries out the liquidation of art as pertaining to an autonomous realm, but behind the veil of politicization it really serves the aestheticizing of naked political violence. It replaces the degraded cult value of bourgeois art with a manipulatively produced one. The cultic spell is broken only to be revived synthetically; mass reception becomes mass suggestion.[14]

Benjamin's theory of art appears to develop a notion of culture proper to the critique of ideology, which Marcuse will take up a year later; however, the parallels are deceptive. I note four essential differences:

• Marcuse deals with the exemplary forms of bourgeois art in accord with ideology critique, inasmuch as he fastens on the contradiction between the ideal and the real. From this critique results an overcoming of autonomous art only as the consequence of an idea. In contrast, Benjamin does not raise critical demands against a culture still unshaken in its substance. Instead, he describes the factual process of the disintegration of the aura, upon which bourgeois art grounds the illusion of its autonomy. He proceeds descriptively. He observes a functional change in art, which Marcuse only anticipates for the moment in which the conditions of life are revolutionized.

• It is thus striking that Marcuse, like most other proponents of idealist aesthetics, limits himself to the periods acknowledged within bourgeois consciousness as classical. He is oriented toward a notion of artistic beauty taken from the symbolic forms within which essence comes to appearance. The classic works of art (in literature this means especially the novel and the bourgeois tragic drama) are suitable objects for a critique of ideology precisely because of their affirmative character, just as in the realm of political philosophy rational natural right is suitable on account of its affirmative character. Benjamin's interest, however, is in the nonaffirmative forms of art. In his investigation of the baroque tragic drama he found in the allegorical a concept that contrasted with the individual totality of the transfigurative work of art.[15] Allegory, which expresses the experience of the passionate, the oppressed, the unreconciled, and the failed (that is, the negative), runs counter to a symbolic art that prefigures and aims for positive happiness, freedom, reconciliation, and fulfillment. Whereas the latter needs ideology critique for decodifying and overcoming, the former is itself suggestive of critique: "What has survived is the extraordinary detail of the allegorical references: an object of knowledge whose haunt lies amid the consciously constructed ruins. Criticism is the mortification of the works. This is cultivated by the essence of such production more readily than by any other." (O, p. 182)

• In this connection, it is furthermore remarkable that Marcuse spares the transformation of bourgeois art by the avant-garde from the direct grasp of ideology critique, whereas Benjamin shows the process of the elimination of autonomous art within the history of modernity. Benjamin, who regards the emergence of the metropolitan masses as a "matrix from which all traditional behavior toward works of art emerges rejuvenated" (I, p. 239), uncovers a point of contact with this phenomenon precisely in the works that seem to be hermetically closed off from it: "The masses are so interiorized by Baudelaire that one searches in vain for clarification of them by him." ("On Some Motifs in Baudelaire," *I*, pp. 155–200) [For this reason Benjamin opposes the superficial understanding of *l'art pour l'art*: "This is the moment to embark on a work that would illuminate as no other the crisis of the arts that we are witnessing: a history of esoteric poetry. . . . On its last page one would have to find the x-ray image of surrealism." (*R*, p. 184)] Benjamin pursues the traces of modernity because they lead to the point where "the realm of poetry is exploded from within." (*R*, p. 178) The insight into the necessity for overcoming autonomous art arises from the reconstruction of what avant-garde art exposes about bourgeois art in transforming it.

• Finally, the decisive difference with Marcuse lies in Benjamin's conceiving the dissolution of autonomous art as the result of an upheaval in techniques of reproduction. In a comparison of the functions of painting and photography, Benjamin demonstrates in exemplary fashion the consequences of new techniques moving to the fore in the nineteenth century. In contrast with the traditional printing methods of pouring, casting, woodcarving, engraving, and lithography, these techniques represent a new developmental stage that may be comparable to the invention of the printing press. In his own day Benjamin could observe a development in phonograph records, films, and radio, which was accelerated by electronic media. The techniques of reproduction impinge on the internal structure of works of art. The work sacrifices its spatio-temporal individuality, on the one hand, but on the other hand it purchases more documentary authenticity. The temporal structure of ephemerality and repeatability, which replaces the uniqueness and duration typical of the temporal structure of the autonomous work of art, destroys the aura, "the unique appearance of a distance," and sharpens a "sense for sameness in the world." (*I*, pp. 222 ff.) Things stripped of their aura move nearer the masses, as well, because the technical medium intervening between the selective organs of sense and the object copies the object more exactly and realistically. The authenticity of the subject matter, of course, requires the constructive use of means for realistic replication, that is, montage and literary interpretation (the inscription of photographs).[16]

2

As these differences make clear, Benjamin does not let himself be guided by the concept of art based on ideology critique. With the dissolution of autonomous art, he has something else in mind than does Marcuse with his demand for the overcoming of culture. Whereas Marcuse confronts ideal and reality and highlights the unconscious content of bourgeois art that legitimates bourgeois reality while unintentionally denouncing it, Benjamin's analysis forsakes the form of self-reflection. Whereas Marcuse (by analytically disintegrating an objective illusion) would like to prepare the way for a transformation of the thus unmasked material relationships of life and to initiate an overcoming of the culture within which these relationships of life are stabilized, Benjamin cannot see his task to be an attack on an art that is already caught up in a process of dissolution. His art criticism behaves conservatively toward its objects, whether he is dealing with baroque tragic drama, with Goethe's *Elective Affinities*, with Baudelaire's *Fleurs du Mal*, or with the Soviet films of the early 1920s. It aims, to be sure, at the "mortification of the works" (*O*, p. 182), but the criticism practices this mortification of the art work only to transpose what is worth knowing from the medium of the beautiful into that of the true and thereby to rescue it.

Benjamin's peculiar conception of history explains the impulse toward rescuing[17]: There reigns in history a mystical causality of the sort that "a secret agreement (comes about) between past generations and ours." "Like every generation that preceded us, we have been endowed with a *weak* messianic power, a power on which the past has a claim." ("Theses on the Philosophy of History," *I*, p. 254) This claim can only be redeemed by an ever-renewed critical exertion of historical vision toward a past in need of redemption; this effort is conservative in an eminent sense, for "every image of the past that is not recognized by the present as one of its own concerns threatens to disappear irretrievably." (*I*, p. 255) If this claim is not met, then danger threatens "both for the continuance of the tradition and for its recipients."[18]

For Benjamin the continuum of history consists in the permanence of the unbearable and progress is the eternal return of catastrophe: "The concept of progress is to be founded within the idea of catastrophe." Benjamin notes in a draft of his work on Baudelaire that

"the fact that 'everything just keeps on going' is the catastrophe."
This is why "rescuing" has to cling "to the little crack within the
catastrophe." (GS, I, p. 513) The concept of a present in which time
stops and comes to rest belongs to Benjamin's oldest insights. In the
"Theses on the Philosophy of History," written shortly before his
death, the following statement is central: "History is the object of a
construction whose site forms not homogeneous and empty time but
time filled by the 'presence of the now' (Jetztzeit; nunc stans). Thus, to
Robespierre ancient Rome was a past charged with the time of the
now, which he blasted out of the continuun of history." (I, p. 261)
One of Benjamin's earliest essays, "The Life of Students," starts off
in a similar sense:

There is an apprehension of history that, trusting in the endlessness
of time, discriminates only the different tempos of humans and epochs,
which roll rapidly or slowly along the highway of progress. . . . The
following treatment, on the contrary, is concerned with a distinct
condition in which history rests as if gathered into one burning point,
as has always been the case with the utopian images of thinkers. The
elements of the final condition do not lie evident as shapeless, progressive tendencies, but are embedded in any present time as the most
imperiled, scorned, and derided creations and ideas. (GS, II, p. 75)

To be sure, the interpretation of the rescuing intervention into the
past has shifted since the doctrine of ideas presented in Benjamin's
book on baroque tragic drama. The retrospective gaze was then supposed to gather the phenomenon rescued, inasmuch as it escaped
processes of becoming and passing away, into the fold of the world
of ideas; with its entry into the sphere of the eternal, the primordial
event was supposed to shed its pre- and post-history (now become
virtual) like a curtain of natural history. (O, pp. 45–47) This constellation
of natural history and eternity later gives way to the constellation of
history and the time of the now; the messianic cessation of the event
takes over the place of the origin.[19] But the enemy that threatens the
dead as much as the living when rescuing criticism is missing and
forgetting takes its place remained one and the same: the dominance
of mythic fate. Myth is the mark of a human race hopelessly deprived
of its vocation to a good and just life and exiled into the cycle of sheer
reproduction and survival.[20] The mythic fate can be brought to a
standstill only for a transitory moment. The fragments of experience
that have been wrung at such moments from fate (from the continuum

of empty time) for the relevance of the time of the now shape the duration of the endangered tradition. The history of art belongs to this tradition. Tiedemann quotes from the Paris Arcades project the following passage: "In every true work of art there is a place where a cool breeze like that of the approaching dawn breathes on whoever puts himself there. It follows from this that art, which was often enough regarded as refractory toward any relationship with progress, can serve its *authentic* distinctiveness. Progress is at home not in the continuity of the flow of time, but in its interferences: wherever something genuinely new makes itself felt for the first time with the sobriety of dawn." (Tiedemann, *Studien*, pp. 103 ff.)

Benjamin's partially carried out plan for a primal history of modernity also belongs in this context. Baudelaire became central for Benjamin because his poetry brings to light "the new within the always-the-same, and the always-the-same within the new." (*GS*, I, p. 673)

Within the headlong processes of antiquation, which understands and misunderstands itself as progress, Benjamin's criticism uncovers the coincidence of time immemorial. It identifies within the modernization of forms of life propelled by the forces of production a mythological compulsion toward repetition which is just as pervasive under capitalism—the always-the-same within the new. However, in doing this, Benjamin's criticism aims—and in this it is distinguished from critique of ideology—at rescuing a past charged with the *Jetztzeit*. It ascertains the moments in which the artistic sensibility puts a stop to fate draped as progress and enciphers the utopian experience in a dialectical image—the new within the always-the-same. The reversal of modernity into primal history has an ambiguous meaning for Benjamin. Myth belongs to primordial history, as does the content of the images. These alone can be broken away from myth. They have to be revived in another, as it were, awaited present and brought to "readability" for the sake of being preserved as tradition for authentic progress.[21] Benjamin's antievolutionary conception of history, in accord with which the *Jetztzeit* runs perpendicular to the continuum of natural history, is not rendered utterly blind toward steps forward in the emancipation of the human race. However, it judges with a profound pessimism the chances that the punctual breakthroughs that undermine the always-the-same will combine into a tradition and not be forgotten.

Benjamin is acquainted with a continuity that, in its linear progress, breaks through the cycle of natural history and thereby menaces the lastingness of tradition. This is the continuity of demystification, whose final stage Benjamin diagnoses as the loss of aura: "In prehistoric times, because of the absolute emphasis on its cult value, the work of art was an instrument of magic. Only later did it come to be recognized as a work of art. In the same way today, because of the absolute emphasis on its exhibition value, the work of art becomes a structure with entirely new functions, among which the one we are conscious of, the artistic function, later may be recognized as incidental." (*I*, p. 225) Benjamin does not explain this deritualization of art, yet it has to be understood as part of the world-historical process of rationalization that the developmental surge of the forces of production causes in social forms of life through revolutionizing the mode of production. Max Weber uses the term *disenchantment* too. Autonomous art became established only to the degree that, with the rise of civil society, the economic and political system was uncoupled from the cultural system and traditionalistic world views were undermined by the basic ideology of fair exchange, thus freeing the arts from the context of ritual.[22] In the first place, art owes to its commodity character its liberation for the private enjoyment of the bourgeois reading, theater-going, exhibition-going, and concert-going public that was coming into being in the seventeenth and eighteenth centuries.[23] The advance of the process to which art owes its autonomy leads to its liquidation as well. In the nineteenth century the public made up of bourgeois private persons gave way to the laboring populace of large urban collectives. Thus, Benjamin concentrates on Paris as the large city *par excellence*. He also concentrates on mass art, since "photography and the film provide the most suitable means" to recognize the "deritualization of art." (*I*, p. 225)

3

On no point did Adorno contradict Benjamin as vigorously as on this one. He regarded the mass art emerging with the new techniques of reproduction as a degeneration of art. The market that first made possible the autonomy of bourgeois art permitted the rise of a culture industry that penetrates the pores of the work of art itself and, along with art's commodity character, imposes on the spectator the attitudes of a consumer. Adorno first developed this critique in 1938, using jazz as an example, in his essay "The Fetish Character in Music and the

Regression of Listening."[24] He summarized and generalized the criticism—since carried out with regard to a number of different objects—in his posthumous volume on aesthetic theory (GS) under the title "Art Deprived of Its Artistic Character":

Of the autonomy of works of art—which stirs the customers of culture to indignation that one should consider it as something better—there is nothing left except the fetish character of the commodity. . . . The work of art is disqualified as the *tabula rasa* for subjective projections. The poles of its deprivation are that it becomes both just one thing among others and the vehicle for the psychology of the beholder. What reified works of art no longer say, the beholder replaces with the standardized echo of himself, which he receives from them. The culture industry sets this mechanism in motion and exploits it. . . . (p. 33)

The ingredient of historical experience in this critique of the culture industry is disappointment, not so much about the history of the decline of art, religion, and philosophy as about the history of the parodies of their overcoming. The constellation of bourgeois culture in the age of its classical development was, to put it rather roughly, characterized by the dissolution of traditional images of the world, first by the retreat of religion into the sphere of privatized faith, then by the alliance of empiricist and rationalist philosophy with the new physics, and finally by an art which, having become autonomous, took up the complementary positions on behalf of the victims of bourgeois rationalization. Art was the preserve for a satisfaction, be it only virtual, of those needs that became, so to speak, illegal within the material processes of life in bourgeois society: the need for a mimetic relation with external nature and the nature of one's own body, the need for life together in solidarity, and, in general, the need for the happiness of a communicative experience removed from the imperatives of purposive rationality and leaving room for fantasy and spontaneous behavior. This constellation of bourgeois culture was by no means stable; it lasted, as did liberalism itself, only a moment; then it fell prey to the dialectic of the enlightenment (or, rather, to capitalism as its irresistible vehicle).

Hegel already announced the loss of aura in his *Lectures on Aesthetics*.[25] In conceiving art and religion as restricted forms of absolute knowledge which philosophy as the free thinking of the absolute spirit penetrates, he set in motion the dialectic of a "sublation" [*Aufhebung*], which immediately transcended the limits of the Hegelian logic. Hegel's disciples achieved secular critiques of religion and then philosophy in order finally to allow the sublation of philosophy and its realization to come to term in the overcoming of political violence; this was the hour when Marxist ideology critique was born. What in the Hegelian construction was still veiled now came into the foreground: the special status assumed by art among the figures of the absolute spirit to the extent that it did not (like religion once it became subjectivized and philosophy once it became scientific) take over tasks in the economic and political system, but gathered residual needs that could not be satisfied in the "system of needs." Consequently, the sphere of art was spared from ideology critique right down to our century. When it finally fell subject to ideology critique, the ironic overcoming of religion and philosophy already stood in full view.

Today not even religion is a private matter, but with the atheism of the masses the utopian contents of the tradition have gone under as well. Philosophy has been stripped of its metaphysical claim, but within the dominant scientism even the constructions before which a wretched reality was supposed to justify itself have disintegrated. In the meantime, even a "sublation" of science is at hand. This destroys the illusion of autonomy, but less for the sake of discursively guiding the scientific system than for the sake of functionalizing it for unreflected interests.[26] Adorno's critique of a false elimination of art should also be seen in this context; it does destroy the aura, but along with the dominative organization of the work of art it liquidates its truth at the same time.

Disappointment with false overcoming, whether of religion, philosophy, or art, can evoke a reaction of restraint, if not of hesitancy, of the sort that one would rather be mistrustful of absolute spirit's becoming practical than consent to its liquidation. Connected with this is an option for the esoteric rescue of moments of truth. This distinguishes Adorno from Benjamin, who insists that the true moments of the tradition will be rescued for the messianic future either exoterically or not at all. In opposition to the false overcoming of religion, Adorno — like Benjamin an atheist, if not in the same way — proposes bringing in utopian contents as the ferment for an uncompromisingly critical thought, but precisely not in the form of a univeralized secular illumination. In opposition to the false overcoming of philosophy, Adorno — an antipositivist, like Benjamin — proposes bringing a transcendent impetus into a critique that is in a certain way self-sufficient, but does not penetrate into the positive sciences in order to become universal in the form of a self-reflection of the sciences. In opposition to the false overcoming of autonomous art, Adorno presents Kafka and Schoenberg, the hermetic dimension of modernity, but precisely not the mass art that makes the auratically encapsulated experience public. After reading the manuscript of Benjamin's essay on the work of art, Adorno (in a letter dated March 18, 1936) objects to Benjamin that "the center of the autonomous work of art does not itself belong on the side of myth." He continues: ". . . Dialectical though your work may be, it is not so in the case of the autonomous work of art itself; it disregards the elementary experience which becomes more evident to me every day in my own musical experience—that precisely the utmost consistency in the technological law of autonomous art changes this art and, instead of rendering it into a taboo or a fetish, approximates it to the state of freedom, of something that can consciously be produced and made."[27] After the destruction of the aura, only the formalist work of art, inaccessible to the masses, resists the pressures toward assimilation to the needs and attitudes of the consumer as determined by the market.

Adorno follows a strategy of hibernation, the obvious weakness of which lies in its defensive character. Interestingly, Adorno's thesis can be documented with examples from literature and music only insofar as these remain dependent on techniques of reproduction that prescribe isolated reading and contemplative listening (the royal road of bourgeois individuation). In contrast, for arts received collectively—architecure, theater, painting—just as for popular literature and music, which have become dependent on electronic media, there are indications of a development that points beyond mere culture industry and does not *a fortiori* invalidate Benjamin's hope for a generalized secular illumination.

Of course, the deritualization of art has an ambiguous meaning for Benjamin too. It is as if Benjamin were afraid of myth's being eradicated without any intervening liberation—as if myth would have to be given up as beaten, but its content could be preserved for transposition into tradition, in order to triumph even in defeat. Now that myth is wearing the robes of progress, the images that tradition can find only within the innermost recesses of myth are in danger of toppling over and being forever lost to rescuing criticism. The myth nesting within modernity, which is expressed in positivism's faith in progress, is the enemy against which Benjamin sets the entire pathos of rescuing. Far from being a guarantee of liberation, deritualization menaces us with a specific loss of experience.

4

Benjamin was always ambivalent about the loss of aura.[28] In the aura of a work of art is enclosed the historical experience of a past *Jetztzeit* in need of revitalization; the undialectical destruction of aura would be a loss of that experience. When Benjamin, as a student, still trusted himself to sketch "The Program of Coming Philosophy" (*GS*, II, p. 159), the notion of an unmutilated experience already stood at the center of his reflections. At that time, Benjamin polemicized against "experience reduced to point zero, the minimum of significance," against the experience of physical objects with respect to which Kant had paradigmatically oriented his attempt at an analysis of the conditions of possible experience. Against this, Benjamin defended the more complex modes of experience of people living close to nature, madmen, seers, and artists. At that time he still had hopes of restoring a systematic continuum of experience through metaphysics. Later he assigned this task to art criticism, supposing that *it* would transpose the beautiful into the medium of the true, by which transposition "truth is not an unveiling, which annihilates the mystery, but a revelation and a manifestation that does it justice." (*O*, p. 31) The concept of aura ultimately takes the place of the beautiful illusion as the necessary outer covering, which, as it disintegrates, reveals the mystery of complex experience: "Experience of aura thus rests on the transposition of a response common in human relationships to the relationship between the inanimate or natural object and human beings. The person whom we look at, or who feels he is being looked at, looks at us in turn. To perceive the aura of an object means to invest it with the capacity to look at us in turn." (*I*, p. 298)

The auratic appearance can occur only in the intersubjective relationship of the I with its counterpart, the alter ego. Wherever nature gets so "invested" that it opens its eyes to look at us in return, the object is transformed into a counterpart. Universal animation of nature is the sign of magical world views in which the split between the sphere of the objectified, over which we have manipulative disposal, and the realm of the intersubjective, in which we encounter one another communicatively, has not yet been achieved. Instead, the world is organized according to analogies and correspondences for which totemistic classifications supply an example. A subjectivistic remainder of the perception of such correspondences are the synaesthetic associations.[29]

In the light of the appearance of aura, Benjamin develops the emphatic notion of an experience that needs to be critically conserved and appropriated if the messianic promise of happiness is ever to be redeemed. On the other hand, he also treats the loss of aura in a positive way. This ambiguity is also expressed in Benjamin's emphasis on just those achievements in autonomous art that are also distinctive of the deritualized work of art. Art fully stripped of the cultic element — and surrealist art, whose proponents have once again taken up Baudelaire's notion of *correspondances*, is exemplary in this regard — has the same aim as autonomous art, namely to experience objects within the network of rediscovered correspondences as a counterpart that makes one happy: "The *correspondances* constitute the court of judgement before which the object of art is found to be one that forms a faithfully reproduced image — which, to be sure, makes it entirely problematic. If one attempted to reproduce even this aporia in the material of language, one would define beauty as the object of experience in the state of resemblance." (*I*, p. 99, n. 13) The ambiguity can be resolved only if we separate the cultic moment in the notion of the auratic appearance from the universal moments. With the overcoming of autonomous art and the collapse of aura, the esoteric access to the work of art and its cultic distance from the viewer disappear. Hence, the contemplation characteristic of the solitary enjoyment of art disappears too. However, the experience released by the shattered shell of aura, namely the transformation of the object into a counterpart, was already contained in the experience of aura as well. A field of surprising correspondences between animate and inanimate nature is thereby opened up wherein things, too, encounter us in the structure of vulnerable intersubjectivity. In such structures, the essence that appears escapes the grasp after immediacy without any distance at all; the proximity of the other refracted in the distance is the signature of a possible fulfillment and a mutual happiness.[30] Benjamin's intention aims at a condition in which the esoteric experiences of happiness have become public and universal, for only in a context of communication into which nature is integrated in a brotherly fashion, as if it were set upright once again, can human subjects open up their eyes to look in return.

The deritualization of art conceals the risk that the work of art also sacrifices the experiential content along with its aura and becomes trivial. On the other hand, the collapse of aura opens up the chance of universalizing and stabilizing the experience of happiness. The absence of a protective shell around a happiness that has become exoteric and has dispensed with auratic refraction grounds an affinity with the experience of the mystic, who in the experience of rapture is more interested in the actuality of the nearness and sensible presence of God than in God himself. Only the mystic closes his eyes and is solitary; his experience as well as its transmission is esoteric. Exactly this moment separates the experience of happiness that Benjamin's rescuing criticism validates from religious experience. Benjamin therefore calls *secular* the illumination he elucidates in terms of the effect of surrealistic works that are no longer art in the sense of autonomous works but manifestation, slogan, document, bluff, and counterfeit. Such works bring us to the awareness that "we penetrate the mystery only to the degree that we recognize in it the everyday world, by virtue of a dialectical optic that knows the everyday as impenetrable, the impenetrable as everyday." (R, p. 190) This experience is secular because it is exoteric.[31]

No interpretation—however insistent in wrestling for the soul of a friend, as is Scholem's contribution to the volume *Zur Aktualität Walter Benjamins*[32]—can dismiss Benjamin's break with esotericism. In the face of the rise of fascism, political insight forced Benjamin to break with that esotericism of the true for which the young Benjamin had reserved the dogmatic concept of doctrine.[33] Benjamin once wrote to Adorno that "speculation sets out upon its necessarily bold flight with some prospect of success only if, instead of donning the waxen wings of esotericism, it sees its source of power in construction alone." (NLR, p. 76) Benjamin turned against the esotericism of fulfillment and happiness just as decisively. His intention—and this sounds like a repudiation of Scholem—is "the true, creative *overcoming* of religious illumination. . . . a *secular* illumination, a materialist, anthropological inspiration" (R, p. 179), for which solitary ecstasy could at most serve as a primer.

If we look back at Benjamin's thesis about the overcoming of autonomous art from this point, we see why it cannot be a thesis of ideology critique: Benjamin's theory of art is a theory of experience (but not of the experience of reflection).[34] In the forms of secular illumination, the experience of aura has burst the protective auratic shell and become exoteric. It does not derive from an analysis that sheds light on what has been suppressed and sets free what has been repressed. It is gained in a manner other than reflection would be capable of, namely by taking up again a semantics that is pried piece by piece from the interior of myth and released messianically (that is, for purposes of emancipation) into works of great art at the same time as it is preserved. What is unexplainable in this conception is the peculiar undertow that must be stemmed by rescuing criticism: Without its permanent exertion, it seems, the transmitted testimony of punctual liberations from myth and the semantic contents wrung from it would have to fall into a void; the contents of tradition would fall victim to forgetfulness without leaving a trace. Why? Benjamin was obviously of the opinion that meaning was not a good capable of being increased, and that experiences of an unimpaired interchange with nature, with other people, and with one's self cannot be engendered at will. Benjamin thought instead that the semantic potential on which human beings draw in order to invest the world with meaning and make it accessible to experience was first deposited in myth and needs to be released from it, and that this potential cannot be expanded but only transformed. Benjamin was afraid that semantic energies might escape during this transformation and be lost to humanity. His linguistic philosophy affords a foothold for this perspective of decline and fall; the theory of experience is founded in it.[35]

5

Throughout his life, Benjamin adhered to a mimetic theory of language. Even in the later works he comes back to the onomatopoetic character of single words and even of language as a whole. It is unimaginable to him that words are related to reality accidentally. Benjamin conceives words as names. In giving names to things, however, we can either hit their essence or miss the mark; naming is a kind of translation of the nameless into names, a translation from the incomplete language of nature into the language of humans. Benjamin did not consider the special property of language to lie in its syntactical organization (in which he had no interest) or in its representational function (which he regarded as subordinate to its expressive function[36]). It is not the specifically human properties of language that interest Benjamin but the function that links it with animal languages. Expressive speech, he thinks, is only one form of the animal instinct that is manifested in expressive movements. Benjamin brings this together with the mimetic capacity to perceive and reproduce similarities. An example is dance, in which expression and mimesis are fused. He cites a statement by Mallarmé: "The dancer is not a woman but a metaphor that can bring to expression an aspect of the elementary forms of our existence: a sword, a drinking cup, a flower, or anything else." (*GS*, p. 478) The primordial mimesis is the representation of correspondences in images: "As is known, the sphere of life that formerly seemed to be governed by the law of similarity was comprehensive; it ruled both microcosm and macrocosm. But these natural correspondences acquire their real importance only if we recognize that they serve without exception to stimulate and awaken the mimetic capacity in the human being that responds to them." (*R*, p. 333) Whatever is expressed in linguistic physiognomy or in expressive gestures generally is not a mere subjective state but, by way of this, the as-yet-uninterrupted connection of the human organism with surrounding nature; expressive movements are systematically linked with the qualities of the environment that evoke them. As adventurous as this mimetic theory of language sounds, Benjamin is correct in supposing that the oldest semantic stratum is that of expression. The expressive richness of the language of primates is well researched, and, according to Ploog, "to the extent that language is entoned emotional expression, there is no basic difference from the vocal expressive capacity of the nonhuman family of primates."[37]

One might speculate that a semantic basis from the subhuman forms of communication entered into human language and represents a potential in meanings that is incapable of being increased and with which humans interpret the world in light of their needs and thereby engender a network of correspondences. Be that as it may, Benjamin counts on such a mimetic capacity with which the species on the verge of becoming human was equipped before it entered upon the process of reproducing itself. It is one of Benjamin's fundamental (non-Marxist) convictions that meaning is not produced by labor, as value is, but can at most be transformed in dependence upon the process of production.[38] The historically changing interpretation of needs feeds from a potential with which the species has to economize, because although we can indeed transform it we cannot enrich it:

> It must be borne in mind that neither mimetic powers nor mimetic objects or referents (which, one could add, have stored away in them something of the releasing qualities of whatever is compelling and pregnant) remain the same in the course of thousands of years. Rather, we must suppose that the gift of producing similarities (for example, in dances, whose oldest function was this), and therefore also the gift of recognizing them, have changed with historical development. The direction of this change seems definable as the increasing decay of the mimetic faculty. (*R*, pp. 333–334)

This process has an ambiguous significance.

In the mimetic capacity, Benjamin sees not only the source of the wealth of meaning that human needs, released in the socio-cultural form of life, pour out in language over a world that is thereby humanized. He also sees in the gift of perceiving similarities the rudimentary form of the once-violent compulsion to become similar, to be forced into adaptation—the animal legacy. To this extent, the mimetic capacity is also the signature of a primordial dependence on the violent forces of nature; it is expressed in magical practices, lives on in the primal anxiety of animistic world views, and is preserved in myth. The vocation of the human species, then, is to liquidate that dependence without sealing off the powers of mimesis and the streams of semantic energies, for that would be to lose the poetic capacity to interpret the world in the light of human needs. This is the secular content of the messianic promise. Benjamin has conceived the history of art, from the cultic to the postauratic, as the history of the attempts to represent in images these insensible similarities or correspondences but at the same time to loose the spell that once rested on this mimesis. Benjamin called these attempts divine, because they break myth while preserving and setting free its richness.

If we follow Benjamin this far, the question arises what is the source of those divine forces that at once preserve and liberate. Even the criticism whose conservative-revolutionary power Benjamin counts on has to be directed retrospectively toward past *Jetztzeiten*; it lights on structures in which contents recovered from the myth (that is, documents of past deeds of liberation) have been deposited. Who produces these documents? Who are their authors? Benjamin obviously did not want to rely, in an idealist way, on an underivable illumination of great authors, and thus on an utterly nonsecular source. Indeed he was close enough to the idealist answer to the question, for a theory of experience grounded in a mimetic theory of language permits no other response. Benjamin's political insights stood opposed to this, however. Benjamin, who uncovered the prehistoric world by way of Bachofen, knew Schuler, studied and appreciated Klages, and corresponded with Carl Schmitt—this Benjamin, as a Jewish intellectual in the Berlin of the 1920s could still not ignore where his (and our) enemies stood. This awareness compelled him to a materialist response.

This is the background to Benjamin's reception of historical materialism, which he naturally had to unite with the messianic conception of history developed on the model of rescuing criticism. This domesticated historical materialism was supposed to supply an answer to the open question about the subject of the history of art and culture, an answer at once materialist and yet compatible with Benjamin's own theory of experience. To have thought he had achieved this was Benjamin's mistake and the wish of his Marxist friends.

Ideology critique's concept of culture has the advantage of introducing the cultural tradition methodologically as a part of social evolution and making it accessible to a materialist explanation. Benjamin went behind this concept, because the kind of criticism that appropriates the history of art under the aspects of rescuing the messianic moments and preserving an endangered semantic potential has to comprehend itself not as reflection on a process of self-formation but as identification and *re-trieval* of emphatic experiences and utopian contents. Benjamin also conceived the philosophy of history as a theory of experience.[39] Within this framework, however, a materialist explanation of the history of art—which Benjamin, for political reasons, does not want to give up—is not possible in any direct way. That is why he tries to integrate this doctrine with basic assumptions of historical materialism. He announces his intention in the first of his "Theses on the Philosophy of History": The hunchbacked dwarf theology is supposed to take the puppet historical materialism into its service. This attempt must fail, because the materialist theory of social development cannot simply be fitted into the anarchical conception of the *Jetztzeiten* that intermittently break through fate as if from above. Historical materialism, which reckons on progressive steps not only in the dimension of productive forces but in that of domination as well, cannot be covered over with an antievolutionary conception of history as with a monk's cowl. My thesis is that Benjamin did not succeed in his intention of uniting enlightenment and mysticism because the theologian in him could not bring himself to make the messianic theory of experience serviceable for historical materialism. That much, I believe, has to be conceded in Scholem's favor.

I would like now to take up two difficulties: the odd adaptation of Marxian critique of ideology and the idea of a politicized art.

6

In 1935, at the behest of the Institute for Social Research, Benjamin prepared an exposé in which he presented for the first time some motifs of the Paris Arcades Project (*Paris, Capital of the Nineteenth Century*). Looking back on the lengthy history of its genesis, Benjamin writes in a letter to Adorno about a process of recasting that "has brought the entire mass of thought, which was metaphysically motivated at the start, to a state in which the universe of dialectical images has been secured against the objections provoked by metaphysics."(B, 2, p. 664) By this he is referring to "the new and incisive sociological perspectives that provide a secure framework for the span of inter-pretation." (B, 2, p. 665) Adorno's response to this exposé and his critique of the first study on Baudelaire that Benjamin offered the *Zeitschrift für Sozialforschung* three years later reflect very exactly the way Benjamin makes original use of Marxist categories—and in terms of both what Adorno understands and what he misunderstands.[40] Adorno's impression is that Benjamin does violence to himself in the Arcades Project in order to pay tribute to Marxism, and that this turns out for the good of neither. He warns against a procedure that "gives to conspicuous individual features from the realm of the superstructure a 'materialist' turn by relating them, without mediation and perhaps even causally, to corresponding features of the base." (NLR, p. 71) He refers particularly to the merely metaphorical use of the category of commodity fetishism, concerning which Benjamin had announced in a letter to Scholem that it stood at the center of the new work in the same way the concept of the tragic drama stood at the center of his book about the Baroque. Adorno lances the superficially materialist tendency to relate "the contents of Baudelaire's work immediately to adjacent features in the social history of his time, and, as much as possible, to those of an economic kind." (NLR, p. 70) In doing so,

Benjamin gives Adorno the impression of a swimmer "who, covered with great goose pimples, plunges into cold water." (Ibid.) This sharp-sighted judgment, which loses none of its trenchancy even when Ador-no's rivalry with Brecht is taken into account, still contrasts oddly with the unintelligent insistence that his friend might wish to make good the "omitted theory" and the "lacking interpretation" so that the dialectical mediation between cultural properties and the overall social process would become visible. Adorno never noticeably hesitated to attribute to Benjamin the precise intention of ideology critique that he followed in his own work, and in this he was wrong. This error is shown in exemplary fashion by the objections that were supposed to have moved Benjamin to revise the notion of dialectical image that was central to his theory of experience so that "a purification of the theory itself might be achieved." (NLR, p. 54) Adorno does not see how legitimate it is to want to carry out the project for a primal history of modernity—which aims at decodifying a semantics that has been buried and is threatened with forgetfulness—by hermeneutical means, through the interpretation of dialectical images. For Benjamin, imaginal fantasies of the primal past are set loose under the impulse of the new, in which the continuity of the always the same is carried on; they "mingle with the new to give birth to utopias." (R, p. 148)

Benjamin's exposé speaks of the collective unconscious as the store-house of experiences. Adorno is rightly put off by this use of language; however, he is quite incorrect in thinking that disenchantment of the dialectical image has to lead back to an unbroken mythic thinking, for the archaic dimension of modernity—in which Adorno would see Hell instead of the golden age—contains just the potentialities for experience that point the way to the utopian condition of a liberated society. The model is the French Revolution's recourse to Roman antiquity. Here Benjamin uses a comparison with the realization of dream elements upon waking, which was developed into a technique in surrealism and which Benjamin misleadingly calls a classic instance of dialectical thinking. Adorno takes Benjamin too literally here. Trans-posing the dialectical image into consciousness as a dream seems to him to be naked subjectivism. The fetish character of commodities, he contends against Benjamin, is no mere fact of consciousness but is dialectical in the eminent sense that it produces consciousness—archaic images—within alienated bourgeois individuals. However, Benjamin has no need to take up this claim of ideology critique; he does not want to reach behind the formations of consciousness to the objectivity of an evaluation process by means of which the commodity as fetish gains power over the consciousness of individuals. Benjamin wants and needs to investigate only "the mode of apprehension of the fetish character in the collective consciousness," because dialectical images are phenomena of consciousness and not (as Adorno thought) transposed into consciousness.

Of course, Benjamin also deceived himself about the difference between his manner of proceeding and the Marxist critique of ideology. In the manuscripts for the Arcades Project he once puts it as follows: "If the base determines the superstructure to a certain extent in regard to the material for thought and experience, and if this determination is, however, not that of a simple mirroring, how then is it to be characterized, quite apart from its causal origin (!) ? As its expression. The superstructure is the expression of the base. The economic conditions under which the society exists come to expression in the superstructure." (cited after Tiedemann, *Studien*, p. 106) Expression is a category of Benjamin's theory of experience; it is related to those insensible correspondences between animate and inanimate nature upon which the physiognomical gaze of the child and of the artist rests. Expression, for Benjamin, is a semantic category that is more akin to what Kassner or even Klages intended than to the base-superstructure theorem. The same misunderstanding is shown in relation to the critique of ideology as practiced by Adorno, when Benjamin remarks about chapters of his later book on Wagner that "*one* tendency of this work interested (me) in particular: situating the physiognomical immediately, almost without psychological mediation, within the social realm." (*B*, 2, p. 741) In fact Benjamin did not have psychology in mind, but neither was he concerned with a critique of necessarily false consciousness. His criticism was concerned with doing justice to the collective fantasy images deposited in the expressive qualities of daily life as well as in literature and art. These images arise from the secret communication between the oldest semantic potentials of human needs and the conditions of life generated by capitalism.

In their correspondence concerning the Arcades Project, Adorno appeals to the goal "for the sake of which you sacrifice theology." (*NLR*, p. 54) Benjamin had surely made this sacrifice, inasmuch as he now accepted mystical illumination only as secular (i.e., universalizable) exoteric experience. However, Adorno, who in comparison with Benjamin was certainly the better Marxist, did not see that his friend was never prepared to give up the theological heritage, inasmuch as he always kept his mimetic theory of language, his messianic theory of history, and his conservative-revolutionary understanding of criticism immune against objections from historical materialism (to the degree that this puppet could not simply be brought under his direction). This can also be seen in Benjamin's assent to the instrumental politicization of art, where he confessed to being an engaged Communist. I understand this assent, which becomes clearest in the lecture "The Author as Producer" (R, pp. 220–238), as a perplexity resulting from the fact that an immanent relation to political praxis is by no means to be gained from rescuing critique, as it is from consciousness-raising critique.

When it uncovers within apparently universal interests the particular interest of the ruling class, ideology critique is a political force. Insofar as it shakes the normative structures that hold the consciousness of the oppressed captive and comes to term in political action, ideology critique aims to dismantle the structural violence invested in institutions. It is oriented toward the participatory eradication of the violence thus set loose. Structural violence can also be released preventatively or reactively from above; then it has the form of a fascist partial mobilization of the masses, who do not eradicate the violence unleashed but "act it out" in a diffuse manner.

I have shown that there is no room in this relational frame of reference of ideology critique for the type of criticism developed by Benjamin. A criticism that sets out to rescue semantic potential with a leap into past *Jetztzeiten* has a highly mediated position relative to political praxis. On this, Benjamin did not manage to achieve sufficient clarity.

In the early essay "Toward a Critique of Violence," Benjamin differentiates law-making violence from law-keeping violence. The latter is the legitimate violence exercised by the organs of the state; the former is the structural violence set loose in war and civil strife, which is present latently in all institutions.[41] Law-making violence, unlike law-keeping violence, does not have an instrumental character; instead it "manifests itself." And, to be sure, the structural violence embodied in interpretations and institutions is manifested in the sphere that Benjamin, like Hegel, reserves for destiny or fate (the fates of wars and families). Of course, changes in the sphere of natural history change nothing: "A gaze directed only at what is close at hand can perceive at most a dialectical rising and falling in the law-making and law-preserving formations of violence. . . . This lasts until either new forces or those suppressed earlier triumph over the hitherto law-making violence and thus found a new law, which is destined in turn to decay." (R, p. 300) Here again we meet Benjamin's conception of fate, which affirms a natural historical continuum of the always the same and excludes cumulative changes in the structures of domination.

This is where the figure of rescuing criticism sets in. Benjamin then shapes the concept of revolutionary violence in accord with this figure; he invests with all the insignia of praxis the act of interpretation that extracts from the past work of art the punctual breakthrough from the continuum of natural history and makes it relevant for the present. This is then the "pure" or "divine" violence that aims at "breaking the cycle under the spell of mythical forms of law." (Ibid.) Benjamin conceptualizes the "pure" violence in the framework of his theory of experience; hence, he has to divest it of the attributes of purposive rational action: Revolutionary violence, like mythical violence, manifests itself—it is the "highest manifestation of unalloyed violence in humans." (Ibid.) In a consistent way, Benjamin refers to Sorel's myth of the general strike and to an anarchistic praxis characterized by the way it bans the instrumental character of action from the realm of political praxis and negates purposive rationality in favor of a "politics of pure means": "The violence (of such a praxis) may be assessed no more from its effects than from its goals, but only from the law of its means." (R, p. 292)

That was in 1920. Nine years later Benjamin wrote his famous essay on the surrealist movement, in which Baudelaire's idea of an intimate connection between dream and deed had in the meantime gained ascendancy. What Benjamin had conceived as pure violence had, in the surrealist provocation, surprisingly taken shape: In the nonsensical acts of the surrealist, art was translated into expressive activity; the separation between poetic and political action had been overcome. Thus, Benjamin could see in surrealism the confirmation of his theory of art. Nonetheless, the illustrations of pure violence offered by surrealism found in Benjamin an ambivalent spectator. Politics as show, or even poeticizing politics—when Benjamin saw these realizations, he did not want after all to close his mind to the difference in principle between political action and manifestation: "This would mean the complete subordination of the methodical and disciplinary preparation for revolution to a praxis oscillating between training for it and celebrating its imminent onset." (R, p. 199) Encouraged by his contact with Brecht, Benjamin thus parted with his earlier anarchist inclinations; he then regarded the relationship of art and political praxis primarily from the viewpoint of the organizational and propagandistic utility of art for the class struggle. The resolute politicizing of art was a concept that he found ready at hand. He may have had good reasons for taking up this notion, but it did not have a systematic relation to his own theory of art and history. Inasmuch as Benjamin accepted it without any bother, he mutely admitted that an immanent relation to praxis cannot be gained from his theory of experience: The experience of shock is not an action, and secular illumination is not a revolutionary deed.[42]

Benjamin's intention was to "enlist the services" of historical materialism for the theory of experience, but that intention had to lead to an identification of ecstasy and politics that Benjamin could not have wanted. The liberation from cultural tradition of semantic potentials that must not be lost to the messianic condition is not the same as the liberation of political domination from structural violence. Benjamin's relevance does not lie in a theology of revolution.[43] His relevance can be seen if we attempt now, conversely, to "enlist the services" of Benjamin's theory of experience for historical materialism.

7

A dialectical theory of progress, which historical materialism claims to be, is on its guard; what presents itself as progress can quickly show itself to be the perpetuation of what was supposedly overcome. More and more theorems of counter-enlightenment have therefore been incorporated into the dialectic of the enlightenment, and more and more elements of a critique of progress have been incorporated into the theory of progress—all for the sake of an idea of progress that is subtle and relentless enough not to let itself be blinded by the mere illusion of emancipation. Of course, this dialectical theory of progress has to contradict the thesis that emancipation itself mystifies.[44]

In the concept of exploitation that was determinative for Marx's critique, poverty and domination were still one. The development of capitalism has taught us in the meantime to differentiate between hunger and oppression. The deprivations that can be provided against by an increase in the standard of living are different from those that can be helped, not by the growth of social wealth, but by that of freedom. In *Natural Right and Human Dignity* Bloch introduced into the concept of progress distinctions that were made necessary by the success of the forces of production developed under capitalism.[45] The more the possibility grows in developed societies of uniting repression with prosperity (that is, satisfying demands directed to the economic system without necessarily having to redeem the genuinely political exigencies), the more the accent shifts from the elimination of hunger to emancipation.

In the tradition that reaches back to Marx, Benjamin was one of the first to emphasize a further moment in the concepts of exploitation and progress: besides hunger and repression, failure; besides prosperity and liberty, happiness. Benjamin regarded the experience of happiness he named secular illumination as bound up with the rescuing of tradition. The claim to happiness can be made good only if the sources of that semantic potential we need for interpreting the world in the light of our needs are not exhausted. Cultural goods are spoils that the ruling elite carries in its triumphal parade, and so the process of tradition has to be disentangled from myth. The liberation of culture is certainly not possible without the overcoming of the repression anchored in institutions. Yet, for a moment the suspicion cannot help but arise that an emancipation without happiness and lacking in fulfillment might not be just as possible as relative prosperity without the elimination of repression. This question is not without risks; however, on the verge of *posthistoire*, where symbolic structures are exhausted, worn thin, and stripped of their imperative functions, neither is it entirely idle.

Benjamin would not have posed this question. He insisted on a happiness at once most spiritual and most sensual as an experience for the masses. Indeed, he was almost terrified by the prospect of the possibility of the definitive loss of this experience, because, with his gaze fixed on the messianic condition, he observed how progress was successively cheated for the sake of its fulfillment by progress itself. The critique of the Kautskian way of viewing progress is therefore the political context of the "Theses on the Philosophy of History." Even if one does not argue with respect to each of the three dimensions discussed above that progress in the increase of prosperity, the expansion of liberty, and the promotion of happiness does not represent real progress as long as prosperity, liberty, and happiness have not become universal, it still can plausibly be argued with respect to the hierarchy of the three components that prosperity without liberty is not prosperity and that liberty without happiness is not liberty. Benjamin was profoundly imbued by this: We cannot be sure about even partial progress before the Last Judgment. Naturally, Benjamin wove this emphatic insight into his conception of fate, according to which historical changes effect no change unless they are reflected in the orders of happiness: "The order of the secular should be erected upon the idea of happiness." (R, p. 312) In this totalizing perspective, the cumulative development of the productive forces and the directional change of the structures of interaction are wound down into an undifferentiated reproduction of the always-the-same. Before Benjamin's Manichean gaze, progress can be perceived only at the solar prominences of happiness; history spreads out like the orbiting of a dead planet upon which, now and then, lightning flashes down. This forces us to construe the economic and political systems in concepts that would really only be adequate to cultural processes: Within the ubiquity of the context of guilt, evolutions are submerged beyond recognition— evolutions that, for all their questionable partiality, take place not only in the dimensions of the forces of production and of social wealth but even in the dimension in which distinctions are infinitely difficult to make in the face of the weight of repression. (I mean progress, which is certainly precarious and permanently threatened by reversal, in the products of legality if not in the formal structures of morality.) In the melancholy of remembering what has been missed and in conjuring up moments of happiness that are in the process of being extinguished, the historical sense for secular progress is in danger of atrophy. No doubt these advances generate their regressions, but this is where political action starts.

Benjamin's critique of empty progress is directed against a joyless reformism whose sensorium has long since been stunted as regards the difference between an improved reproduction of life and a fulfilled life (or, better, a life that is not a failure). But this criticism becomes sharp only when it succeeds in making this difference visible in connection with the uncontemptible improvements of life. These improvements create no new memories, but they dissolve old and dangerous ones. The step-by-step negations of poverty and even repression are, it has to be conceded, oddly without traces; they make things easier, but they do not fulfill, for only alleviation that was remembered would be a preparatory stage for fulfillment. In the face of this situation, there are in the meantime two overworked positions. The counter-enlightenment based on a pessimistic anthropology would have us realize that utopian images of fulfillment are the life-serving fictions of a finite creature that will never be able to transcend its mere life to reach the good life. On the other side, the dialectical theory of progress is quite sure of its prognosis that successful emancipation also means fulfillment. Benjamin's theory of experience could—if it were not the monk's cowl but the core of historical materialism—oppose to the one position a grounded hope and to the other a prophylactic doubt.

Here we are talking only about the doubt that Benjamin's semantic materialism suggests: Can we preclude the possibility of a meaningless emancipation? In complex societies, emancipation means the participatory transformation of administrative decision structures. Is it possible that one day an emancipated human race could encounter itself within an expanded space of discursive formation of will and yet be robbed of the light in which it is capable of interpreting its life as something good? The revenge of a culture exploited over millennia for the legitimation of domination would then take this form: Right at the moment of overcoming age-old repressions, it would harbor no violence but it would have no content either. Without the influx of those semantic energies with which Benjamin's rescuing criticism was concerned, the structures of practical discourse—finally well established—would necessarily become desolate.

Benjamin comes close to wresting the reproach of empty reflection from the counter-enlightenment and appropriating it for a theory of progress. Whoever looks for Benjamin's relevance in this direction is of course open to the objection that emancipatory efforts, in the face of an unshaken political reality, should not be encumbered so lightheartedly with further mortgages, however sublime they might be—first things first. I of course think that a differentiated concept of progress opens a perspective that does not simply obstruct courage but can make political action more sure of hitting its mark, for under historical circumstances that prohibit the thought of revolution and give one reason to expect revolutionary processes of long duration, the idea of the revolution as the process of forming a new subjectivity must also be transformed. Benjamin's conservative-revolutionary hermeneutics, which deciphers the history of culture with a view to rescuing it for the upheaval, may point out one path to take.

A theory of linguistic communication that wanted to bring Benjamin's insights back into a materialist theory of social evolution would need to conceive two of Benjamin's theses together. I am thinking of the assertion that "there is a sphere of human agreement that is nonviolent to the extent that it is wholly inaccessible to violence: the proper sphere of 'mutual understanding,' language." (R, p. 289) And I am thinking of the warning that belongs with this: " . . . pessimism all along the line. Absolutely . . . , but above all mistrust, mistrust, and again mistrust in all reciprocal understanding between classes, between nations, between individuals. And unconditional trust only in I.G. Farben and the peaceful perfection of the Luftwaffe."(R, p. 191)

Notes

1. W. Benjamin, *Schriften*, 2 vols., T. W. and Gretel Adorno, eds. (Frankfurt am Main, 1955). Citations and references in the text use available English translations where possible. Abbreviations to the editions used are as follow:

Briefe (B), Gershom Scholem and T. W. Adorno, eds. (Frankfurt, 1966).

"Correspondence with Benjamin" (NLR), *New Left Review* 81 (1972): 55–80.

"Edward Fuchs, Collector and Historian" (F), *New German Critique* 5 (1975): 27–58.

Gesammelte Schriften I–V (GS), Rolf Tiedemann and Hermann Schweppenhäuser, eds. (Frankfurt am Main, 1972–).

Illuminations (I), Hannah Arendt, ed. (New York, 1969).

The Origins of German Tragic Drama (O) (London, 1977).

Reflections (R), Peter Demetz, ed. (New York, 1978).

2. G. Scholem, "Walter Benjamin," in *Über Walter Benjamin* (Frankfurt, 1968) [English translation in Scholem, *Jews and Judaism in Crisis* (New York, 1976)]. See also "Walter Benjamin and His Angel" and "Two Letters to Walter Benjamin," *ibid.*, and Scholem, "Nachwort," in W. Benjamin, *Berliner Chronik* (Frankfurt, 1970).

3. T. W. Adorno, *Über Walter Benjamin* (Frankfurt, 1970). In English, see "A Portrait of Walter Benjamin," in Adorno, *Prisms* (Cambridge, Mass., 1982).

4. P. Szondi, "Nachwort," in W. Benjamin, *Städtbilder* (Frankfurt, 1963).

5. R. Tiedemann, *Studien zur Philosophie W. Benjamins* (Frankfurt, 1965); Tiedemann, "Nachwort," in Benjamin, *Charles Baudelaire* (Frankfurt, 1969); Tiedemann, "Nachwort," in Benjamin, *Versuche über Brecht* (Frankfurt, 1966); H. Schweppenhäuser, "Einleitung," in Benjamin, *Über Haschish* (Frankfurt, 1972).

6. H. Brenner, "Die Lesbarkeit der Bilder. Skizzen zur Passagenentwurf," *alternativ* 59/60 (1968): 48 ff.; H. Lethen, "Zur materialistischen Kunsttheorie Benjamins," *ibid.* 65/67 (1967): 225–232; M. Scharang, *Zur Emanzipation der Kunst* (Neuweid, 1971).

Walter Benjamin

7. W. Benjamin, *Briefe*, vol. I, pp. 120 ff.

8. H. Arendt, *Benjamin, Brecht. Zwei Essays.* (Munich, 1971); "Introduction: Walter Benjamin 1892–1940," in *I*.

9. P. Bürger, *Der Französische Surrealismus* (Frankfurt, 1971); K. H. Bohrer, *Die gefährdete Phantasie oder Surrealismus und Terror* (Munich, 1970); E. Lenk, *Der springende Narziss* (Munich, 1971). Adorno's critique of surrealism may be found in *Noten zur Literatur* I (Frankfurt, 1958), pp. 153–160. Following him is H. M. Enzensberger, "Die Aporien der Avantgarde," in *Einzelheiten* (Frankfurt, 1962). On the status of the secondary literature see W. S. Rubin, "The D-S Expedition," *New York Review of Books* 18 (1972): 9–10.

10. See *Text und Kritik* 31/32 (1971), the issue dedicated to Benjamin, which has essays by B. Lindner, L. Wiesenthat, and P. Krumme and an annotated bibliography (pp. 85 ff.) with references to uncompleted dissertations on Benjamin.

11. H. Marcuse, *Kultur und Gesellschaft* I (Frankfurt, 1965), pp. 56–101 [English translation: *Negations* (Boston, 1968), pp. 88–133)].

12. H. Marcuse, *An Essay on Liberation* (Boston, 1969), especially chapter II. Marcuse has developed and also partially modified this perspective in "Art and Revolution," in *Counterrevolution and Revolt* (Boston, 1972). Cf. G. Rohrmoser, *Herrschaft und Versöhnung. Aesthetik und die Kulturrevolution des Westens* (Freiburg, 1972).

13. "Certain Madonnas remain covered nearly all year round; certain sculptures on medieval cathedrals are invisible to the spectator on ground level. With the emancipation of various art practices from ritual go increasing opportunities for the exhibition of their products." (*I*, p. 225)

14. "Fascist art is executed not only for the masses but also by the masses ... [It] casts the ones performing as well as the recipients under a spell. Under this spell they must appear monumental to themselves, i.e., incapable of well-considered and independent actions.... Only in the attitude imposed on them by the spell, so Fascism teaches us, do the masses find their expression." (*GS* III, p. 488)

15. "Whereas in the symbol destruction is idealized and the transfigured face of nature is fleetingly revealed in the light of redemption, in allegory the observer is confronted with the *facies hippocratica* of history as a petrified, primordial landscape....This is the heart of the allegorical way of seeing, of the baroque, secular explanation of history as the Passion of the world. Its importance resides solely in the stations of its declines." (*O*, p. 166)

16. Here, too, Benjamin sees Dadaism as a precursor of the technical arts by other means: "The revolutionary strength of Dadaism lay in testing art for its authenticity. One made still-lifes out of tickets, spools of cotton, cigarette butts, and mixed them with pictorial elements. One put a frame around the whole thing. And in this way one showed the public: Look, your picture frame explodes time; the smallest authentic fragment of everyday life says more than a painting. Just as a murderer's bloody fingerprint on a page says more than the book's text. Much of this revolutionary content has been rescued and redeemed by passing into photomontage." (*R*, p. 229)

17. Tiedemann, *Studien*, pp. 103 ff.; H. D. Kittsteiner, "Die Geschichtsphilosophischen Thesen," *alternativ* 55/56 (1966): 243–251.

18. The rescuing power of a retrospective criticism is, of course, not to be confused with the empathy and reexperiencing that historicism took over from Romanticism: "With Romanticism begins the hunt for false wealth, for the assimilation of every past, not by a progressive

emancipation of the human race in virtue of which it takes its own history into view with even more heightened awareness and constantly gets new angles on it, but by imitation, which ferrets out all the works from all the nations and world epochs that have ever lived." (*GS* II, p. 581) On the one hand, this is not a recommendation to apprehend history hermeneutically as a continuum of effective history or to reconstruct it as the self-formative process of the human species. Over against this stands the most profoundly antievolutionary conception of history.

19. B. Lindner, "Natur-Geschichte—eine Geschichtsphilosophie und Welterfahrung in Benjamins Schriften," *Text und Kritik* 31/32 (1971), at 56.

20. In this sense, enlightened sciences such as systems theory and behaviorist psychology conceive human beings as "mythic" natures.

21. [I]ndeed this attainment of readability is a distinctive critical point interior to them (i.e., the dialectical images). Each present is determined by those specific images which are synchronic with it: Each now is the now of a distinctive recognizability. In the now the truth is changed with time to the explosion-point." (Cited in Tiedemann, *Studien*, p. 310)

22. "Autonomy" here designates the independence of the works of art in relation to the intentions of employing them, which are extrinsic to art. The autonomy of the *production* of art could already develop earlier, namely in the forms of support connected with patronage.

23. A. Hauser, *Sozialgeschichte der Kunst*, 2 vols. (Munich, 1953); J. Habermas, *Strukturwandel der Öffentlichkeit*, fifth edition (Neuweid, 1971), pp. 46 ff.

24. T. W. Adorno, in *Dissonanzen* (Göttingen, 1969).

25. "Art in its beginnings still leaves something mysterious, a secret foreboding and a longing. . . . But if the perfect content has been perfectly revealed in artistic shapes, then the more farseeing spirit rejects this objective manifestation and turns back into its inner self. This is the case in our time. We may hope that art will always rise higher and grow to perfection, but the form of art has ceased to be the supreme need of the spirit. No matter how excellent we find the statues of the Greek gods, no matter how we see God the Father, Christ, Mary so estimably and perfectly portrayed, it is no help; we bow the knee no longer." (G. W. F. Hegel, *Aesthetics, Lectures on Fine Art I* (Oxford, 1975), p. 103)

26. J. Behrmann, G. Böhme, and W. van den Daele put forward this thesis in the manuscript *Alternativen in der Wissenschaft*.

27. T. W. Adorno, "Correspondence with Benjamin," *New Left Review* 81 (Sept.–Oct. 1972): 55–80, at 65.

28. "For the last time the aura emanates from the early photographs in the fleeting expression of a human face. This is what constitutes their melancholy and incomparable beauty." (*I*, p. 226)

29. "The important thing is that the *correspondances* record a concept of experience that includes ritual elements. Only by appropriating these elements was Baudelaire able to fathom the full meaning of the breakdown that he, a modern man, was witnessing. Only in this way was he able to recognize in it the challenge meant for him alone, a challenge he incorporated into the *Fleurs de Mal*." (*I*, p. 181) "Baudelaire describes eyes of which one is inclined to say that they have lost their ability to look." (*I*, p. 189)

30. On Adorno's speculations about reconcilation with nature, especially those presented in *Minima Moralia*, see my essay "Theodor W. Adorno, Ein philosophierende Intellektueller (1963),"

in *Philosophisch-politische Profile* (Frankfurt, 1971). See also my essay on Adorno in the present volume.

31. This is why Benjamin does not accept private ecstasy or hashish as a model for this experience: "The reader, the thinker, the loiterer, the flâneur, are types of illuminati just as much as the opium eater, the dreamer, the ecstatic. And more profane." (*R*, p. 190)

32. *Zur Aktualität Walter Benjamin. Aus Anlass des 80. Geburtstages von Walter Benjamin*, S. Unseld, ed. (Frankfurt, 1972). See also "Walter Benjamin and His Angel," listed in note 2 above.

33. [T]hus the demands on future philosophy can finally be put into words: to fashion a notion of knowledge on the basis of the Kantian system that corresponds to the concept of experience for which the knowledge is doctrine" (*GS*) II, p. 168)

34. "It would be worth demonstrating that the theory of experience represents the by no means secret center of all Benjamin's conceptions." P. Krumme, "Zur Konzeption der dialektishen Bilder," *Text und Kritik* 31/32 (1971), p. 80, n. 5.

35. Already in the "Program of Coming Philosophy" there is the following suggestion: "A notion of [philosophy] gained through reflection on the linguistic nature of knowledge will create a corresponding notion of experience, which will also comprise areas whose true systematic ordering Kant did not achieve." (*GS* II, p. 168) Hamann had already attempted this during Kant's lifetime.

36. "The word must communicate *something* (other than itself). That is really the Fall of the spirit of language. The word as something externally communicating, as it were a parody of the expressly mediate word. . . ." (*R*, p. 327)

37. D. Ploog, "Kommunikation in Affengesellschaften und deren Bedeutung für die Verständesweisen des Menschen," in *Neue Anthropologie*, vol. 2, H.-G. Gadamer and P. Vogler, eds. On Benjamin's philosophy of language, which has been relatively neglected in the discussion until now, see H. H. Holz, "Prismatisches Denken," in *Über Walter Benjamin*.

38. The thesis "that meaning, significance, etc.—in a Marxist fashion—gets engendered only by the world-historical labor processes of the human species—in which it produces itself—Benjamin never made his own." (Lindner, "Natur-Geschichte," at 55)

39. Among other things, the fourteenth thesis on the philosophy of history proves this. Benjamin is interested in the experiential content of the French Revolution rather than the objective changes to which it led: "The French Revolution understood itself as Rome returned. It cited Rome precisely the way fashion cites a costume of the past." (*I*, p. 261)

40. I am referring to two letters from Adorno to Benjamin, dated August 2, 1935, and November 10, 1938 (*B* 1, pp. 671 ff. and 782 ff.; *NLR*, pp. 55–80). For Benjamin's answer, see *B* 1, pp. 790 ff. On this whole complicated matter see Jacob Taubes, "Kultur und Ideologie," in *Spätkapitalismus oder Industriegesellschaft?* (Stuttgart, 1969).

41. In this context, Benjamin put forth a critique of parliamentarianism that drew Carl Schmitt's admiration: "They [the parliaments] offer the familiar, woeful spectacle because they have not remained conscious of the revolutionary forces to which they owe their existence. Accordingly, in Germany in particular, the last manifestation of such forces bore no fruit for parliaments. They lack the sense that a lawmaking violence is . . . a supposedly nonviolent manner of dealing with political affairs." (*R*, p. 288)

42. On this see Bohrer, *Die gefährdete Phantasie*, especially pp. 53 ff., and B. Lypp, *Ästhetischer Absolutismus und politische Vernunft* (Frankfurt, 1972).

43. See H. Salzinger, "W. Benjamin—Theologe der Revolution," *Kürbiskern* (1969): 629–647.

44. From this perspective, critical theory is viewed as "modern sophistry." See, for example, R. Bubner, "Was ist kritische Theorie?," in *Hermeneutik und Ideologiekritik* (Frankfurt, 1971).

45. "Social utopia aimed at human happiness, natural right, and human dignity. Social utopia portrayed relationships in which the miserable and heavy-laden were no longer to be found; natural right constructed relationships in which the downtrodden and the degraded disappear." [E. Bloch, *Naturrecht und menschliche Würde* (Frankfurt am Main, 1961), p. 13] See my references in the article on Ernst Bloch (in this book).

Herbert Marcuse: On Art and Revolution (1973)

Herbert Marcuse's next-to-last book, *An Essay on Liberation*, appeared just as the protest movement had passed its high point: in 1968 in the United States and a year later in German translation. The paradoxical title of his new book, *Counterrevolution and Revolt* (Boston, 1972), reflects the fundamentally changed situation; Marcuse now measures the coming revolution in a time span of generations, whereas the massive countermovement seems to take on the ironic form of a preventive counterrevolution. Even in West Germany, which this image does not seem to fit so well (despite the decree against employing "radicals"), one can find evidence of the latter. Consider the pathetic haste with which both the opposition and the government take at its word a little group that trumpets itself as a powerful cadre—a self-stylization with a pretense to power is preventively labeled as a reality. Marcuse's book took shape in 1970–71, when the protest movement had already entered the doldrums. It contains a sharp criticism of the pseudo-Marxist orthodoxy that has been revived once again within the ranks of the New Left. This orthodoxy expresses itself in a ritualized conceptual apparatus and leads to a fetishizing of the working class (in Marcuse's dry remark, a "new dimension of commodity fetishism"). On the other side, however, Marcuse's critique is directed against clowning and letting oneself go, against the trifling with violence of "revolutionary suicide." This appeal to the self-control of the militants strikes a novel tone.

These tactical remarks do not, however, constitute the theme of the book. Since the 1930s, Marcuse has never let go of the problem of the relationship of art and revolution (more precise, the role art can play in revolutionizing a stunted sensuality and a repressive structuring of the drives or instincts)—a problem that now, by reason of the experiences of the 1960s, shifts into a different light. Because the existing society is reproduced not only in the consciousness of the people but even in their senses, the emancipation of consciousness has to go along with the liberation of the senses—the "repressive familiarity with the given world of objects" has to be dissolved. It is no accident that this onetime student of Heidegger uses the language of phenomenology when he postulates a radical transformation of the "preconscious constitution of the experienced world." Behind this stands an empirical assumption that it is precisely capitalism's capacity for achievement—the unparalleled dynamism of a society oriented toward prosperity and consumption—that will bring forth "transcending," nonmaterial needs, which late capitalism cannot satisfy. These new needs are manifested in the values and modes of conduct of the subversive countercultures, in which the potential of art and that of aesthetic experience are released into a political force. What is new about these theses is the emphasis with which Marcuse still stresses the tension between art and revolution.

We get to know a Marcuse who turns away in horror before the consequences of a lack of differentiation between art and life. Art should not carry out the surrealistic imperative to pass over, desublimated, into life. Only as art can it express its radical potential. The subversive truth of art appears only in the transformation of reality into illusion. If Marcuse once criticized the affirmative character of the beautiful illusion as the ideological element in bourgeois art, he now sees in the affirmative power of a symbolic universe set off from life the source of the negation of what currently exists as well. In the face of an anti-art, which could appeal to Marcuse's earlier theses about the overcoming of art, Marcuse revokes his indictment: "When we confront a disintegration of bourgeois culture, which results from the inner dynamism of contemporary capitalism and the adaptation of culture to its demands, does not then the cultural revolution, insofar as it aims at the destruction of bourgeois culture, accord with the capitalist adaptation and redefinition of culture?"

Marcuse is very close to the fundamental position of Adorno's aesthetics. He disagrees with the theses about the end of art once propagated in *Kursbuch*; even under socialism art must maintain its transcendence: "An end to art is imaginable only if humans are no longer capable of distinguishing between true and false, good and evil, beautiful and ugly, present and future. That would be the state of utter barbarism at the high point of civilization." Here Marcuse repeats nightmares of Vico and Nietzsche. In this turning against cultural anarchism may also be hidden a bit of unresolved antimodernism. I am not sure whether Marcuse does justice to the experimental logic of the artistic avant-garde, which, in the wake of surrealism, using extreme means (even to the point of demonstrative muteness), lays bare the petrified forms of speech and interaction, i.e., negates them up to the very threshold of a self-negation of art. Just how rooted in the traditions of German Romanticism Marcuse's sensibility is can be seen through a comparison with Benjamin and Adorno, who, for all their opposition to classicism, were also not completely untouched by it. All the same, it would be a mistake to attribute Marcuse's warning against destroying art as an independent universe simply to backsliding into culturally conservative attitudes.

Marcuse can hardly count on an understanding reception in West Germany today, and this is the case not only among his usual opponents but also among those who have become his opponents or have turned away from him in indifference. The unorganized remnants of the New Left, among whom some resonance is possible, no longer have much room for action. For the scenes Marcuse and the protest movement have left behind there are—if one leaves aside the Communists who are loyal to the party and the militants who have settled down between Mao and Stalin—two characteristic fields of force. On the one side are the diffuse and apolitical youth cultures whose mood—already commercialized again—is documented by the fad word *nostalgia*. A new historicism runs through the modern world (which has become old rather quickly) looking for charms and decorations that are suitable for the private enjoyment of values that run counter to, and of experiences that are complementary to, the everyday qualities of an achieving society. Since the time of *Jugendstil*, a veritable treasure has been plundered; the quest goes forward into the 1920s and the 1930s and backward to the post-Romanticism of Visconti. On the other side, the Young Socialists have fashioned a tactically successful political opposition that, for the first time in postwar Germany, has necessitated a politically fruitful confrontation with socialist analyses of society. Marcuse does not believe that the current competitive democracy affords a suitable field of operations for a transition to democratic socialism. In contrast, the Young Socialists try to make clear to the establishment parties that the capacities of the late-capitalist economic system have to be put to the test in terms of politically set priorities and, in case of an expected negative outcome, be open to structural transformation. The Young Socialists see that radical reforms ought not to be started before the democratic government has at its disposal legal means for opposing a foreseeable politics of obstruction, which would exploit the freedom of investment of giant private enterprises to prevent change. On the other hand, what unites the Young Socialists with Marcuse is expressed in their declared 'double strategy": Successes within the current institutions will bureaucratically seep away unless a simultaneous politicizing of the consciousness of larger segments of the populace creates new needs that legitimate, implement, and sustain altered social priorities.

The remains of the unorganized New Left, hemmed in between nostalgic culture consumption and successful competition from the Young Socialists—if indeed that is the scene here in Germany upon which Marcuse's new book enters, then resonance is not at all probable, but the essence of Marcuse's idea stands out clearly against this background.

Since the rise of the modern state, the political sphere has been delimited by international and civil wars and filled out by the routines of public bureaucracies. Against this concept of politics, which is confined to the distribution of power and the administrative processing of social matters, Marcuse and the New Left have posed the concept of a constant and all-embracing politicizing that is to take hold of the consciousness and the sensibility of the subjects themselves and change the value structures of the society. This means a categorial shift in political activity. As soon as the nonmaterial needs for the new relationships of solidarity between groups, generations, and sexes and between subjects and nature were brought into the collective formation of consensus, politics and life practice would have entered into a new constellation. This degovernmentalization of politics is making headway in public processes of planning. Such a dedifferentiation of previously separate media always presents itself as the destruction of a relatively autonomous realm. Now the movement of cultural revolution has brought to awareness the meshing of various processes of dedifferentiation; the well-defined limits between illness and normality, between art and life, between politics and art, between private and public conflicts, and between adaptation and criminality have shifted at the same time. Governmental politics and the system of science can look ahead to what is fully underway in other realms. Peter Gorsen has dealt instructively with two of these media shifts in his contribution to the fourth volume of *Neue Anthropologie* (edited by Hans-Georg Gadamer): the deaestheticizing of art by action-reaction games, mixed media, concept art, land art, happening, science fiction, the equation of kitsch and literature, etc.; and the depathologizing of the ill by the new antipsychiatry movement (Basaglia, Cooper), the shakeup of the compulsive autonomy of bourgeois normality in relation to madness (Foucault), and the political revaluation of schizophrenic regression into a constructive resolution of repressive living conditions (Laing).

Marcuse was one of the first to analyze the questionable autonomy of the beautiful illusion; he developed striking arguments for a new political praxis that integrates sensuality, fantasy, and desire. His chapter on nature and revolution deals with this once again. Against this background, however, Marcuse's more recent turn against the destruction of the transcendence of the beautiful and against the dissolution of political action into activism gains special weight. Marcuse stresses that the dedifferentiation of the old cultural articulations is not supposed to lead to the desublimation of passionate reason and of creativity. The constellations of bourgeois culture that were taken for granted for three or four centuries have been set in motion, but only at the price of humanity could this movement ignore that, even in a new social universe, art, politics, and life practice remain differentiated from one another.

At first glance, this defensive message stands in contradiction with the uninterrupted revolutionary rhetoric. Here, as always, Marcuse defends rebellion against "the whole," the qualitative leap, the break with the continuum of previous history. Here, as always, the discourse is affirmative; its theoretic content is somewhat meager. The book contains only the one hypothesis that the satisfaction of elementary needs creates needs of a new sort, which late capitalism cannot satisfy. It may be correctly said that this hypothesis is not grounded but is presupposed as valid. However, objections on this level miss the point, for the investigation of social-scientific hypotheses is not Marcuse's goal. Marcuse's arguments have to be construed instead as part of a grand practical discourse in which the point is not the verification of

Herbert Marcuse

empirical assertions but the identification and justification of universalizable interests. The point here is the radically new interpretation of needs and the diagnostic question whether the masses acknowledge in these interpretations what they really want, whether they recognize themselves in them.

Hannah Arendt: On the Concept of Power (1976)

Max Weber has defined power as the possibility of forcing one's own will, whatever it may be, on the conduct of others. Hannah Arendt, by contrast, understands power as the capacity to agree in uncoerced communication on some community action. Both authors discuss power as a potency realized in actions, but each relies on a different model of action.

Power in Max Weber, Talcott Parsons, and Hannah Arendt

Max Weber proceeds from the teleological model of action in which an individual subject or a group has a set purpose and chooses the means suitable for realizing it. The success of the action consists in bringing about a condition in the world that fulfills the purpose set. To the extent that this success depends on the conduct of another subject, the agent has to dispose of the means that instigate the desired conduct on the part of the other. This manipulative power over the means that afford influence on the will of another Max Weber names power. Hannah Arendt reserves for it the term violence. Since the purposively rational agent, who is exclusively interested in the success of his action, has to dispose of the means by which he can coerce a subject capable of decision (whether by the threat of sanctions, by persuasion, or by skillful manipulation of alternatives for action), "power means every chance within a social relationship to assert one's will even against opposition."[1] The single alternative to coercion is the voluntary agreement of the participating subjects. The teleological model of action nevertheless considers only agents who are oriented toward their own success and not toward agreement. It admits of processes focused on agreement only when they seem to the participants to be functionally required for the successful outcome. However, this sort of agreement, which is sought one-sidedly under the proviso of being instrumentally useful for one's own success, is not intended in earnest; it does not fulfill the conditions for a consensus arrived at without compulsion.

Hannah Arendt proceeds from a different model of action, the communicative: "Power corresponds to the human ability not just to act but to act in concert."[2] The basic phenomenon is not the instrumentalizing of another's will for one's own purposes but the formation of a common will in a communication aimed at agreement. This could, of course, be construed as if *power* and *violence* designated merely two different aspects of the same exercise of political domination. Then *power* would mean the consent of the governed mobilized for the sake of collective goals (that is, their readiness to support the political leadership), whereas *violence* would signify manipulations of resources and coercive means in virtue of which a political leadership reaches and implements normative decisions in order to realize collective goals. This conception has in fact inspired the system-theoretic concept of power. Talcott Parsons understands by *power* the overall capacity of a social system "to get things done in the interest of collective goals."[3] The mobilizing of consent engenders the power that is transformed into normative decisions by the exploitation of social resources. Talcott Parsons can bring the two phenomena contrasted with one another by Hannah Arendt as power and violence into a unified concept of power, because he construes power as the property of a system that behaves in relation to its own components according to the same scheme as the purposively rational acting subject does in relation to the external world: "I have defined power as the capacity of a social system to mobilize resources to attain collective goals."[4] He repeats on the level of a systems theory the same teleological conception of power (power as the potential for realizing purposes) followed by Max Weber on the level of action theory. In both instances, the specific factor that separates the power of unifying discourse from instrumentally exercised violence is lost. The consensus-building force of communication aimed at agreement is an end in itself and cannot be instrumentalized for other purposes.

The agreement of those who deliberate together in order to act communally, which Arendt calls "an opinion upon which many publicly are in agreement,"[5] signifies power insofar as it rests on conviction and hence on that peculiarly coercion-free force with which insights prevail. Let us try to clarify this. The soundness of a consensus brought about by coercion-free communication is not measured in terms of any kind of success except that of the claim to rational validity immanent within speech. Even convictions formed publicly in the give and take of discussion can be manipulated, but effective manipulation still has to take the claims of reason into account. We allow ourselves to be persuaded by the truth of a statement, the rightness of a norm, or the truthfulness of an utterance; the authenticity of our conviction stands and falls with the awareness that the acknowledgment of these validity claims is rational (that is, motivated by reason). Convictions are manipulable, but the rational claim from which they draw their subjective force is not.

In brief: The communicatively engendered power of common convictions goes back to the fact that the parties are oriented toward agreement and not just toward their own respective success. To this end, they employ language not in a "perlocutionary" way (i.e., not just to instigate the desired conduct in the other subjects), but in an "illocutionary" way (i.e., to establish intersubjective relationships free from violence). Arendt dissociates the concept of power from the teleological model of action: Power is formed within communicative action; it is a group effect of speech in which agreement is an end in itself for all parties. However, if power is no longer conceived as a potential for the realizing of purposes, if it is not actualized in purposively rational action, then in what does it issue and what end can it serve?

Arendt treats the unfolding of power as an end in itself. Power serves the preservation of praxis, out of which it emerges itself. It solidifies into political power in institutions that secure forms of life centered upon reciprocal speech. Power is manifested in orders that protect political freedom, in resistance against forces that threaten political freedom from within or without, and in those revolutionary acts that found new institutions of freedom: "It is the people's support that lends power to the institutions of a country, and this support is but the continuation of the consent that brought the laws into existence to begin with. . . . All political institutions are manifestations and materializations of power; they petrify and decay as soon as the living power of the people ceases to uphold them. This is what Madison meant when he said 'all government rests on opinion.' "[6]

It becomes clear at this point that the communications concept of power also has a normative content. Is such a concept scientifically useful? Is it at all suited to descriptive purposes? I will try to answer this question in several steps. I will first show how Arendt introduces and grounds her concept. Then I would like to offer a reminder of how she employs it. Finally, I want to deal with a few weaknesses in the concept, which in my view derive less from its normative status than from the fact that Arendt remains bound to the historical and conceptual constellation of Aristotelian thought.

The Structure of Unimpaired Intersubjectivity

Arendt's chief philosophical work, *The Human Condition* (1958), serves the systematic renewal of the Aristotelian concept of praxis. The author does not rely on the exegesis of classic texts; she sketches an anthropology of linguistic action—a counterpart to Arnold Gehlen's anthropology of purposive action, *Der Mensch* (1940). Whereas Gehlen examines the functional circuit of instrumental action as the most important reproductive mechanism of the species, Arendt analyzes the form of intersubjectivity engendered in the practice of speech as the basic trait of culturally reproduced life. Communicative action is the medium in which the intersubjectively shared life world takes shape. This is the "realm of appearance" which the agents enter and in which they meet and are seen and heard. The spatial dimension of the life world is determined by the "fact of human plurality": Each interaction joins the multiple perspectives of perception and action of those present, who as individuals assume incontrovertible standpoints. The temporal dimension of the life world is determined by the "fact of human birth": The birth of any individual indicates the possibility of a new beginning, and to act means to take an initiative and to be able to do something unforeseen. For the rest, the life world is determined by the task of securing the identity of individuals and groups in social space and in historical time. In communicative action individuals become actively visible as unique beings and are disclosed in their subjectivity. At the same time they have to acknowledge one another as accountable, as beings capable of intersubjective agreement—the rational claim immanent in speech grounds a radical equality. Finally, the life world itself is, so to speak, fulfilled by praxis, by the "relational network of human affairs" (that is, the histories in which agents are caught up in doing and suffering).[7]

One might hold the phenomenological method by which Arendt's philosophy of praxis is carried out to be inadequate, but the intention is clear: She wants to read off the general structures of an unimpaired intersubjectivity in the formal properties of communicative action or praxis. These structures fix the conditions for the normality of an existence at once human and humanly worthy. Because of its innovative potential, the realm of praxis is highly unstable and in need of protection. The political institutions of a society organized in a state take care of this. They are nourished by the power that issues from unimpaired structures of intersubjectivity, and they must protect the relevant structures of intersubjectivity from deformations if they themselves are not supposed to deteriorate. From this arises the central hypothesis that Arendt tirelessly repeats: Political leaderships cannot replace power by violence with impunity, and they can gain power only from a public sphere that has not been impaired. Others have conceived the public-political sphere as the generator, if not of power, then at least of the legitimation of power, but Arendt insists that a public sphere as political can engender legitimate power only as long as it gets expressed in the structures of an undistorted communication:

What first undermines and then kills political communities is loss of power and final impotence; and power cannot be stored up and kept in reserve for emergencies, like the instruments of violence, but exists only in actualization. Where power is not actualized, it passes away, and history is full of examples that the greatest material riches cannot compensate for this loss. Power is actualized only where word and deed have not parted company, where words are not empty and deeds are not brutal, where words are not used to violate and destroy but to establish relations and create new realities. Power is what keeps the public realm, the potential space of appearance between acting and speaking men, in existence.[8]

Some Applications of the Communications Concept of Power

Arendt did not try to test her hypothesis on examples of the downfalls of great empires. Her historical investigations revolve instead about two extreme cases: the annihilation of political freedom under totalitarian rule and the revolutionary founding of political freedom. *The Origins of Totalitarianism* (New York, 1951) and *On Revolution* (New York, 1960) both apply the communications concept of power in such a way that the deformations of Western mass democracies are illuminated from opposite sides.

Every political order that isolates its citizens from one another through mistrust and suppresses the public exchange of their opinions degenerates into a domination based on violence. It destroys the communicative structures without which power cannot emerge. Fear heightened to terror compels each person to shut himself off from every other and at the same time eliminates the distances between individuals. It takes the force of initiative away from them and robs their linguistic interaction of the force for spontaneous unification; "pressed together with everyone, each is totally separated from all."[9]

Of course, the totalitarian rule investigated by Arendt in the examples of the Nazi regime and Stalinism is not merely a modern form of tyranny; otherwise it would simply silence the communicative movement of the public realm as political. Its specific achievement is the mobilizing of the depoliticized masses: "On the one hand, the police state destroys all relations between men that still remain after the discontinuance of the public-political sphere; on the other hand, it demands that those who have been fully isolated and forsaken by one another be able to be brought into political actions (even if not to genuine political action). . . ."[10]

The totalitarian rule of the Nazi regime may be conceived as a heightened form of tyranny only from a typological standpoint; historically, it arose upon the groundwork of a mass democracy. This circumstance provides Arendt with the occasion for a vigorous critique of the privatism embedded within modern societies. Whereas the theoreticians of a democratic elite (following in the footsteps of Schumpeter) praise representative rule and the party system because they supply narrow channels for the political participation of a depoliticized populace, Arendt sees the menace precisely in this system. It is the mediation of the population by way of highly bureaucratized public administrations, parties, associations, and parliaments that enlarges and fortifies the privatistic forms of life that first makes possible the social-psychological conditions for mobilizing the apolitical and that leads to totalitarian rule.[11] Thomas Jefferson, the radical democrat among the fathers of the American constitution, had "at least a foreboding of how dangerous it might be to allow the people a share in public power without providing them at the same time with more public space than the ballot box and with more opportunity to make their voices heard in public than election day."[12] What Jefferson perceived to be the mortal danger to the republic was "that the Constitution had given all power to the citizens, without giving them the opportunity of *being* republicans and of *acting* as citizens." "In other words," Arendt continues, "the danger was that all power had been given to the people in their private capacity, and that there was no space established for them in their capacity of being citizens."[13]

Here is expressed the motif that inspired Arendt's investigations of the bourgeois revolutions of the eighteenth century, the Hungarian revolt of 1956 and the civil disobedience and student protest movements of the 1960s. As regards emancipatory movements, she is interested in the power of common conviction: the withdrawal of obedience in relation to institutions that have lost their legitimacy, the confrontation of power generated by free coalition with the physically coercive means of a violent yet impotent state apparatus, the originative act of a new political power and the attempt—the pathos of the new beginning—to hold onto the revolutionary point of departure, to prolong institutionally the communicative engendering of power. It is fascinating to see how Arendt notices the same phenomenon again and again. When revolutionaries seize power that lies in the streets, when a populace resolved upon passive resistance confront alien tanks with their bare hands, when convinced minorities dispute the legitimacy of current laws and organize civil disobedience, when in the course of the protest movement there is manifest a "pure pleasure in action" on the part of the students—in all this there seems to be confirmed again and again that no one really possesses power; it "springs up between men when they act together and vanishes the moment they disperse."[14] This emphatic concept of praxis is more Marxist than Aristotelian; Marx called it "critical-revolutionary activity."

Limits of Classical Theory

There have been initiatives toward the institutionalization of direct democracy: in the American town hall meetings of 1776, in the *Sociétés populaires* in Paris between 1789 and 1793, in the sections of the Paris Commune in 1891, in the Soviets in Russia in 1905 and 1917, and in the Revolutionary Councils in Germany in 1918. In these various forms of parliamentary systems Arendt sees the only attempts toward a constitution of liberty under the conditions of mass society. She traces the failure of these attempts in the nineteenth and twentieth centuries back to the political defeats of the labor movement and to the econ-omistic success of the unions and the labor parties: ". . . with the transformation of a class society into a mass society and with the substitution of a guaranteed annual wage for daily or weekly pay . . . the workers today are no longer outside of society; they are its members, and they are jobholders like everybody else. The political significance of the labor movement is now the same as that of any other pressure group."[15] In its context, this thesis seems a bit too facile. It is not the result of well-balanced investigations; it issues instead from a philo-sophical construction. Because Arendt stylizes the image she has painted of the Greek polis into the essence of the political, she forms rigid conceptual dichotomies between "public" and "private," state and economy, liberty and welfare, political-practical activity and production, which the modern bourgeois society and the modern state escape. So the mere fact that the establishment of the capitalist mode of production produces a characteristically new and complementary relationship be-tween state and economy amounts to an indication of pathology, of harmful confusion: "The functionalizing [of politics] makes it impossible to perceive any serious gulf between the two realms. . . ."[16]

Arendt quite rightly insists that by no means does the technical-economic conquest of poverty signify the practical-political securing of public liberty, but she becomes a victim of a concept of politics that is not applicable to modern relationships when she asserts that "the intrusion of social and economic matters into the public realm, the transformation of government into administration, the replacement of personal rule by bureaucratic resources, and the attending trans-mutation of laws into decrees"[17] has to negate any initiative toward a politically active public sphere and toward radical democracy. She views the French Revolution in this dim light, whereas in America the foundation of liberty may have been successful at first because "the politically insoluble social question did not stand in the way."[18] I cannot go into this interpretation here;[19] I will only recall the peculiar per-spective by which Arendt lets herself be guided: A state relieved of the administrative handling of social affairs, a politics cleansed of all questions of social politics, an institutionalizing of public liberty that is independent of the organization of welfare, a radically democratic formation of consensus that puts a stop to social repression—that is not a conceivable path for any modern society.

So we stand before a dilemma. On the one hand, the communications concept of power discloses modern limiting phenomena to which political science has become practically insensitive; on the other hand, it grounds a conception of the political that, as soon as one approaches modern societies with it, leads to absurdities. For this reason I return to the analysis of the concept of power.

The concept of communicatively engendered power developed by Arendt can be made into a sharp instrument only if it is dissociated from the theory of action inspired by Aristotle. Arendt can reduce political power exclusively to praxis, the mutual speech and mutual action of individuals with one another, because she sets off praxis against the apolitical activities of production and labor on one side and of thought on the other. In contrast with the production of objects and with theoretic knowledge, communicative knowledge has to appear as the single political category. This basic conceptual narrowing of the political to the practical permits illuminating contrasts with the elimination of essentially practical contents from the political process so visible today. For this, however, Arendt pays the price of screening all strategic elements out of politics as "violence," severing politics from its ties to the economic and social environment in which it is embedded via the administrative system, and being incapable of coming to grips with appearances of structural violence.

Strategic Competition for Political Power

The conduct of war is the classic model of strategic action. For the Greeks, strategic action took place outside the city's walls; for Arendt, too, it is essentially apolitical, an affair for experts. This example is naturally suitable for demonstrating the opposition between political power and violence. The craft of making war is obviously a matter of the calculated employment of means of violence, whether to threaten or to physically conquer the enemy. The accumulation of the means of annihilation, however, does not make the superpowers mightier— military might (as the Vietnam War has shown) is often the counterpart of internal weakness. In addition, the example of strategy is ideal for subsuming strategic action under instrumental action. *The Human Con-*

dition, aside from communicative action, considers only the essentially asocial activities of production and labor. And, since the purposive deployment of military means seems to have the same structure as the use of instruments for producing objects or transforming the goods of nature, Arendt, in a kind of shorthand, equates strategic action with instrumental action. She demonstrates that in the waging of war strategic action is as violent as it is instrumental; an action of this type stands outside the realm of the political.

The matter looks somewhat different if we place strategic action between opponents alongside communicative action as another form of social interaction (oriented not, of course, toward agreement but toward success) and if we set it off from instrumental action, which can also be executed by a solitary subject as an asocial activity. Then it becomes clear that strategic action has taken place also within the city walls, as in power struggles in competition for positions connected with the exercise of legitimate power. The acquisition and maintenance of political power must be distinguished from rule or the exercise of political power as much as from the engendering of political power. The concept of praxis comes to our aid in the last case, but only there. No holder of a leadership position can exercise power and no one else can dispute this political power if the position is not anchored in the laws and political institutions whose existence ultimately rests upon commonly held convictions, on "the opinion upon which many are publicly in agreement."

Without a doubt, the elements of strategic action have increased in scope and importance in modern societies. The type of action that was dominant in premodern societies (especially in foreign relations) is admitted as the normal case for economic commerce in internal affairs as well with the establishment of the capitalist mode of production. Modern private law (or right) makes room for formally equal realms of strategic action for all possessors of property. Beyond this, in the modern state, which supplements this society based on economics, the struggle for political power through institutionalization of strategic action (through the admission of an opposition party, competition among parties and associations, the legalizing of labor conflicts, and so on) is normalized. These phenomena pertaining to the acquisition and assertion of power have led theoreticians from Hobbes to Schumpeter to make power interchangeable with a potential for successful strategic action. Against this tradition (in which Weber stands as well),

Arendt can correctly make the case that the strategic contests for political power have neither called forth nor maintained the institutions within which they have their moorings. Political institutions live not by violence but by recognition.

Be that as it may, we cannot exclude the element of strategic action from the concept of the political. We want to understand the violence exercised by way of strategic action as the capacity to keep other individuals or groups from perceiving their interests.[20] In this sense, violence has always belonged to the means for acquiring and holding onto power. This struggle for political power has even been institutionalized in the modern state; it thereby becomes a normal component of the political system. On the other hand, it does not make good sense that someone should be able to generate legitimate power just because he is in a position to keep others from perceiving their interests. Legitimate power arises among those who form common convictions in communication free from coercion.

Deploying Power in the Political System

Though the communicative engendering of power and the strategic competition for political power can be apprehended in terms of action theory, the structures of action in virtue of which this happens are not essential to the exercise of legitimate power. Legitimate power permits the holders of leadership positions to make binding decisions. This use of power is more interesting from the perspective of systems theory than from that of action theory. Questions of what the organizational performances of a state are related to and what functions they play for the various environments of the political system can be well formulated and examined within the framework developed by Talcott Parsons. Arendt has resisted moving beyond her framework of action theory in order to insert a functionalist analysis into it. The spheres of human affairs ought not to be dislocated in accord with the standards of a social scientific objectivism, because the sort of knowledge that is gained with this attitude is incapable of flowing back into the praxis of the relevant subjects. In this respect, Arendt would see no difference between Hegel and Parsons; both investigate historical and social processes that pass over the heads of those involved.[21] She tries to capture this processual aspect of social life once again in a category of action, by differentiating within instrumental action between work and labor. Labor is distinguished from work not in the structure of the action, but in that the concept "labor" represents productive activity as an expenditure of a reproducible labor power and so locates it in the functional context of production, consumption, and reproduction.

With her reservations and her conceptual framework restricted to action theory, Arendt unnecessarily disadvantages herself with respect to the systems analysis that is usual today. On the other hand, her mistrust is only too justified as soon as systems theory becomes in-dependent of action theory. This is demonstrated by Parsons when he discusses C. Wright Mills's zero-sum concept of power. Parsons wants to understand power as an augmentable good, such as credit or buying power. When one side gains political power, the other need not lose any. A zero-sum game results only when different parties struggle for available positions of power, but not under the aspect of the rise and fall of the power of political institutions. Parsons and Arendt are in agreement here, yet they have rather divergent ideas concerning the enhancement of power. Parsons treats this process as an increase in the level of activity, which can be sketched just about as follows: In order for the output in the performances of the state organizations to be able to grow, the "scope of action" of the ad-ministrative system has to be enhanced. This in turn requires a strengthened influx of unspecified support or mass loyalty. Thus, the enhancement of power is initiated from the input side. The political leaders must arouse new needs in the electorate so that increasing demands arise that can be resolved only by mounting state activity.[22]

From the perspective of systems theory, the generation of power appears as a problem that can be solved by the political leadership's having a stronger influence on the will of the populace. In the measure that this occurs by the means of psychic compulsion, with persuasion and manipulation, it is in Arendt's terms a matter of an increase of violence but not of a growth in the power of the political system, for according to her hypothesis power can arise only within structures of communication free from compulsion; it cannot be generated "from above." Parsons would dispute this hypothesis; given the cultural values, for him there cannot be any structural limits to the engendering of power. On the other hand, Parsons would like to distinguish, in concrete cases of power inflation and deflation, between serious and unserious credit of power: "There is a fine line between solid, responsible and constructive political leadership which in fact commits the collectivity beyond its capacities for instantaneous fulfillment of all obligations, and reckless overextendedness, just as there is a fine line between responsible banking and 'wildcatting.' "[23] However, it is difficult to see just how these "fine lines" may be grasped in terms of the concepts of systems theory. Arendt affords a solution for precisely this task. She tries to derive the conditions of the public political sphere from the structures of undistorted subjectivity that have to be fulfilled in order for power to be communicatively engendered or expanded.

Communicative Engendering of Power—a Variation

Let me summarize my considerations thus far. The concept of the political has to be extended to include the strategic competition for political power and the use of power within the political system. Politics cannot, as with Arendt, be identical with the praxis of those who discourse together in order to act communally. Conversely, the dominant theory narrows this concept to the phenomena connected with the competition for and the allocation of power and does not do justice to the peculiar phenomenon of the engendering of power. Here the distinction between power and violence becomes sharp and makes it evident that the political system cannot dispose of power arbitrarily. Power is a good for which political groups compete and with which a political leadership economizes. However, both political groups and leaderships find this good, in a certain manner, already there; they do not produce it. That is the weakness of the powerful—they have to borrow their power from those who engender power. That is Hannah Arendt's credo.

The objection to all this is obvious. Even if in modern democracies it is periodically necessary for the leadership to procure legitimation, history is replete with evidence that political domination must have functioned otherwise and does function otherwise than Arendt claims. Certainly the circumstance that political domination can only last so long as it is recognized as legitimate speaks in favor of her thesis. Against it speaks the experience that the relationships that are stabilized by political domination can only in rare cases be the expression of an "opinion upon which many are publicly in agreement"—at least if, like Arendt, one has an ambitious concept of the political sphere. The two facts may be brought to a common denominator only if one assumes that structural violence is built into political institutions (and not only into political institutions). Structural violence is not manifest as violence; instead it blocks in an unnoticed fashion those communications in which are shaped and propagated the convictions effective for legitimation. Such a hypothesis about unnoticed yet effective barriers to comunication can explain the formation of ideologies; they can make plausible how convictions are formed by which the subjects deceive themselves about themselves and their situation. Illusions that are afforded the power of common convictions are what we name *ideologies*.

This suggestion attempts to give a realistic reading to the communicative engendering of power. In systematically restricted communications, the participants form convictions that are free from compulsion from a subjective point of view but are illusionary; thereby they communicatively engender a power, which, as soon as it is institutionalized, can also be turned against the participants. If we wanted to accept this suggestion, we would have to lay down a standard of criticism and be able to discriminate between illusionary and nonillusionary convictions. This possibility is just what Arendt disputes. She holds onto the classic distinction between theory and praxis, which is that praxis is based on opinions and convictions that are incapable of being true in the strict sense: "No opinion is self-evident. In matters of opinion, but not in matters of truth, our thinking is truly discursive, running, as it were, from place to place, from one part of the world to the other through all kinds of conflicting views, until it finally ascends from all these particularities to some impartial generality."[24] With this outmoded concept of theoretical knowledge that builds upon ultimate evidence, Arendt abstains from conceiving the coming to agreement about political questions as a rational formation of consensus. On the other hand, if "representative thought" in her sense[25] (which tests the generalizability of practical perspectives—and this means the correctness of norms) is not separated by an abyss from argumentation, a claim can also be made for a cognitive foundation for the power of common convictions. Then power is discursively resolvable in factual recognition and is moored in fundamentally criticizable claims to validity.

Arendt, however, sees a yawning abyss between knowledge and opinion that cannot be closed by arguments. She seeks another foundation for the power of opinion, and she finds it in the capacity of the subject able to speak and to make and keep promises: "We mentioned before the power generated when people gather together and 'act in concert,' which disappears the moment they depart. The force that keeps them together . . . is the force of mutual promise or contract."[26] She regards as the basis of power the contract concluded between free and equal persons, by which the parties are mutually obligated to one another. In order to ensure a normative equivalent between power and liberty, in the end she puts more trust in the venerable figure of the contract than in her own concept of a communicative praxis.

So she retreats into the tradition of natural right.

Notes

1. Max Weber, *Economy and Society*, 2 vols. (Berkeley, 1978). Talcott Parsons distinguishes four types of the exercise of power: persuasion, activation of commitments, inducement, and coercion in "On the Concept of Power," in *Sociological Theory and Modern Society* (New York, 1967), pp. 310 ff.

2. Hannah Arendt, *On Violence* (New York, 1970), p. 41.

3. Talcott Parsons, "Authority, Legitimation and Political Action," in *Structure and Process in Modern Societies* (New York, 1960), p. 181.

4. Parsons, "Voting and the Equilibrium of the American Political System," in *Sociological Theory and Modern Society*, p. 193.

5. Arendt, *On Revolution* (New York, 1963), p. 71.

6. Arendt, *On Violence*, p. 41.

7. Arendt, *The Human Condition* (Chicago, 1958), pp. 181 ff.

8. Ibid., p. 200.

9. Arendt, *Elemente und Ursprünge totaler Herrschaft* (Frankfurt, 1955), p. 745. See Arendt, *The Origins of Totalitarianism*.

10. Arendt, *Elemente*, p. 749.

11. The thesis of the "banality of evil" that Arendt illustrated in *Eichmann in Jerusalem* (New York, 1963) is based on this insight. It can be found already in her essay "Organized Guilt," written in 1944 and published immediately after the war in *Die Wandlung* [English translation: *Jewish Frontier*, January, 1945]:

Henrich Himmler does not belong to the intellectuals who come from the dark no-man's-land between bohemian and "five-penny" existence, and whose significance for the formation of the Nazi elite has recently been pointed out again and again. He is neither a bohemian like Goebbels, nor a sex criminal like Streicher, nor a perverted fanatic like Hitler, nor an adventurer like Göring. He is a "Babbitt" with all the appearance of respectability, with all

Hannah Arendt

the habits of the good family man, who does not cheat on his wife and who wants to secure a decent future for his children. And he consciously built up his newest organization of terror, which encompasses the entire country, on the assumption that most men are not bohemians, not fanatics, not adventurers, not sex criminals, and not sadists, but in the first place "jobholders" and good family men. I think it was Peguy who called the family man the "grand adventurier du 20ᵉ siecle"; [Peguy] died too soon to experience in him the great criminal of the century. We have become so accustomed to admiring or smiling at the good-natured solicitude of the family man, the serious concentration on the welfare of the family, the solemn commitment to devote his life to wife and children, that we scarcely perceived how the caring father, who was concerned above all for security, was transformed against his will, under the pressure of the chaotic economic conditions of our time, into an adventurer who with all his anxiety could never be sure of the next day. His pliability was already demonstrated in the homogenization at the start of the regime. It turned out that he was willing to sacrifice conscience, honor, and human dignity for the sake of pension, life insurance, the secure existence of wife and children. [Arendt, *Die verborgene Tradition* (Frankfurt, 1976), pp. 40 ff.]

It is this insight that turned Hannah Arendt and her mentor Karl Jaspers into intrepid radical democrats, their undeniably elitist mentality notwithstanding.

How Arendt conceived the peculiar blend of participatory democracy and elitist structures she held to be necessary is expounded in the following passage:

It would be tempting to spin out further the potentialities of the councils, but it certainly is wiser to say with Jefferson, "Begin only for a single purpose; they will soon show for what others they are the best instruments"—the best instruments, for example, for breaking up the modern mass society, with its dangerous tendency toward the formation of pseudo-political mass movements, or rather, the best, the most natural way for interspersing it at the grass roots with an "elite" that is chosen by no one, but constitutes itself. The joys of public happiness and the responsibilities for public business would then become the share of those few from all walks of life who have a taste for public freedom and cannot be "happy" without it. Politically, they are the best, and it is the task of good government and the sign of a well-ordered republic to assure them of their rightful place in the public realm. To be sure, such an "aristocratic" form of government would spell the end of general suffrage as we understand it today, for only those who as voluntary members of an "elementary republic" have demonstrated that they care for more than their private happiness and are concerned about the state of the world would have the right to be heard in the conduct of the business of the republic. However, this exclusion from politics should not be derogatory, since a political elite is by no means identical with a social or cultural or professional elite. The exclusion, moreover, would not depend on an outside body; if those who belong are self-chosen, those who do not belong are self-excluded. And such self-exclusion, far from being arbitrary discrimination, would in fact give substance and reality to one of the most important negative liberties we have enjoyed since the end of the ancient world, namely freedom from politics, which was unknown to Rome or Athens and which is politically perhaps the most relevant part of our Christian heritage. (*On Revolution*, pp. 283 ff.)

12. Arendt, *On Revolution*, p. 256.

13. Ibid.

14. Arendt, *The Human Condition*, 200.

15. Ibid., p. 219.

16. Ibid., p. 33.

17. *On Revolution*, p. 86.

18. Ibid., pp. 62 ff.

19. Compare my review of the book *Über die Revolution* in *Kultur und Kritik* (1973).

20. On this concept, see my elaborations in Habermas, Luhmann, *Theorie der Gesellschaft oder Sozialtechnologie?* (Frankfurt, 1967), pp. 250–257.

21. *On Revolution*, pp. 45 ff.

22. See Parsons, "On the Concept of Power," p. 340.

23. Ibid., p. 342.

24. Arendt, "Truth and Politics," in *Philosophy, Politics and Society*, third series, P. Laslett and W. G. Runciman, eds., (Oxford, 1967), pp. 115 ff.

25. "Political thought is representative. I form an opinion by considering a given issue from different viewpoints, by making present to my mind the standpoints of those who are absent, that is, I represent them. This process of representation does not blandly adopt the actual views of those who stand somewhere else and hence look upon the world from a different perspective; this is a question neither of empathy, as though I tried to be or feel like somebody else, nor of counting noses and joining a majority, but of being and thinking in my own identity where actually I am not. The more people's standpoints I have present in my mind while pondering a given issue and the better I can imagine how I would feel and think if I were in their place, the stronger will be my capacity for representative thinking and the more valid my final conclusions, my opinion. (It is this capacity for an 'enlarged mentality' that enables men to judge; as such, it was discovered by Kant—in the first part of this *Critique of Judgment*—who, however, did not recognize the political and moral implications of his discovery.) The very process of opinion formation is determined by those in whose places somebody thinks and uses his own mind, and the only condition for this exertion of imagination is disinterestedness, the liberation from one's own private interests. Hence, even if I shun all company or am completely isolated while forming an opinion, I am not simply together only with myself in the solitude of philosophic thought; I remain in this world of mutual interdependence where I can make myself the representative of everybody else. To be sure, I can refuse to do this and form an opinion that takes only my interest, or the interests of the group to which I belong, into account; nothing indeed is more common, even among highly sophisticated people, than this blind obstinacy which becomes manifest in lack of imagination and failure to judge. But the very quality of an opinion as of a judgment depends upon its degree of impartiality." (Arendt, "Truth and Politics," p. 115)

26. Arendt, *The Human Condition*, pp. 244 ff.

Hans-Georg Gadamer: Urbanizing the Heideggerian Province (1979)

[This laudatio for Gadamer was delivered on the occasion of Gadamer's reception of the Hegel Prize of the city of Stuttgart on June 13, 1979.]

1

On Pentecost Sunday, 1940, Gadamer opened a meeting in Weimar devoted to Hegel with a lecture on "Hegel and the Ancient Dialectic." The reaction set off there by this outsider among Hegel scholars (according to the still half-shocked reminiscence of the 77-year-old Gadamer) must not have been very friendly: "I was not numbered among the Hegelians. But after all, it was not forbidden to understand something of Hegel even so. Or was it? . . . I refreshed myself from this spiritually exhausting experience by visiting the graves of our great poets at the Weimar cemetery."[1] In the meantime, Gadamer is still not a Hegelian, but he is the one who called the German Hegel Society into life in the 1960s, he is the one who instigated important international meetings at which Hegel specialists discussed their work, and it was on his initiative that the Hegel Congress in Stuttgart took place in the jubilee year of 1970. Today the same lecture that met with rejection at Gadamer's debut in Hegel circles (surely because he situated Hegel too close to Plato) opens a volume that brings together Gadamer's Hegel studies;[2] the book ends with a treatment of "Hegel and Heidegger." As a matter of fact, these are the two lodestars that have illuminated the path of Gadamer's thought.

When the city of Stuttgart resolved to found a Hegel Prize, Gadamer, whose initiative was unmistakable here as well, made his influence felt in order to ensure that Heidegger would be the first to receive the prize. However, the first recipient was Bruno Snell. This history must have been taken into consideration by the curators when this time, in interchange with significant scholars in the *Geisteswissenschaften*, they bestowed the prize once again on a philosopher, and indeed this philosopher, who has been accustomed to characterize himself with the remark that he is a student of Heidegger and has learned the craft of classical philology. In our day no one could span the ever greater distance between philosophy and the *Geisteswissenschaften* as convincingly as Gadamer.

Bridge building distinguishes the mentality and the cast of thought of this learned man generally: "One has to make distinctions, to be sure, but even more one has to see things in their interrelatedness."[3] This maxim comes from Gadamer's own mouth, but formulated in a still more Gadamerian fashion it would have read "One has to bridge not only the distances between disciplines, which have become remote from one another, but especially the temporal distance that separates those born later from the texts passed down, the distance between different languages that challenges the technical skill of the interpreter, and the distance that engenders the violence of radical thought." Now, Heidegger was just such a radical thinker who has dug a gorge about himself. I see the greatness of Gadamer's philosophic achievement in this, that he has bridged over this gorge. The image of the bridge, of course, brings along with it misleading connotations; it awakens the impression that here someone is furnished with a pedagogical crutch for the purpose of getting closer to an unreachable place. I do not intend it in this way. Hence, I would rather say that Gadamer urbanizes the Heideggerian province. One has to bear in mind that in German we associate with "the provinces" not only the confining element but also a thick-skinned uniqueness and originality.

To be sure, Gadamer regards the matter quite differently. He once thought that Heidegger needed a Marx. (Marx, though he was an opponent of Hegel, kept thinkers of his time from treating Hegel like a dead dog.) If I am correct in interpreting the late 1970s, Heidegger does not need his Marx; the subcultural wanderers are already breaking into the quadrate [*Geviert*] and the extravagant [*Verstiegene*]. All the more needed is someone who forges paths over which Heidegger can return from his self-chosen isolation. This can only be someone who— at a certain distance, to be sure—still follows Heidegger far enough to promote his thought productively and on a sound basis. I should say that Gadamer's productivity is of this type.

2

Gadamer's relationship to Heidegger is marked by a distance engendered by outward circumstances. Gadamer came to know Heidegger (who was only eleven years his elder) after he had a foot planted in the world of Marburg neo-Kantianism and had already received his doctorate, a student of Natorp, a friend of Nicolai Hartmann, his older colleague. In his autobiography, which bears the ambiguous title *Lehrjahre* [Years of Apprenticeship, or Years of Teaching], Gadamer depicts the world into which Heidegger irrupted. He portrays the circle surrounding the art historian Richard Hamann, the radiance cast by Stefan George over youthful spirits, the walks with E. R. Curtius, the intense debates of the Protestant theologians, and the private circles that gathered regularly (the circle surrounding Rudolf Bultmann, in which one read the Greek classics each Thursday evening, and the one in which Gerhard Krüger read aloud the great works of world literature. For more than fifteen years, this entire ambience was separated, as if by a glass wall, from the political events of the Weimar Republic. In this world, Heidegger must have struck like a bolt of lightning. As Gadamer recalled in his later years, "One cannot imagine Heidegger's entrance into Marburg in terms that are dramatic enough."

When we inquire as to the biographical significance of Heidegger's entry on the Marburg scene, perhaps we can start from the series of contrasts Gadamer used to characterize himself. Gadamer comes from Silesia, a province of Prussia, and when he was young the career of an officer was planned for him—but Gadamer is as un-Prussian as can be, and quite thoroughly civilian. Gadamer comes from an academic household stamped by the natural sciences (his father was a self-assured chemist), but in his first semester Gadamer let himself be drawn by literary and artistic interests into the field of the *Geisteswissenschaften*, and then to Marburg, at that time the locale of a philosophy with worldwide pretensions and an active center of the *Geisteswissenschaften* and theology. Even in relation to this world of academic philosophy and self-confident humanism Gadamer set himself apart, thanks to the stimulus he received from Heidegger. He had looked upon the Western tradition with the eyes of the historicist nineteenth century; then along came Heidegger, who made this tradition real and present in a more radical way by undertaking a precipitous retrieval of its beginnings. Gadamer swore by this tradition, but from then on he wanted to get beyond the "bourgeois *Bildungsreligion* in which it lived on."[4]

This is indeed the fundamental drive behind Gadamer's major philosophical work, which ripened through the decades—the drive to clarify for himself and others what the encounter with eminent texts means, what the binding character of the classic is all about. In this clarification Gadamer knows that he can no longer have recourse to a canon, but has to get behind every canon in order to elucidate the effective-historical conditions under which classic significance can accrue to a work:

It is part of the elemental experience of philosophy when we try to understand the classics of philosophical thought. . . . they posit, of themselves, a claim to truth that the contemporary consciousness can neither reject nor transcend. The naive self-respect of the present moment may rebel against this. . . . But it is undoubtedly a far greater weakness of philosophical thinking not to face this kind of investigation . . . but to play the fool on one's own. It is clear that in understanding the texts of these great thinkers, a truth is recognized *that could not be attained in any other way*, even if this contradicts the standard of research and progress.[5]

3

The preceding statement comes from the introduction to *Truth and Method*, the book with which the sixty-year-old Gadamer attained literary stature and gained international recognition—relatively late, after years of influential activity as a teacher at Leipzig, at Frankfurt, and especially in the chair of Jaspers at Heidelberg. (One can still discern in the discursive style of this text the oral context of teaching.) The philosophical hermeneutics that Gadamer projects is not intended as a methodological doctrine but as an attempt to renew the truth claim of philosophy in the wake of Hegel and hence the truth claim of the ambiguous end of metaphysics. Hence, philosophical hermeneutics poses itself the acute task of reestablishing the continuity of this truth claim beyond a threefold break in the tradition, of bridging three chasms that have opened up between ourselves and the philosophy of the Greeks: the breaks brought about in the nineteenth century by historicism, in the seventeenth century by physics, and at the start of modernity by the transition to the modern apprehension of the world.

Gadamer sets about building the first bridge in the form of a critique of Dilthey's theory of the *Geisteswissenschaften*. He bridges the putative opposition between merely historical reconstitution and systematic knowledge. The blow is directed against a historical consciousness that, in appropriating traditions, isolates them in the museum and robs them of their persuasive force. In opposition to this objectivism Gadamer propounds the thesis "that the effective-historical moment remains operative in all understanding of tradition, even where the methodology of the modern historical sciences has taken hold . . . and makes what has been transmitted historically into an object."[6]

Gadamer establishes the second bridge in the form of a reconstruction of the humanistic tradition of thought that appeals to the power of judgment [*Urteilskraft*]. He bridges the putative opposition between methodologically rigorous science and practical reason. The blow is directed against a concept of objective knowledge and method that is supposed to reserve for the modern empirical sciences a monopoly on possibilities for human knowledge. In contrast to this, Gadamer wants to establish the legitimacy of an understanding that precedes objectifying thought and joins the experiential modes of everyday praxis with the experience of art, philosophy, the *Geisteswissenshaften*, and history.

Finally, Gadamer promises to rehabilitate the substance of the philosophies of Plato and Hegel. He wants thereby to bridge the (as he supposes) false opposition between the metaphysical and the modern apprehension of the world. The alternatives that separated the camps in the famous *querelle des anciens et des modernes* are to be exposed as merely illusory alternatives. In doing this Gadamer makes use of a chess maneuver that reminds one in an ironic way of Wittgenstein's overcoming of illusory problems in philosophy: If we analyze the fact of our dependence on historical traditions rigorously enough, we hit on the ground of our almost natural [*naturwüchsige*] interest in these traditions, which is that the tradition has something to say to us that we cannot know on our own. The argument is lodged in the following questions: "Is this conversation with the whole of our philosophical tradition, in which we stand, and which as philosophers we are, groundless? Is there any need for grounding what already bears us along?"[7] Just as Wittgenstein invokes the fact of the functioning of ordinary language, Gadamer invokes the experience of being unable to exhaust the substantive content of eminent texts. Gadamer clings to the authority of this experience as a positivist clings to that of sense perception.

4

This conception contrasts in the most remarkable way with Heidegger's lordly destruction of Western thought, with the project that devalues the history of philosophy from Plato through Thomas down to Descartes and Hegel as the drama of a mounting forgetfulness of being. Can a more stark contrast be imagined than that between this turn away from every articulate figure of the tradition in the interests of a mysticism of being and Gadamer's quest to renew the humanistic tradition, from Plato to the Renaissance, from Vico through Scottish moral philosophy down to the *Geisteswissenschaften* of the nineteenth century, in terms of such key concepts as cultural formation [*Bildung*], common sense, judgment [*Urteilskraft*], and taste? (This humanistic tradition arose from the experiential context of urbane citizens, and the endangering of it has always been connected with the decline of urbanity.)

Gadamer has followed Heidegger farther than most; he participated in performing the "turning" [*Kehre*] by which Heidegger revised the transcendental self-understanding of *Being and Time*. In this connection the brief report of a dispute that Gadamer had with Löwith in the 1950s while they were holding a joint seminar on Heidegger's *Vom Wesen der Wahrheit* is rather telling. Löwith "had discovered the young Heidegger for himself" and "naturally did not fail to recognize the importance of *Being and Time*," but "the 'turning' and the talk about the being that was not supposed to be the being of a circumscribable entity—this he took for mythology or pseudo-poetry." "But"—thus Gadamer defends the master—"it is not mythology and not poetry, but *thinking*, even if the poetizing speaking in parables or indeed the poetic quest arising from the linguistic needs of a novel way of thinking, furnished an often confusing testimony. I have tried *in my own manner* to let myself be helped along by Heidegger's thought *even so*."[8] If my view of the matter is correct, Gadamer can so emphatically defend as thinking the meditation that characterizes the speechlessness of the mystic only because he renders an account of being as tradition, because he does not deliver himself up to the shapeless undertow of an ethereal being, but, casting his gaze back to Hegel, takes into account the massive stream of the tradition of words that have become objective and concrete, actually spoken in their place at their time. Whether we have before us an objective misunderstanding is perhaps not so important; how could a tradition remain vital if it were not transmitted through misunderstandings?

It remains that the author of *Truth and Method*, as the afterword to the third edition makes clear, has given a meditative slant to one circumstance. Gadamer has repeatedly pointed out that philosophical hermeneutics ought not to be foreshortened into a theory of science; that the phenomenon of understanding characterizes the relationships, prior to all science, with the world of a communicatively constituted form of life. Actually, though, the effective history of his book has left profound traces in the theory of the sciences and in the social sciences and *Geisteswissenschaften* themselves. The discussion connected with this book has not so much relativized the sciences in respect to the experiential realms of philosophy and art as they have laid bare the hermeneutical dimension within the sciences (especially the social and natural sciences). In recent years, philosophical hermeneutics has had a delayed effect on the Anglo-Saxon discussion—an effect fostered by the English translation of *Truth and Method* and promoted by its author's numerous guest lectureships at American universities. Its influence has not been confined to the divinity schools. It has also been joined to the impulses released by the protest movement. Interpreters have noticed things in common with the linguistic analysis of the later Wittgenstein and with the postempiricist theory of science of Thomas Kuhn, and it has been fused with the phenomenological, interactionist, and ethnomethodological approaches of interpretive sociology. This effect in no way accentuates the polemical meaning imbedded in the title *Truth and Method*; it demonstrates, on the contrary, that hermeneutics has contributed precisely to the self-enlightenment of methodological thinking, to the liberalizing of the understanding of science, and even to the differentiation of the practice of research.

5

It must surely be granted that hermeneutics can be exhausted neither by its own intentions nor by its effectiveness in transforming the self-understanding of modern scientists and scholars. Like phenomenology and linguistic analysis, it shifts everyday life relations into the foreground and furthers the enlightenment concerning the depth structures lying at the base of the life world. In the tradition of Humboldt's philosophy of language, and in a certain way parallel to the pragmatism (schooled in Hegel) of Peirce, Royce, and George Herbert Mead, Gadamerian hermeneutics highlights the linguistic intersubjectivity that unites all communicatively socialized individuals from the outset. It stubbornly pursues the question of the form and content of "the solidarity that unites all the speakers of a language,"[9] a question that has taken on supreme relevance in our day, when threats to historic life forms— the perils of a colonization of the life world through the imperatives of uncontrolled economic growth, through bureaucratic attacks, and through the external costs of the legalized, formally organized spheres of our society—press on a sensitized everyday consciousness. Gadamer does not shy away from extending Heidegger's critique of the "self-crucifying subjectivism of modernity" to social reality. He observes the growing independence of social subsystems whose characteristic is "a type of self-regulation that is conceivable . . . along the lines . . . of life organized in regulated cycles," and this for the sake of warning: "It would still be a mistake to disregard the desire for mastery expressed in these new methods for dominating nature and society."[10] Here the critique of technology of Heideggerian provenance is brought into contact with a critique of instrumental reason fed from other sources. Both are in agreement that the violence and exclusivity of objectifying thought correlates with the philosophical prominence of subjectivity, and under subjectivity both understand a self-awareness become rigid, a hardened autonomy instrumentalized for the purposes of self-assertion. Here Gadamer takes his stand in a very German tradition, following a self-interpretation of modernity against which second thoughts have been raised from the other side in the name of the legitimacy of modernity.

If I should undertake to locate Gadamer's philosophical effectiveness in the political context of German postwar history, I would emphasize as its most significant element, and as a purifying element, his magnificent actualization of the humanist tradition, which is oriented to the formation of the free spirit and is pervasive as a secret competitor and as a complement to the characteristic force of modern science throughout modernity. However, Gadamer himself points to the fact that in Germany, which has not set one revolution in motion by its own power, aesthetic humanism was always more strongly developed than political humanism. If one keeps in mind that in the nations of Western Europe more political awareness has entered into the *humaniora*,[11] the question arises in our context as to what harbors the greater danger: degrading the tradition of the Greeks to a prefiguration of the modern, or undervaluing the dignity of the modern itself. In the end, Gadamer would reject these alternatives in favor of the dignity of the tradition—not of tradition in general, to be sure, but of the traditions whose power is grounded in their reasonableness: "In truth, tradition that is not the defense of what has been handed down but the continual shaping of the ethical life in general constantly depends upon raising awareness, which takes over in freedom."[12] At any rate, we take over traditions in freedom only when we can say both Yes and No. I mean that one cannot simply strain the Enlightenment, the universalist eighteenth century, out of the humanist tradition. With this addition, however, I will not retain the last word. Gadamer is the first one to stress the openness of the conversation. From him we all can learn the basic hermeneutic wisdom that it is an illusion to suppose one could retain the last word.

Notes

1. Hans-Georg Gadamer, *Philosophische Lehrjahre* (Frankfurt, 1977), p. 115.

2. Gadamer, *Hegel's Dialectic* (New Haven, 1976).

3. Gadamer, *Philosophische Lehrjahre*, p. 23.

4. Ibid., p. 181.

5. Gadamer, *Truth and Method* (New York, 1975), p. xii.

6. Ibid., p. xxi.

7. Ibid., p. xxiv.

8. Gadamer, *Philosophische Lehrjahre*, p. 177.

9. Gadamer, *Reason in the Age of Science* (Cambridge, Mass., 1981), p. 3.

10. Ibid., p. 14.

11. Gadamer, *Truth and Method*, p. xvii.

12. Gadamer, "Nachwort," in *Wahrheit und Methode*, third edition (Tübingen, 1978), pp. 533 ff.

Gershom Scholem: The Torah in Disguise (1978)

[This address was delivered on the occasion of Scholem's eightieth birthday.]

Dear, most esteemed Mr. Scholem,

On the invitation of the German Embassy, we citizens of the Federal Republic of Germany come to Israel to celebrate you. Even though we might count on the friendly agreement of the one whose jubilee is being celebrated, we cannot avoid the delicate question of what really entitles us to this step. Who would think of sending a similar contingent to Paris for the eightieth birthday of Jean-Paul Sartre? If, without being presumptuous, we claim a special kind of right to offer congratulations in Scholem's case, then this must be based on a simple fact. Today we have—and I do not shy away from the possessive turn of phrase—nine books written by Scholem in the German language, and the author's flawless scholarly prose demonstrates that he was born into this language.

This would be a simple fact, of course, only if the commonality of mother tongue meant that we shared the same culture, the same traditions, and the same historical circumstances. Jews and Germans had a piece of history in common, but they did not so much share as divide up the risks, the pain, and the sacrifice involved, and in a quite unequal manner. This was going on long before the physical violence of the latter against the former extinguished any thought of commonality. You, Mr. Scholem, have made this clear to me and to us all.

Allow me to speak for a moment about "us," that is, the generation whose spiritual development began after the war with the recollection of the catastrophe. For us, your speech of 1966 in which you uncovered the profound asymmetries in German-Jewish relations was a shock. Hadn't we just recognized the streams of Jewish productivity in the best traditions—the only ones that outlasted the corruption—and hadn't we acknowledged them without reservations for the first time? Did we not stand under the dominant intellectual influences of Marx, Freud, and Kafka? Were we not accepted as students by those (such as Bloch, Horkheimer, Adorno, Plessner, and Löwith) who had returned from exile? Had we not, thanks to Adorno's and your help, discovered Walter Benjamin? And this was only the most dramatic instance. Other lines led to Hannah Arendt, Norbert Elias, Eric Erickson, Herbert Marcuse, and Alfred Schütz, and back to Karl Kraus, Franz Rosenzweig, Georg Simmel, and the Freudian Marxists of the 1920s. In addition, there fell into my hands a remarkable book[1] about major trends in Jewish mysticism that surprised me with the family affinities between the theosophy of Jacob Böhme and the teaching of a man by the name of Isaac Luria. Behind Schelling's *Ages of the World* and Hegel's *Logic*, and behind Baader, loomed not only the Swabian spiritual predecessors, not only Pietism and Protestant mysticism, but also (mediated by Knorr von Rosenroth) that version of the Kabbalah in whose antinomian consequences were anticipated, more clearly than anywhere else, the figures of thought and preoccupations of the great dialectical philosophy. Scholem was the name of the author who opened up these insights for me, and from this Scholem we heard a few years later that the assimilation of the Jews into German culture—the Jews to whom we had to be grateful for so much—had been "a false start from the beginning": "As a price of emancipation, the Germans demanded a resolute disavowal of Jewish nationality—a price the leading writers and spokesmen of the Jewish avant-garde were only too happy to pay."[2]

In this truth I still sense a defensive reaction, but it is a truth; indeed it is the historical truth from which your life's work draws its justification. Today I believe myself capable of seeing both sides. After everything was over, a last generation of Jewish scholars, philosophers, writers, and artists returned and developed as scarcely ever before an intellectual influence in Germany. To these German-Jewish traditions we acquire the right—even and precisely after Auschwitz—in the measure that we can in carrying them forward productively, make use of them so as to direct at ourselves a gaze of those exiles who were schooled in Marx, Freud, and Kafka, upon ourselves, in order to identify the estranged, the repressed, the rigidified parts in ourselves as something split off from life. This is the future of the assimilation of the German-Jewish spirit that has become a part of the past, but the future for which you, Mr. Scholem, take responsibility is quite another one. In Johann Peter Hebel you find the great exception, the single person who let the Jews be Jews, who "saw in the Jews what they had to give and not what they had to give up."[3] It belongs to your deepest convictions that the symmetry of give and take could be brought about only by a turning back of the Jewish spirit and the Jewish nation to their own history.

So it is that you have done your utmost to see that the world of Jewish mysticism—treasures that the Jews have to give from their own selves—is recovered from obscure sources and now lies spread out before the eyes of all. With this, you have clarified the situation of give and take. My task, therefore, is not, as the protocol stipulates, to deliver an encomium, but rather to give a speech of gratitude. Whoever says thanks has to be able to say what it is that he is grateful for. This I will attempt, but the task is not simple.

The transparency of Scholem's erudite discourse is perspicuous only at first glance; his historical-philological presentation has many levels. I am incapable of assessing Scholem the philologist and historian, but whoever is engrossed in Scholem's writings notices other kinds of philologist behind the scholar: the lover, the discoverer, the battling Zionist, and finally the philologist who begins to theorize about his subject matter.

Mr. Scholem, to recognize in you the lover of philology one need not have accompanied you to Ackermann's, the old and rare book shop you have visited every time you have gone to Munich over more than fifty years. Out of the mouth of the eighty-year-old Scholem speaks someone simply mad about books when he recalls how, as a seventeen year old, he came across a 50-pfennig copy of Lichtenberg's satire on Lavater's attempt to convert Moses Mendelssohn, and then adds with a smirk that last year a copy of this writing was offered for 1,500 marks.[4]

Further, the passion of the philological discoverer breaks through when Scholem recalls finding a manuscript in 1938 in the Jewish Theological Seminary in New York. With it he was able to explain the generations-old puzzle of Reuchlin research: "It was an hour for me to celebrate as I gazed on these pages, which included what amounted to a collection of the citations in Reuchlin's work."[5] [It was not known before then how Reuchlin had come by his many (and often erroneously cited) Kabbalah sources.] A still further impulse was needed for Scholem to become a discoverer in the tradition of Jewish studies, an unbiased investigator of the symbolic world of Jewish mysticism.

In the indefatigable effort of this great philologist there is the intellectual drive, the historical experience, and the sensibility of the generation of the pre–World War I youth movement. The turn that Scholem gave Kabbalah research was inspired by the consciousness the Zionist movement had awakened in him. He himself regards the opening up of Jewish mysticism as a part of this "movement oriented to the rebirth of the Jewish people, in virtue of which a new vision of Jewish history became possible."[6]

However, what fascinates me still more than the incorruptible scholar, the foolish lover, the passionate discoverer, and more than the historically conscious educator of a people is the theoretician that Scholem does not intend at all to be and that takes shelter behind the many walls of philology.

Philologists also have to understand the subjects with which a text deals; otherwise they cannot make their texts intelligible. The more these subjects are removed from everyday awareness, the less philological handicraft can be exercised in a merely instrumental fashion and the more the philologist has to become an expert in his subject matter. Hence, the great philologists and historians are always in part jurists, theologians, or philosophers. But how is the philologist who deals with mystical texts to conduct himself? He has to bridge a twofold distance. The texts themselves already express a sort of irony on which the Romantics right down to Kierkegaard have reflected: These texts are supposed to articulate the ineffable; they are supposed to communicate truth precisely as something incommunicable. This distance could be overcome if the interpreter of indirect communications could become a religious adept, if he could become a mystic. However, such a thing is not at his disposal; even Scholem is not a mystic. For this reason, the philologist here has to draw near his subject by way of a theory of the subject. The theoretical appropriation of the content of traditions of mysticism is the single bridge over which the philologist of mysticism has to go if he wants to understand something and make it intelligible. To the extent that I have an overview of Scholem's works, I can say that Scholem has spoken as a theoretician only once, and of course under a pretext that belies the bad conscience of the historian-philologist. I am referring to the "Ten *Unhistorical* Statements Concerning the Kabbalah."[7] This short text is distinguished from Scholem's other writings by the fact that the Cartesian clarity of the language yields to dialectical concepts, and almost to dialectical imagery. In this one place, Scholem deploys that diction of revealing enigma that he so admired in his friend Walter Benjamin. The text begins with a reference to the ironic element that attaches to the philology of a mystical discipline such as the Kabbalah: "Does there visibly abide in him, the philologist, something of the law of the subject matter itself, or does just what is essential in this projection of the historical disappear from sight?" The answer is ambiguous. Only a tradition in decline can become an object of philology and has any need of that discipline, but even the grandeur of a tradition becomes visible only through the medium of objectifying appropriation—"authentic tradition remains hidden." In the nine sections that follow this first one, Scholem identifies all the theoretical motifs that one rediscovers in his substantive works as pivotal for his systematic interpretation. Permit me to highlight at least two of these motifs, an epistemological one and one having to do with the history of philosophy.

The first motif is circumscribed by the terms *revelation, tradition,* and *teaching.* The rabbinic parable that the Holy Scriptures are like a large house with many chambers and with a key lying in front of each door affords us a starting point, but it is not the right one; all the keys have changed places.[8] Here the tradition is bathed in a Kafkaesque light. What is the meaning of tradition? First of all, teaching. The teaching of the prophetic word is the medium for the transmission of knowledge that arose with the great world religions. Rabbinic Judaism has elaborated the practice of teaching, the exegesis of the Holy Scripture, into a highly stylized form. It was in this form that the sixteen-year-old Scholem became acquainted with it when he took up his Hebrew studies with Rabbi Isaac Bleichrode and "learned Talmud,"[9] but was that still teaching, still tradition in an unbroken sense?

In the nineteenth century the *Geisteswissenschaften* developed. An ambiguous product of the Enlightenment, they formed the modern system of locks by which the streams of tradition were interrupted. The structure of tradition was brought to awareness hermeneutically, and traditional teaching was perceived as a dogmatic form of thought. On the other hand, it lay in the interests of the *Geisteswissenschaften* that the traditions they promoted (in however reflective a fashion) not be dissolved into sheer opinions, and so they operated in the ambivalence between elucidating documents from which we were still able to learn things of importance for our living and demystifying their dogmatic claims to validity. This ambivalence has remained unsettling to a philology that actually participates in its objects right down to our own day. From Schleiermacher to Gadamer, philosophical hermeneutics has sought to resolve this by trying to hold together what the methodology of the *Geisteswissenschaften* makes possible and destroys at once, namely the appropriation of the tradition. This same problem is posed for Scholem, but he shows himself unperturbed; he can meet the problem of historicism, of which I am now speaking, by means of a concept of tradition that has been schooled and sharpened in the Kabbalah.

The mystic who appeals to illuminations—and that means to an immediate, intuitive access to the divine life process—is the born competitor to the official administrators of the authentic divine word, the priesthood, even though Jewish mysticism has emerged for the most part as orthodox and has been effective as a conservative force. The kabbalists have a natural interest in raising the value of the oral Torah over the Bible; they give an important place to the commentaries through which each generation appropriates the revelation anew. They no longer identify revelation with the written Torah. For them, truth is not fixed, not expressed positively in a well-circumscribed group of propositions, so that tradition could be exhausted in the truest possible reproduction. Instead revelation is the Torah's process of tradition itself; revelation is intrinsically related to the creative commentary. The written Torah becomes complete only through the oral; the voice of God speaks through the conflict of interpretations of scripture scholars of every generation, until the last day.[10] If this conflict were to cease, the divine source would be dried up. Later this kabbalistic conception is radicalized yet again. The written Torah stands already as a translation of the divine word into the language of human beings; it is already simply a disputable interpretation. The oral Torah is everything; the written Torah is a mystical notion referring to the messianic state of a future knowledge.[11] We know about the revelation, but all the keys have changed places. Scholem's thinking circles persistently around this point, which Jewish mysticism varies in many symbols and parables. Here he seems to seek the solution for the problems of how the fallibility of human knowledge and the historical multiplicity of interpretations can be united with the unconditional and universal claim to truth.

The Torah, in the overflowing fullness of its meaning, turns to each generation and even each individual another face, and yet it is one and the same. The Torah of the tree of knowledge is a hidden Torah. It changes its clothing, and these sets of clothing *are* the tradition. Only in the state of redemption—when theory and practice, the tree of knowledge and the tree of life, have been joined together—does the Torah enter the light in an unhidden way. Only in this light will the multiplicity of the disputing interpretations make known their secret unity. Thus, the mystical concept of tradition includes a messianic concept of truth that proves to be the equal of historicism. The dimension of time—the centuries throughout which the instructional conversation remains unbroken, and which is headed toward the vanishing point of a consensus achieved in the end ("in the long run," as the secularized formula of Peirce has it)—makes it possible to reconcile the fallibilism of the process of knowledge with a view of the unconditional character of knowledge itself. From this vantage point, even the objectifying *Geisteswissenschaften* lose the terrifying aspect of relativizing all claims to validity. Like human knowledge in general, these scholarly disciplines share with the traditions they appropriate the ambiguous status of a Torah in disguise that harbors sparks of the truth without affording the bright light of certitude before the irruption of the last day.

Of course, this theory of truth accounts for a concept of tradition that is not only turned backward. Tradition no longer counts as the continuous transcription and renewal of an old truth; just as in the mystical illumination, truth can break into the tradition and explode its continuity. Tradition is grounded not in an unequivocally obvious knowledge but in an idea of knowing whose messianic resolution is still outstanding; hence it lives from the tension between its conservative and utopian contents. This notion of tradition assimilates into itself revolutions no less than restorations; it strips what we once called tradition of its dogmatic character.

Here the motifs of epistemology and philosophy of history intertwine. Like the complex of knowledge, tradition, and teaching, the idea of the creative force of negation, of the self-negation of God, can serve as an example for the systematic outcome of an "unhistorical" way of reading the Kabbalah. Among Scholem's "Ten Unhistorical Principles" the following is to be found: "The materialist language of the Lurianic Kabbalah, especially in its deduction of the *Zimzum* (the self-contraction of God), gives rise to the thought as to whether the symbolism that uses such imagery and modes of discourse could not be the reality itself."[12]

Processes of creation had always been thought of in the mythological realm and even in that of metaphysical thought, as a creation out of something preexistent, out of chaos or out of some matter antecedent to the creative principles. However, with the Judeo-Christian formula of *creatio ex nihilo* a radically new idea came to the fore: that the nothingness out of which the absolute will creates the world can no longer be imagined as a potency outside the creative power. It is precisely mystical thought, which immerses itself in the divine life process, that attaches itself firmly to this formula.[13] The concept that God descends into his own primordial grounds in order to fashion himself out of them can be taken up by Isaac Luria (as well as Jacob Böhme) for the sake of conceiving the creation from nothing according to the dialectical image of a God who withdraws into himself or contracts; he thereby engenders an abyss within himself into which he descends, into which he withdraws, and only in this way does he set free the space the creatures are going to take over. The first act of creation is a self-negation, by which God, so to speak, calls forth the nothing—a doctrine that is posited in strict opposition to the Neo-Platonic conceptions of emanation. This model offers the single coherent solution to the theodicy problem: "A perfect world cannot be created, because then it would be God himself, who does not multiply himself but can only contract himself. The naiveté that expects God to repeat himself is remote from the kabbalists. Precisely because God can never repeat himself, what must underpin any creation on the part of this

God—if I may state it in a Hegelian manner—is alienation, in which the godhead, in order to be itself, has to expel evil from itself."[14]

The self-contraction of God is the archetypal form of the exile, of the self-banishment, which explains "why it is that since that primordial act, all being has been a being in exile, in need of being led back and redeemed."[15] From this conception of the abyss or the matter or the wrath into which God in his egoism (taken quite literally) withdraws, various lines lead through Schelling and Hegel to Marx. One line ends in the materialist dialectic of nature: For the Lurianic mystic the everlasting creation means that the contraction of God is renewed in each process of nature, that in each and every creative process the contact with nothingness is repeated. A second line leads to the revolutionary theory of history, and a third to the nihilism of a postrevolutionary enlightenment. Scholem has been intensively preoccupied with the last two motifs.

It goes without saying that a God who banishes himself invests the historical experiences of exile with a grave significance—and indeed with an apocalyptic significance wherever the violence of the negative— persecution, repression, and isolation—are construed as indications of the creative power of the negative, of a turn to the good. Hölderlin's saying about the greatest peril, in which the redemptive element mounts up, is anticipated here. If even creation itself begins with the self-exiling of God, then the moment of the supreme catastrophe points toward the chance of redemption: "If you have sunk to the lowest level, in *that* hour I redeem you."[16]

To be sure, Isaac Luria's world of ideas undergirded the apocalyptic notions of the spontaneity and incalculability of redemption less than it did the messianism of those who wished to "compel" the redemption. The act of self-banishment indeed means also that God withdraws and clears out a realm of freedom and responsibility for others. His withdrawal is the condition for the catastrophes that were initiated with the "shattering of the vessels" within the divine life process itself and were repeated in the history of the nations with the fall of Adam. God has withdrawn to such an extent that the leading of things back to their primordial place is surrendered to humans. Just as each sin repeats the primordial process of the divine self-banishment, so each good act contributes to the leading home of the exiled one: "To Luria the coming of the Messiah means no more than the signature under a document that we ourselves write."[17] The mystic was ever accustomed to the idea of a magical power of contemplation that can coerce movements in the heart of the Godhead and prepare in the inmost part of the world the process of reestablishing a fallen nature. The later Kabbalah turns this inner movement outward, into a messianic activism that ultimately takes on the more profane meaning of a political liberation from exile. From the early Marx on down to Bloch and the late Benjamin, it takes the form "no resurrection of nature without a revolutionizing of society."

Sabbatai Zevi and his prophet, Nathan of Gaza, made not merely a messianic but a antinomian use of this idea.[18] Sabbatai Zevi was offered the choice by the sultan of suffering martyrdom or going over to Islam. He resolved upon apostasy, and this fall of the messiah came to be understood and justified in accord with the model of Zimzum as a creative act of descent into the darkness. The fall is a tragic component of the mission that is to rout the power of the antigodly from its innermost realm. Scholem has made a study of the nihilistic consequences of this doctrine in the Frankish sects. He has traced the manifestations of religious nihilism through the history of the heretics among the Taborites amd Adamites, among the Begins and the Begards, the Brothers and Sisters of the Free Spirits, all the way back to the early Gnostic sects.[19] By breaking the law they wanted to fulfill its true, messianic meaning. The model of the descent of God into the abyss provided the warrant for monstrous visions of the redemptive power of the subversive in the heretical messianism of the Sabbatians; it covered as well the pertinent rituals which were supposed to manifest the power of negation in the performance of actions at once destructive and liberating.

One cannot read Scholem's presentation of the religious nihilism of the eighteenth century without having parallels with the present day come to mind. (Naturally, these parallels should be drawn only with great care.) Scholem stresses, and documents in biographical instances, the tendency toward a reversal of mysticism into enlightenment. The nihilism of Joseph Frank seemed to push Jewish mysticism to a point where the religious shell was burst open so that deeper impulses could combine with the novel ideas of the French Revolution. This transposition of religious into political contents took place so often without any specific mediation that one wonders whether antinomianism might itself not have been reacting to the decline of the religious factor, much as Surrealism reacted to the decline of auratic art in the modern age. We are familiar with Benjamin's interest in Surrealism; did there exist parallels with Scholem's interest in antinomianism?

The cases of religious and, if you will, aesthetic nihilism are also alike in that the authentic content of religion and the content of art—the substance of these spheres of value, as Max Weber put it—are supposed to be salvaged by means of a radical supersession or destruction. This explains the exhibitionism of the kabbalists' self-consuming actions and the shock at which they were aiming. Incidentally, similar traits show up in the current version of terrorism, which from the standpoint of the participants could well be directed toward saving the pure content of revolution by means of shocking exhibitions of pure destructiveness at the exact moment when the possibility of revolution wanes—when the modern state and the style of revolutionary practice that corresponds to it fall apart or at any rate undergo a transformation that is difficult to underestimate.

I have highlighted only two motifs—the theory of knowledge and the philosophy of history—of Scholem's multifaceted thought. Both motifs affect Scholem's appraisal of Zionism and Judaism today. The political and spiritual energy of many generations of Jewish intellectuals has been deposited in the universalist values of emancipatory movements, bourgeois as well as socialist. In this regard, Scholem insists that this universalism is in need of embodiment. He praises Zionism for not being a messianic movement but for, rather, taking historical-political constraints into account. On the other hand, Scholem identifies Judaism as little with the political figure of Israel as with the traditional shape of its traditions. He sees in it primarily a moral concern, a historical project that cannot be defined once and for all. Judaism is a spiritual enterprise and lives out of religious sources, but it may survive even the secularization of those sources. This notion of Judaism is vague and is related to a historical particularity, and yet there is expressed a more universal problem: How, under the conditions of modernity, can a people maintain its identity?

In an interview in 1970, Mr. Scholem, you were questioned about the significance kabbalistic thought could have for Judaism today. At that time you doubted that the Kabbalah could still have a vital answer to our situation. At that time you made use of a kabbalistic figure of thought in your reply: "God will appear as non-God. All the divine and symbolic things can also appear in the garb of atheistic mysticism."

Once the authority of the voice that said "I am the Lord, thy God" no longer holds as unquestionably true, there remains only a (in your terms) transformed tradition that knows no crime but one: Whoever cuts off the living bond between the generations commits a crime. Among modern societies, only those who can bring essential elements of their religious tradition, which points beyond the merely human, into the spheres of the profane will be able to save the substance of the human as well.

For Judaism, for Israel, Scholem poses the question of identity as follows:

The blazing landscape of redemption (as if it were a point of focus) has concentrated in itself the historical outlook of Judaism. Little wonder that overtones of Messianism have accompanied the modern Jewish readiness for irrevocable action in the concrete realm, when it set out on the utopian return to Zion. It is a readiness which no longer allows itself to be fed on hopes. Born out of the horror and destruction that was Jewish history in our generation, it is bound to history itself and not to meta-history; it has not given itself up totally to Messianism. Whether or not Jewish history will be able to endure this entry into the concrete realm without perishing in the crisis of the Messianic claim which has virtually been conjured up—that is the question which out of this great and dangerous past the Jew of this age poses to his present and to his future.[20]

Notes

1. Scholem, *Major Trends in Jewish Mysticism* (New York, 1946).

2. Scholem, "Jews and Germans," in *On Jews and Judaism in Crisis: Selected Essays*, ed. W. Dannhauser (New York, 1976), p. 75.

3. Scholem, *Judaica* 2, p. 40.

4. Scholem, *From Berlin to Jerusalem* (New York, 1980), pp. 50–51.

5. *Judaica* 3, p. 52.

6. Ibid., p. 261.

7. Ibid., pp. 264 ff.

8. Scholem, *On the Kabbalah and Its Symbolism* (New York, 1969), pp. 12 ff.

9. *From Berlin to Jerusalem*, p. 63.

10. Scholem, *Grundbegriffe des Judentums*, pp. 90 ff.

11. *On the Kabbalah*, pp. 71 ff.

12. *Judaica* 3, p. 266.

13. *Grundbegriffe*, pp. 53 ff.

14. Scholem, *Von der mystischen Gestalt der Gottheit*, p. 79.

15. *On the Kabbalah*, p. 112.

16. *Grundbegriffe*, p. 135.

17. *On the Kabbalah*, p. 117.

18. *Major Trends*, pp. 287–324.

19. Scholem, "Der Nihilismus als religiöses Phänomen," *Eranos Jahrbuch*, 1974.

20. Scholem, *The Messianic Idea in Judaism* (New York, 1971), pp. 35–36.